THE COMMON YEARS

Jilly Cooper comes from Yorkshire and was educated at Godolphin School in Salisbury. For twenty-five years she lived in London and for thirteen of them she wrote for the *Sunday Times*, during which time her column was one of the most widely read features in the paper. In 1982 she moved to Gloucestershire and began writing a column for the *Mail on Sunday*. Recently she has devoted more of her time to writing books, ten of which have been published by Mandarin; she is also the author of six romances, three bestselling novels, *Riders*, *Rivals* and *Polo*, a book of short stories, two anthologies and several children's books. She makes frequent appearances on television and has done many radio broadcasts.

Paul Cox was born in 1957. He studied illustration at Camberwell and the Royal College of Art. His work has appeared in numerous publications including *Outing* by Dylan Thomas, *The Irish R.M.* and editorial assignments for *The Times*, *Daily Telegraph* and *Observer*.

JILLY COOPER

The Common Years

With illustrations by Paul Cox

Mandarin

A Mandarin Paperback

THE COMMON YEARS

First published in Great Britain 1984
by Methuen London Ltd
This edition published 1989
Reprinted 1990 (twice), 1991
by Mandarin Paperbacks
an imprint of Reed International Books Ltd
Michelin House, 81 Fulham Road, London SW3 6RB
and Auckland, Melbourne, Singapore and Toronto

Reissued 1992
Reprinted 1995

Text copyright © 1984 Jilly Cooper
Drawings copyright © 1984 Paul Cox

ISBN 0 7493 0178 3

A CIP catalogue record for this title is available
from the British Library

The lines of poetry on page 28 are from
'The Garden' from Ezra Pound's *Collected Shorter Poems*,
and the lines on page 75 are from T.S. Eliot's *Four Quartets*,
both quoted by kind permission of Faber and Faber Ltd.
The lines on page 256 are from John Betjeman's 'Slough',
quoted by kind permission of John Murray Ltd.

Design based on the design for the original hardcover edition
by James Campus

Printed and bound in Great Britain
by Cox & Wyman Ltd, Reading, Berkshire

To George Humphreys
with love
because he always believed in me

Also by Jilly Cooper

FICTION
Polo
Riders
Rivals

NON-FICTION
Animals in War
Angels Rush In
Class
Hotfoot to Zabriskie Point
(with Patrick Lichfield)
How to Stay Married
How to Survive Christmas
How to Survive from Nine to Five
Jolly Marsupial
Jolly Super
Jolly Super Too
Jolly Superlative
Men and Super Men
Mongrel Magic
Super Cooper
Super Jilly
Super Men and Super Women
Turn Right at the Spotted Dog
Women and Super Women

CHILDREN'S BOOKS
Little Mabel
Little Mabel Saves the Day
Little Mabel Wins
Little Mabel's Great Escape

ROMANCE
Bella
Emily
Harriet
Imogen
Lisa & Co
Octavia
Prudence

ANTHOLOGIES
The British in Love
Violets and Vinegar

CONTENTS

———

INTRODUCTION	*page* 9
THE TWO WALKS	15
1972	20
1973	23
1974	26
1975	49
1976	72
1977	91
1978	120
1979	142
1980	164
1981	196
1982	247

INTRODUCTION

For ten years, sometimes two or three times a day, I walked my dogs on Putney and Barnes Commons. Often my children, Felix and Emily, who were two and a half years and nine months respectively when we moved to Putney in 1972, came with me. Occasionally on Sunday, I was accompanied by my husband, Leo. But normally I set out alone.

Because I spent so much time on the Common, and because when the children were young, it was really the only quiet place to think, I started taking a note book and pen out with me, and jotting down random thoughts, impressions of people I met, and any changes in the seasons.

To begin with the entries were sporadic. There were periods when I was writing a book or working on some *Sunday Times* piece, during which I didn't write a word in the diary for weeks. But gradually it became a fascination to see that the same chestnut tree, two down from the slide in the children's playground, was always the first to turn gold in the autumn; or that one year the snowdrops would appear much earlier than others; or that certain muggy kinds of weather brought out flashers and undesirables like a rash.

This book is based on that diary but many of the main characters who appear in it are fictitious, although modelled in part on the people I met on the Common in those years.

Putney and Barnes Commons are situated five miles from Hyde Park. I should also explain that, although merging into one another, they are run by different bodies. Barnes Common is looked after by the London Borough of Richmond and Twickenham.

Putney Common, on the other hand, which consists of some forty acres, belonged to the Earl Spencer, whose ancestors over the centuries repeatedly tried to enclose the land. Happily the local people resisted and, in 1871, a Bill was passed which vested control of the Common in the hands of eight Conservators, who were to be elected every three years by the people who lived within three-quarters of a mile of the Common. It is still the same today. Each year Common rates are paid by people living near the Common and every three years they elect eight Conservators, who meet regularly to decide how the Common should be run. (They also control Wimbledon Common.) Part of the money raised by these Common rates pays the salary of a ranger, who takes care of Putney Common, mowing, picking up litter, supervising the planting of trees, reporting undesirables to the police and refereeing fearful squawking matches between dog walkers.

During the ten years we lived in Putney, I mainly took two routes round the Commons, usually walking anti-clockwise, but sometimes clockwise – so as to avoid and fox those people and dogs I didn't want to meet. Both routes are shown on the map on pages 12 and 13 and described in the following pages.

Ten years is a long time to walk over the same small area. I still miss the friends I made on the Common. They were a merry, gallant bunch, who braved tempests, hail and the bitterest cold rather than let their dogs go unwalked. Some of them, as will be seen from the pages that follow, drove me demented, and I them. But a diary is a convenient dumping ground for one's grievances, and, having once dumped them, I would usually be falling on my temporary foes' necks within twenty-four hours.

I think even now, eighteen months after we've left Putney, I could find my way along those routes with my eyes shut, guided by the raw soapy scent of the hawthorns, or the rank smell of the elder, or the sweet elusive fragrance of the wild roses. I never got bored with the Common – each day there was something new to look at, violets suddenly appearing by the railway line, or the return of the toadflax by the football pitch. Each day, however badly I or my dogs behaved, the Common, given the chance, would restore my sanity. Familiarity never bred contempt. I can only look back on the ten years we were acquainted with love and gratitude.

J.C.

Gloucestershire 1984

THE TWO WALKS

On my favourite walk, you set out to the north down Egliston Road, passing on the right a group of modern houses, known as 'Alimony Villas' because at one time there were so many divorced women and their children living there. Through an archway formed by two huge plane trees lies the first Common. It is divided into two squares by a little road up the centre. The left-hand western square is occupied by the cricket pitch. On the right-hand square on the south-east corner stands All Saints' Church, a solid Victorian pile consecrated in 1874. It has a little white bell tower rising out of the trees like a Cape Canaveral rocket, and several very beautiful windows designed by William Morris and Edward Burne-Jones. The churchyard has no tombstones and is framed by a square of limes, a straggling privet hedge and, on the outside, an iron spiked fence.

Leaving the church, you pass All Saints' School, the 22 bus shelter, and the Spencer Arms public house (named after Earl Spencer) on your right, and cross the first Common, until you reach the fork where the Lower Richmond Road splits in two and continues under the same name on the right, but becomes Queen's Ride on the left. In the fork between the two roads, lies a stretch of grass known as the 'Fair Triangle', because in May every year the Fair arrives and parks here for a month.

Crossing Queen's Ride and the Lower Richmond Road (both busy main roads) at the tip of the Fair Triangle, you reach the Big Common, a stretch of open land, divided by a line of plane trees, and bordered on the boundary by a sluggish overgrown stream called Beverley Brook.

To reach the Brook you pass, on the right, first the ranger's hut, with its little garden, then Putney Hospital rising from a sea of green grass like a great pink liner, then the nurses' home, the bowling green with its crinkly red-roofed pavilion, and finally a block of council flats known as the Ranelagh Estate, past which, to the north-east, Beverley Brook continues its meandering way down to the River Thames.

Between the Brook and the Thames lie the fenced-in Barn Elms Playing Fields. At the extreme north-east corner of the Common, just before the Brook reaches the Ranelagh Estate, grows a clump of trees and nettles known as 'Cat Corner'; this clump swarms with stray cats and also cats from the estate, who become the target of every passing dog. In the early days, before the two footbridges across to the playing fields and the two paths were built, you could not walk along the north side of the Brook, which was lined with elms. Instead, you turned left when you reached Cat Corner, away from the council estate, and walked along the south bank of the Brook, which was lined with willows, poplars, hawthorns and lush vegetation.

To the south as you walk lie the 'Hillocks', two undulating swells of grass under which piles of bomb rubble were buried after the Second World War. At the end of the Hillocks, you come to the football pitch, and leaving Beverley Brook you swing left along the side of the pitch. Ahead lies an enchanted square of land known as the 'Flower Garden', because it was once allotments, and today is crammed with wild flowers, brambles, dog roses and oak and sycamore saplings. But, instead of entering the Flower Garden, you turn right again, with the football pitch on your right, and a splendid colonnade of plane trees, which border the Flower Garden, on your left, and walk down the grassy path until you reach 'Oedipus Corner' – so named because it is marked by three tall Lombardy poplars, where three paths meet. To the left here, on the north-west corner of the Flower Garden, lies a dense sycamore copse, known as 'Flashers' Point', because so many flashers lurk there in high summer waiting to startle unsuspecting lady dog-walkers.

Leaving Flashers' Point, you can take a right path through low hanging oak trees, or the left path known as the 'Nettle Tunnel', because it is flanked by treacherous beds of nettles, which close over the top in summer.

At the end of both the oak path and the Nettle Tunnel, you come to the grassy boundary of Putney and Barnes Commons. As you carry on westward onto Barnes Common, on the right lie the tennis courts, the putting green, with its little thatched pavilion, and the children's playground. To the left is Barnes Graveyard, which is unfenced and open to the public and every passing vandal. Many gravestones have been broken, stone angels lie battered and armless in the long grass. Most of the more august female statues have black eyes or broken noses. Untended, except (rarely) by morose Richmond council workers, it remains a place of haunting, if desolate, beauty, a forsaken garden beloved of film crews.

On the far west end of the Graveyard, you come to a triangle of parking space, flanked by chestnut trees, known locally as the 'Eternal Triangle', because so many lovers – usually adulterers who can only meet during the day – park their cars there during the lunch hour.

Beyond the Eternal Triangle lies a stretch of rough grass, leading to Rocks Lane, another main road, which crosses the Lower Richmond Road, and later Queen's Ride; but our walk turns left past a stretch of marshy ground, known unromantically as Barnes Bog, and curving back round the other side of the graveyard into the 'Squirrel Wood'. Filled with oaks, thorns, sycamores, and one very beautiful poplar, the wood is inhabited by dozens of grey squirrels and usually rings with the excited barks of dogs chasing them.

Emerging from the Squirrel Wood, you reach the Barnes-Putney boundary again. On the right lies a magnificent avenue of chestnuts. We, however, go straight on, crossing the blackthorn copse on the boundary into the Flower Garden. On the right, beyond the Chestnut Avenue, lies Putney Cemetery, which is framed by an ancient russet wall, and which (in contrast to the lush wilderness of Barnes Graveyard) is beautifully kept.

At the end of the Cemetery wall, the Flower Garden merges into the Big Common down a gentle slope known as 'Dogger Bank', because it is pitted with holes, made by all the dogs frenziedly burrowing after voles and shrews.

By Dogger Bank, you can either cross the Big Common diagonally which will bring you back to the ranger's hut again, or turn right along the Cemetery wall, until you reach another wooden hut on the edge of Lower Richmond Road.

Known locally as 'the 'Ut', it is the place where Putney Cricket Club have their tea and booze-ups with opposition teams after cricket matches. The 'Ut is always a good place to catch recalcitrant dogs, because, while they investigate the dustbins for the remains of last Saturday's cricket tea, you can often sneak up on them and catch them by the tail.

From the 'Ut, you cross the Upper Richmond Road and Queen's Ride at the base of the Fair Triangle, which brings you back onto the first Common but on the cricket pitch side. On the right of the pitch lies Chester Close, a row of modern houses. Ahead, to the south, stretching the length of the first Common stands a row of solid, handsome red-brick Victorian houses, called Lower Common South. Each one has its own individual character, because they (like the houses in Egliston Road) were all designed completely differently by the same imaginative architect. They are splendid family houses, with big gardens filled in the spring with apple blossom and bluebells.

Turning left along Lower Common South, you reach Alimony Villas once more, and turn right back into Egliston Road. This walk, depending on whom I met or on the caprices of the dogs, or whether the muse struck, would take between thirty minutes and an hour and a half.

A variation on this route, but one I took less often, was to cross the first Common and turn left along the Fair Triangle, across the Putney-Barnes boundary, which is marked here by an oblong copse of grey poplars and silver birches.

From the boundary, you enter the 'Yarrow Meadow', which like most of Barnes Common – as opposed to Putney Common – is made up of sandy heath, covered with bracken, gorse bushes, oak trees, silver birches and beautiful grasses. In late summer, this stretch is dotted with white yarrow, hence its name.

From the Yarrow Meadow, you cross Common Road to 'Peter's Meadow', so named because, when I first explored it on a glorious summer morning, it reminded me of the meadow Peter goes out into, to the accompaniment of that haunting theme tune at the beginning of *Peter and the Wolf*. Once again this area is dotted with gorse, bracken, oak trees and long lush grass, which is mowed in summer for the local children's school sports. Since we left Putney it has been used in winter as a football pitch.

Along the south side of Peter's Meadow runs the railway line, and on the south-west corner, through a hawthorn copse, you enter a red-brick tunnel, known as 'Mugger's Tunnel', because it contains a blind corner, where bag snatchers lurk and jump out on unwary passers-by.

Through the tunnel, on the left, stands Barnes Station: a Gothic folly with its four mulberry red chimneys. Turning right, you plunge into a chestnut wood, which gives way to more open heathland. Ahead lies a group of splendid houses in the middle of the Common, called Mill Hill.

Turning left towards home, you can either cross Rocks Lane, then bear left over the Lower Richmond Road and follow the route of the first walk home past the Eternal Triangle and Barnes Graveyard, or turn right across the bottom of Peter's Meadow, back into the Yarrow Meadow and home across the grey poplar boundary and the Fair Triangle.

1972

Sunday, February 27th

Tomorrow we move to Putney. Fed up with our smart friends telling us we cannot live south of the river. Go over to the new house to talk to the plumbers. They inevitably don't turn up, so I go upstairs onto the balcony and gaze down Egliston Road – soon to be *our* road. At the bottom lies Putney Common, a glorious stretch of rain-rinsed green. Suddenly out of the gate opposite comes a Thelwell child on a gleaming skewbald pony, followed by a golden retriever. They all set off briskly towards the Common. Putney seems to combine the best of both town and country. Feel convinced we are right to move. Make momentous decision to get a dog.

Saturday, July 22nd

Drive down to Maidstone to collect new English setter puppy. He has a black patch over one eye, and is beautifully marked like a baby seal. I fall totally in love with him, which is a good thing, as he is sick fifteen times on the way home.

The minicab driver sits behind the wheel phlegmatically peeling off one page of the *Sporting Life* after another and handing them to me in the back. Having exhausted the *Sporting Life*, he starts on the *Daily Mirror*. Despite this early setback, the puppy perks up the moment he gets home, and endears himself to everyone. He is to be called 'Smith'.

Thursday, August 10th

We all dote on the new puppy, but have gone off the name Smith. Everyone calls him 'Puppy' which is ludicrous, as he is getting larger every day.

Tuesday, October 10th

Puppy still called 'Puppy'. Together we have started exploring the delights of Putney Common. The only problem is that he will not come when he is called. Hardly surprising when he hasn't got a name yet.

Thursday, November 2nd

Puppy is finally named 'Maidstone'. Nervous of his escaping across Queen's Ride and the Lower Richmond Road, which are both main roads, I walk with him on the lead half-way down the Big Common past Putney Hospital and the bowling green before letting him loose. He promptly rushes off and plunges into Beverley Brook. Fortunately it isn't deep, but he emerges with thick black stockings of mud, like a tart, and whisks about, refusing to be caught.

Suddenly a tight-lipped woman with a Persil-washed West Highland terrier puppy on a long training lead comes over the hill. Scenting sport, Maidstone flattens. Imagining a little dog, the West Highland puppy approaches until she is nose to nose with Maidstone, who promptly rears up to his full height and pounces. The Westie screams her head off. Maidstone gets inextricably caught up in the long training lead. By the time he is extracted the Westie is also thickly covered in black mud.

Her tight-lipped mistress is understandably incensed. Can I not control my dog, she snaps; don't I realise that setters need proper training, and stalks off.

1973

Friday, February 23rd

An exquisite morning. Notice crimson blur on the five tallest elm trees on the north side of Beverley Brook. On closer examination, I am enchanted to discover the blur is made up of tiny rose-pink flowers. Maidstone takes advantage of my studying nature to vanish. I comb the Common yelling. He is nowhere to be seen. In the end, as I have a *Sunday Times* piece to finish by the afternoon, I give up in despair and go home.

On the doorstep, I find the Persil-white West Highland terrier and her owner, who, I have discovered, is called Rachel. She has brought Maidstone home, using her mackintosh belt as a lead.

'How dare you let your dog roam the streets?!' she says furiously, her face twitching like milk coming up to the boil. 'What happens if a lorry swerves to avoid him and crashes into another car, or mounts the pavement and knocks down a little kiddie?'

Escape inside the house muttering apologies and feeling deeply depressed. I know it is entirely my fault Maidstone is so ungovernable, and that, instead of working out the plots of novels and brooding on the beauties of nature, I should spend my time on the Common training him to sit and walk to heel. But as the children are only four and one and three quarters, and neither of them is yet at school, the din at home is so frightful that the only time I get to think seems to be on the Common.

Tuesday, June 12th

Woken up by Maidstone licking my face, which means he wants to go out. I put on my dressing-gown and take him out into the garden. The birds are singing their heads off, the roses brim with rain from a recent storm. Maidstone, perfidious creature, takes advantage of my Wordsworthian reverie to escape through a hole in the fence, and, dodging the milkman and the postman, who make valiant attempts to stop him, is now hell bent for the Common. I chase him, trying to keep my dressing-gown within the bounds of decency. People walking their dogs look at me incredulously. Naturally I bump into Rachel. Such is her disapproval, I am forced into telling the frightful lie that I've actually been up for hours, writing. Finally I corner Maidstone in a neighbour's garden, where he is giving heart attacks to two hamsters in a cage.

By the time I get home, my Irish housekeeper who comes in daily has arrived and been told Maidstone has broken down the fence again. Muttering and armed with hammer and nails, she goes off into the garden.

Later, as it is quite hot, I take my typewriter into the garden. Maidstone buries an old pork chop he had found in the dustbin. My Irish housekeeper has now mended the fence; it looks like some sort of *objet trouvé* – nailed-on orange boxes, prams and the remains of an old typewriter blocking up the holes. Maidstone inspects it with interest; I suspect he's working on a book on great escapes. Any moment, he'll have all our cats vaulting over a wooden horse.

Just as I am leaving for lunch, my Irish housekeeper screams that Maidstone has bashed the fence down again. We all surge out onto the Common, including the mini-cab driver who's come to collect me, and finally corner him under a plane tree.

Later I arrive home from lunch to find six children having tea. The din is hideous. My Irish housekeeper informs me proudly that Emily, who is nearly two, has just spoken her first full sentence.

'What is it?' I ask.

23

'Puppy get out on the Common,' replies my Irish housekeeper.

Saturday, December 8th

Maidstone is now eighteen months. Utterly devoted to him, but cannot pretend his behaviour is improving with age. He is still impossible to catch if he doesn't choose.

Today I receive a delightful letter from a fellow setter owner, who says all setters are deaf on a walk. The only answer is to go out on the downs, lie down on the heather and enjoy the larks singing, and wait for your setter to exhaust himself. He will then come back. Feel this is impractical in the middle of winter in Putney when the main roads and Rachel are so near.

1974

Tuesday, February 12th

Two years ago, just before we moved to Putney, I left 50,000
words of a novel about show jumping behind on a bus after a
drunken lunch. I hadn't taken a carbon and I never got the 50,000
words back. So great was the trauma that only now do I feel able to
start re-writing it. As all the main characters in the novel live in the
country, I need to get the rural details right. I will look an idiot if I
have my hero chasing through a field of cow parsley in the middle of
winter. Since I have so much time on my hands when I go out,
waiting for Maidstone to come back, in future I am going to take a
notebook and a pen onto the Common every day, so that I can jot
down the changes in the seasons.

Today I notice once again the rosy blur on the five tallest elms
along Beverley Brook which I noticed last year. Thank God it
means spring is on the way. Also coltsfoot is out, a sudden explosion
of sulphur yellow, on the second hillock by the football pitch.

Thursday, March 21st

Take Maidstone out at dusk. In the copse near Barnes
Graveyard a hawthorn is putting out leaves like tiny green flames.

Down by the Brook, I find the first yellow celandine on the bank. Above, the starlings are gathering in my five beloved elms, blackening them against a soft lilac sky. In and out and round about the starlings wheel, with a high-pitched buzz, that can be heard for miles around. Maidstone runs down to the Brook, and gazes up at them with his mouth open and his speckled head on one side.

Thursday, March 28th

Creeping cold and damp. Yellow crocuses, like blackbirds' bills, and mud-splattered daffodils are out in Barnes Graveyard. The blackthorn is also out, and looks as though its sooty branches have been dipped in flour. Coke tins litter the ground after the mild weekend. Maidstone charges about, guzzling chip paper.

'Don't you ever feed him?' asks Rachel as she passes me. When she is not biting my head off, she assumes an arch, slightly hectoring manner, like someone out of *The Archers*.

I have discovered her dog is called Bridie, and that she is the highly efficient part-time secretary of a local solicitor. She is about forty, with a blonde curly perm, blue eyes and flicked-up spectacles. She has the permanently discontented, beady look of a baby bird whose mother is late with the worm.

Monday, April 1st

Very warm – out without a jersey for the first time. Notice the poplars by the bowling green are thickening with scarlet catkins and bronze leaves. All the young greens are so beautiful: the saffron of the oaks, the buff of the planes, the pale jade of the willows, the acid green of the limes, and the darker inky green of my five lovely elms. But most beautiful of all is a pear tree in one of the back gardens of Lower Common South, which I can see from my study, moonlit green just before dawn, or dancing in the noon sunshine, its white garlanded arms rising and falling.

The blackthorn is already over and the colour of old lace. Progress round the Common is very slow, as Maidstone keeps getting plugged into vole holes.

Saturday, April 6th

Dandelions and coltsfoot already have clock heads. And cow

26

parsley is swathing Beverley Brook with white. The pink flowers on the elms have been supplanted by new acid-green papery flowers with crimson hearts. On studying my tree book, however, I discover that these paper flowers are actually the fruits of the elm – and the equivalent of acorns on an oak tree, or sycamore keys.

Friday, April 12th

Very cold. Along the banks of Beverley Brook, the east wind is scattering the papery green elm fruits like confetti. Notice they are heart-shaped with tiny rose-pink centres. The hawthorn is about to flower, white buds rise from each branch like tiny clusters of balloons.

Today the Common is deserted except for a girl with a Peke. She seems to wander aimlessly. Approaching closer, I find she is dark and extraordinarily beautiful, with huge haunted, violet-ringed eyes. She starts, seems about to speak, then runs away.

I am reminded of Ezra Pound:

> She would like someone to speak to her,
> And is almost afraid that I will commit that indiscretion.

Wednesday, April 24th

Birds are nesting – each tree is a noisy green musical box. Today I bump into the beauty with the Peke a second time. I admire the Peke. She says he is called Michelin, because of his rolls of loose skin. Walking on the Common with another person is rather like having one's hair washed, or sitting behind a taxi driver: there is no eye contact, so people tend to talk about themselves more than they would normally.

The beauty, whose name is Rosie, tells me she split up from her solid reliable husband a year ago, to run off with a handsome lover, who was starting up a garden centre. The garden centre was a flop, all the plants died and so did their passion for one another. Now she lives in a pretty flat off the Upper Richmond Road, with no one pretty to put in it.

She says she is working for a degree in physics at London University. Find this hard to believe, like one of those claims made by prospective Miss Worlds, or nudes in *Playboy*, that their chief

interests are archaeology and Japanese court poetry. But there is a vulnerability about her that is very appealing.

On the way home, Maidstone and I pass a single blue suede glove hanging forlornly from the wire fence surrounding the Common ranger's hut. It reminds me of Rosie – no good without a partner.

Tuesday, April 30th

Exquisite day. Every chestnut candle blazing. The hawthorn blossom is out at last, exploding like white-hot stars from a rocket. Charmed by the piping of birds in every tree, mare's-tails are pushing up their snaky heads all over the Flower Garden. The newly mown Hillocks are a dazzling white-green in the sun, with the tracks of the mower disappearing into the inky-blue shadows cast by my five elms. A very late game of football is being played on the football pitch. A starling keeps imitating the referee's whistle. Maidstone is running everywhere after it. Wish he reacted to my summons with such alacrity.

Wednesday, May 1st

The Fair has arrived, and is set up as usual on the triangle of grass lying in the fork of Queen's Ride and Lower Richmond Road.

The scarlet and yellow merry-go-rounds, and the pink and hyacinth-blue turret of the helter-skelter rise out of the angelic spring-green trees like a fairy city.

Thursday, May 2nd

Torrential rain. Hellish, hellish morning, searching for Maidstone. In the end, Patty, my kind next-door-neighbour drives me round Putney looking for him. We finally track him down at the Fair. He is not buying a bunch of blue ribbons, but has been laboriously losing his virginity to a plump geriatric ginger bitch. He evidently took forty-seven minutes to do so. All the stallholders had bets on how long he would keep going. Appropriately the youth who mans the Big Dipper came closest. Maidstone is nearly black with rain and exhaustion. When he gets home, he sleeps for the rest of the day. Perhaps sex is the answer.

Saturday, May 11th

Sex is not the answer. Yesterday, Maidstone bashed another hole in Patty's fence, dug up some carefully tended regalia lilies, then chased Patty's cat back into the house through the cat door, and got stuck. Extracting himself, he brought the entire cat door with him, and charged around the garden, cat flap flying, like a galvanised sandwich-board man.

Sunday, May 12th

With the warm weather, the season of sleeping out has begun on the Common. Every night visiting tramps stretch out on the vaults in Barnes Graveyard. Pursuing Maidstone, I discover Rachel clicking her tongue over a splendid orgy that must have occurred last night. A copy of *The Sunday Times* is spread as bedding under a great holm oak, and on a nearby grave lie two chewed raw onions, a ball of yellow wool, an empty bottle of VP wine and a suspender belt.

'Disgusting,' snorts Rachel, then adds that she can't understand why I cannot catch Maidstone, when she finds it so easy.

Refrain from replying that in his new Lothario role, Maidstone is determined to seduce Bridie, who never leaves Rachel's heels – so now he doesn't either.

Monday, May 13th

A splendid row has broken out over the Common. In the middle of this perfect spring, the gas board has suddenly decided to lay a huge pipe, under Barnes Common, the Flower Garden, the two Hillocks, Beverley Brook, and down to the Thames. A big red crane already hangs like a malignant stork over my five tall elms. Today the workmen moved their bulldozers in, crashing through speedwell, buttercups and cow parsley, knocking down little hawthorns and oak trees in their green prime.

Even though I've only been walking on this Common for eighteen months, I feel all the outrage of a mother whose child has been raped. The workmen – who are Irish – come in for a lot of flak from the dog walkers, particularly Rachel, who seems to regard them as additionally responsible for all the troubles in Northern Ireland. Every time she passes them a flurry of 'Disgusting's or 'Trust the I R A's fall from her pursed lips.

Tuesday, May 14th

Walk with Rosie, who says she has been mugging up on the quantum theory, the meaning of which she tries but fails to explain to me. Say that I'm too cross about the bulldozers to concentrate. Rosie says gas boards don't even have to get planning permission. It's like *Alice in Wonderland*. Action first, permission afterwards.

Wednesday, May 15th

Out on the Common, I find all the Irish work-force in a high state of dudgeon. All their bulldozers have been wrecked by an overnight saboteur. Work will be held up at least a week.

Sunday, May 19th

Bulldozers still inoperative. Meet Rosie. She asks me with a smirk if I've noticed anything odd about the bulldozers. Then confesses she was the saboteur. On Friday, she crept out at twilight with wire cutters. Jolly brave of her, considering the bulldozers are parked on the edge of Barnes Graveyard, which is not only reputed to be haunted but always swarming at night with undesirables.

Suddenly, she says, she fell in with a posse of thugs, full of beer and bad intent, who were shambling towards the Graveyard, hell-bent on bashing up the stone angels. Catching the eye of the leader, Rosie asked him if he had any idea how to immobilise a bulldozer.

After several 'Yer wot's, the penny dropped, and, seizing the wire cutters, the youth led his troops on the three bulldozers. A good time ripping out wires was had by all – no one bothered to bash up the stone angels that night and everyone, including Michelin, the Peke, ended up in the pub.

I am so impressed by Rosie's daring, that I ask her to dinner next week, rashly promising that I will find a delicious man for her.

Monday, May 20th

Out on the Common, an Irish workman tells me that, on account of the vandalisation of bulldozers, the pipeline will be diverted round rest of the hawthorn copse. Highly delighted, but wish I could think of a delicious man for Rosie.

Sunday, May 26th

Spare man proving most elusive. Perhaps it's the weather, and the lush bosky greenness outside, but all the spare men I know seem suddenly to have got hitched up. They'd all love to come to dinner but can they bring Caroline/Fiona/Georgina/Rowena? The result is a colossal dinner party, but, alas, no one for Rosie.

In despair, I telephone an impossibly good-looking, jet-setting art dealer, who has such an exquisite house in the Boltons that I'm convinced he must be queer. By some miracle, he happens to be in London and is delighted to come. Perhaps Rosie can detach one of the single men from Caroline, Fiona, Georgina or Rowena.

Tuesday, May 28th

Disastrous dinner party. Jet-setting art dealer takes no interest in Rosie, who is looking stunning. He leaves early. Everyone else stays until three o'clock in the morning until we run out of drink. Feel I have utterly failed as Cupid.

Out on the Common holding my aching head together. Notice the trees are changing, the acid-green variations of spring are giving way to the uniform dark green of high summer. Next minute Rosie bounces up saying thank you for a super evening and a frightful hangover. I say I'm sorry about the art dealer.

'He was perfect,' says Rosie in surprise. 'He took my telephone number in the first five minutes, so we didn't have to bother to talk to each other for the rest of the evening, and he's taking me out on Thursday night.'

Add cautiously that I still suspect he may be queer.

Friday, May 31st

Dying to find out how Rosie got on with the art dealer. Walk out on the Common, slap into Rachel in her most belligerent mood. Maidstone, she says, broke into her neighbour's garden yesterday and leapt on her cocker spaniel bitch who is 'in season'. Rachel's lecture is fortunately cut short by Rosie, who has black rings under her eyes.

'How was last night?' I ask.

'I went to a lecture on Rutherford,' says Rosie firmly.

'But I thought. . . .' I blurt out.

'It was excellent,' Rosie goes on, and proceeds to describe a lecture in such abstruse detail, that eventually Rachel stalks off to examine the progress of the wild roses on the Flower Garden.

'I'm not going to let that cow know what I'm up to,' says Rosie. 'Now about last night. Your art dealer friend is definitely not gay.'

Evidently he took her back to dine at his exquisite house, and her suspicions about his masculinity were aroused not only by the perfectly arranged flowers, but also because he cooked new potatoes dripping in mint and butter, but never touched one. Nor did he touch her – all evening – until, positively beady with desire, she started picking on him. Whereupon he told her not to be a bloody bitch. She was about to flounce out of his exquisite house (without the taxi money home) when he gathered up all eight stone of her, carried her upstairs without panting, threw her on his Jacobean four-poster, and took her, added Rosie with a shiver of delight, most gloriously.

As bonus points, Rosie goes on, he didn't even bat an eyelid when he had to drive her home afterwards, because she doesn't like leaving Michelin alone all night. Feel I have played Cupid with consummate skill.

Ahead we see Rachel, making Bridie sit for five seconds, before they cross the Lower Richmond Road. I ask Rosie if she knows anything about Rachel's home life.

'Three children and a husband called Alastair who thinks he married down because he went to a minor public school,' says Rosie. 'Alastair has great charm but doesn't believe a gentleman should work, so he spends his time walking round his estate, which in his case is a three-bedroomed house off the Upper Richmond Road, which leaves him unoccupied and under Rachel's feet for most of the day. Rachel was once very pretty, but is now soured with life's vicissitudes. They are evidently very poor.'

Feel I must be nicer to Rachel in future.

Saturday, June 1st

Dull, gentle, sweaty day. Young bracken is uncurling under the trees in the squirrel wood. Wild roses are out on the Flower Garden. Dotted pale pink over the bushes, they hang like faded rosettes in a tackroom. Also find knapweed, and clover, and bird's-foot trefoil, known as 'bacon and eggs', because of its orange and yellow flowers. Just trying to describe a bank of fat white cumulus clouds gathered above Rocks Lane, when Henrietta sails into view.

Henrietta lives in one of the big houses in Egliston Road. A Virginia Wolverine with a long, pale predatory face and light brown hair drawn back in a bun, she has great organising ability, and considers herself very well bred. Her husband, Ned, who is a stockbroker, always insists on telling everybody that Henrietta was a Wilson-Twickenham before he married her. Henrietta insists on telling everybody that Ned never stops talking in bed. She is very clever, with a second in English, but chooses to stay at home discontentedly, and bring up her five pale, tremendously clever children. If she hadn't made such sacrifices for Ned and the children, she is fond of implying, she would by now be editing *The Times Literary Supplement* or writing definitive biographies. I suspect that, if put to the test, she wouldn't have come up with the goods. People who can write a book usually do.

As with Rachel, I think her bitchiness stems from deep unhappiness. One is reminded of Browning – a 'bitter heart that bides its time and bites' – but this doesn't make her jibes any less painful. Because she has read somewhere that it is good for children to be

33

brought up with animals, she owns a depressed field spaniel called Lady Glencora, after the Trollope heroine, who is walked on the Common about once a fortnight. Today Henrietta is trailing Lady Glencora, and two of her pale children (who always bury their faces in her crutch when one speaks to them).

'What are you writing down in that notebook?' she demands.

I reply brightly that I am studying cloud formations.

'Isn't there going to be too much weather in your novel?' asks Henrietta.

She then goes on to say that she is thinking of buying a horse and stabling it near Ham Common. Why don't I buy a half-share in it, then I can have first-hand experience of horses, which would be far more useful to my novel than rabbiting on about cloud formations?

Mutter that I'll think about it, but that with producing *Sunday Times* pieces every other week, as well as the novel, I don't think I'll have time for a horse.

'What are you working on for *The Sunday Times*?' she asks.

'A piece on housework,' I reply.

'But you never do any,' says Henrietta with a snort of derision.

Gritting my teeth, I break off a plantain.

'Oh look,' I add, admiring its domed brown head with the Saturn ring of white seeds, 'It looks like Lord Longford.'

Henrietta snorts with more derisive laughter, and, putting on a broad West Country accent, says: 'Aaaaaaah, this way they be known as Lard Larngfords.'

Resist temptation to push her into a wild rose bush.

Sunday, June 2nd

White valerian flowering by Dogger Bank. Despite its rather boring exterior it has a beautiful smell – mignonette crossed with wild roses. Along Beverley Brook, I notice young emerald green dock leaves growing by a bed of nettles. Reflect that people can be divided into nettles and docks. Nettles sting and provoke you, like Rachel and Henrietta. Patty, my dear next-door-neighbour, and Rosie, on the other hand, are both docks, because they're soothing, kind, and always leave you feeling happier after five minutes in their company.

Monday, June 10th

Patty once more proves that she is definitely a dock. This morning Maidstone took a running jump at her patched-up fence, landing sideways on all fours. Next minute thirty feet of fence collapsed, flattening my gentle neighbour's newly planted herbaceous plants. Having made our gardens open plan, Maidstone proceeded to disinter several guinea pigs and rabbits which were buried at the bottom of the garden. I wish the gas board would give him a job digging trenches for the pipeline; I'm sure he would be infinitely quicker than the bulldozers.

Over several drinks in the evening, Leo and I promise Patty we will instal new fence to contain Maidstone.

Thursday, June 13th

Lovely walk with Emily. It is her third birthday today, and her pace round the Common is about as slow as Maidstone's. We blow dandelion clocks, and look for the two pairs of fairies' shoes, which lie neatly together under the lid of the white dead-nettle flower.

Emily's favourite games, however, are to wash 'the Lady', and put flowers in the Fairies' Swimming Pool. 'The Lady' is the lovely bronze of a woman's profile set in a broken-off tombstone, lying in the long grass on the edge of Barnes Graveyard. The lady's name is Maria Kathleen Ayoub. According to the tombstone, the bronze was cast by her husband, an artist who outlived her by twenty-five years. She has a fine, long-suffering face, not unlike a kind Henrietta. I always have the fantasy that she was one of those high-principled Edwardian ladies, married on impulse to this talented but feckless Middle-Eastern gentleman, who gave her a hard time when she was alive, but missed her when she died.

Rain-water often gathers in the hollows of the bronze. Emily likes to wash Maria Kathleen's face with it, then give her a muffler of grass or leaves to keep her warm – although she hardly needs keeping warm in this weather.

Our other ritual is to float flowers in the Fairies' Swimming Pool, which is a six-inch hollow in the fork of the huge holm oak on the south of the Graveyard. In wet weather it fills up and overflows like a rain gauge. Today we float two white dog daisies in the pool.

Thursday, June 20th

Rosie is still madly in love with her art dealer. He appears to have given up jet-setting in favour of staying in London and sleeping with Rosie. It's so sweet, she says, the way he folds up both his clothes and her clothes before getting into bed.

Monday, July 1st

The Common has reached the tatty stage when it needs sun. All the long grasses are turning yellow. Lime tree wings litter the churchyard. Emily and I collect some today and float them in the Fairies' Swimming Pool, in case the Fairies need spare pairs.

Thursday, July 4th

Oh dear, oh dear. Leo went off to the country to play cricket today. I went to a local party, and drank too much wine on no breakfast, then Henrietta asked me back to lunch. She always makes me feel such a lousy and superficial writer, and after three hours in her company, she really convinced me that part-owning a horse would be the only way of bringing authenticity to my show-jumping novel.

In the afternoon we went to see a charming chestnut gelding and I was horrified to hear myself saying what fun it would be to buy him.

Now back home I am feeling depressed and deeply apprehensive. When will I have time to exercise and look after a horse every day? I can't afford it, and he's bound to bash the stable door down like Maidstone with the fence and cavort all over Ham Common. Darling Leo returns from cricket. I confess that I have given Henrietta the impression I will buy a half-share in the horse.

'Well, you'll get the back half,' says Leo. 'Ring her at once and say you can't.

Telephone Henrietta. Can tell she's absolutely livid.

Five minutes later she is on the doorstep trailing five pale children and Lady Glencora. Leo answers the door and blocks Henrietta's entrance. She insists on having it out with me.

'Well you can't,' says Leo.

'Well fuck you,' says Henrietta, all in front of the pale children, Lady Glencora and Maidstone, and storms off.

Sunday, July 7th

After sleepless night, I spend the day not answering the telephone. Alas, the perfidious Maidstone keeps escaping through the hole in Patty's fence, always along Egliston Road, so I have to crawl after him on my hands and knees in front of Henrietta's house, so that she won't see me over her wall.

Monday, July 8th

Crawling on my hands and knees after Maidstone, I go slap into Rachel's stockinged kneecaps. If she's so broke, I think irritably, why doesn't she wear trousers and save on the expense of tights?

'What *are* you doing? she demands.

'Going to Canossa,' I mutter

Wednesday, July 10th

Beautiful warm day. My five elms arch in the sunlight like dark green paperweights. Sorrel, rusted the colour of dried blood, stabs the cool green, newly mown Hillocks like murderers' daggers. Why do poplars always shiver – even in high summer? Meet Rosie who tells me that Henrietta has bought the horse with another Putney housewife. They have found livery stables near Richmond Park, and the horse is to be called Phineas, after the Trollope hero.

Monday, July 15th

Solid new fence is installed between our garden and Patty's. It is both hideous and hideously expensive. Take Maidstone out to admire it. Within minutes, he has bounded onto the rubbish heap, and is tightroping gaily along the wall at the bottom of our garden. Now he looks into neighbouring gardens, with the triumphant air of some mountaineer who has scaled the peak, can see into five counties and is making up his mind which to drop into. He chooses a garden on the far left and lands on a lot of rhubarb, to the outraged shrieks of the garden's sunbathing owner.

Monday, August 5th

Very depressed. The moment we finish impregnably barricading off Maidstone's access to the rubbish heap and the back wall he starts examining the fence on the left-hand side of the garden, trampling down clematis and plants at 50p a throw. We go out on the Common not speaking. Maidstone chases butterflies and gets covered in burrs.

It is extraordinary how our attitude has changed towards the Irish workmen on the Common. Over the past months, we have become firm friends, they always talk to the children, and help me catch Maidstone. One of them who drives a gas board van has even become my admirer. He has a squint, brushed-forward black hair and a fund of stories about previous conquests. As he sweats round the Common after me, reeking of Brut, he keeps saying: 'Why are you so scruffy, Jill? I cannot understand why you're so scruffy.'

He might be echoing Rachel.

Today he tells me that last night he scored with a barmaid who had nipples which stuck out like acorns. Feel he may have taken the simile from the acorns which are already crunching underfoot at the entrance to the Flower Garden.

On the way home, I meet Henrietta's husband coming home from the City. To my relief, he is very matey.

'You're well out of it,' he says gloomily. 'Phineas has already tossed Henrietta off fifteen times,' which sounds most dubious.

Saturday, August 10th

Go out early on the Common. I am accosted by Old Dick, a local stalwart, who winter and summer wears a black beret like an onion man, and who lovingly tends the garden round the ranger's hut. Today he gives me a bunch of yellow roses, and asks me if I'm coming to the meeting tomorrow.

When I look blank, he says the Putney Improvement Society, backed up by the local cricket club, are planning to build a second cricket pitch on the Big Common. Tomorrow at the local Methodist hall, the Improvement Society will reveal the findings of their working party. Dick is dead against another cricket pitch, and says he needs my support.

Sunday, August 11th

Leo and I attend meeting in the Methodist hall, together with assorted dog walkers, including Rosie, Rachel, and Henrietta, who has brought along her daily woman, Mrs Bond. Henrietta nods frostily at me and Leo. Sitting beyond Henrietta are Old Dick in his black beret breathing fire, and Ken, the ranger of Putney Common, a charming, gentle, blond young man, who dropped out of advertising, and who now spends his time watching out for flashers, picking up litter on the Common and mediating between the dog walkers. Presumably he will now be expected to look after a second cricket pitch as well.

Also present, but sitting on the other side of the hall, are a depressed-looking curate, representatives from the Scouts, a militant lobby from the local cricket club, and a posse of vigorous lady botanists. Leo and I are not speaking to one another because he is supporting the local cricket club, and is in favour of a second pitch.

Feelings run high, as a handsome grey-haired man with a commanding manner, looking not unlike Gary Cooper, gets up onto the platform. 'That's Judge Hamilton – high Tory,' snorts Henrietta, disapprovingly.

Judge Hamilton then outlines the proposals of the Putney Improvement Society's working party.

After a preamble on how the working party was set up, which sends Mrs Bond, Henrietta's daily woman, fast asleep, the Judge produces a map of Putney Common.

Pointing with a stick to the two Hillocks south of Beverley Brook, he says: 'We feel there is much room for improvement here, for more interesting trees and shrubs to give the area an appearance of natural beauty as on Barnes Common.'

This is a red rag to a bulldozer. There is colossal rivalry between the two Commons, and although Putney Common may lack the rather stylised lushness of Barnes Common, no one who has seen the sun slanting on the newly mown Hillocks or my beloved five elms rising out of the Brook could call the area deficient in natural beauty.

Judge Hamilton's stick then passes over the lovely green stretch of the Big Common, rumoured to be the site of the second pitch.

'Now this area,' he says with deep cunning, 'could never become an area of natural beauty.' He then becomes as lyrical as Edmund Blunden: 'But what better sight here than lots of people in white flannels playing cricket?'

'And losing matches,' chorus the dog walkers.

He then points to the section of the first Common next to the church.

'Nor is there any facility for young people to play football. A properly laid out football pitch for boys – and if necessary for girls,' he adds hastily, 'is a reasonable thing.'

He then proceeds to stun the meeting by saying the working party intend to turn the Common into a sports arena, with not merely a new cricket pitch, but two football pitches, a putting green, and two kiddies' adventure playgrounds.

'There'll be balls everywhere,' says Henrietta in a ringing voice.

'Bloody Wembley,' shouts Rosie.

A coffee break follows. Cabals gather in every corner muttering furiously. For once Rachel, Henrietta, Rosie and I are on the same side. After the interval the fun becomes fast and furious.

Now it is the turn of the residents of the adjacent flats to kick up a fuss about the noise from the proposed Kiddies' Adventure

Playgrounds. A bright spark suggests putting the Adventure Playground near Beverley Brook so it won't disturb anyone.

'Won't the kiddies drown in the Brook?' asks an anxious mother.

'Not the sort of children we have in mind,' says Judge Hamilton blandly.

'Inflatable ones,' mutters Leo.

With feelings running high, we move on to the cricket pitch.

'Why do the cricket club need a second cricket pitch?' asks Rosie.

Because, she is told, the clubhouse (which everyone else in Putney calls the 'Ut) is too far away from the present pitch, and it means that the little colts have to cross dangerous roads to get to it.

'They'll be allowing horses on the Common soon,' snaps Rachel, earning a filthy look from Henrietta, who is obviously hoping to be tossed off by Phineas nearer home.

'Why not move the 'Ut then?' suggests Rosie.

'The reason they want a pitch near the 'Ut,' says Old Dick, 'is because they drink so much Red Barrel beforehand, they don't like to have to run across two main roads every time they go to the toilet.'

Rousing cheers all round, counterpointed by loud snores from Mrs Bond. Someone then asks Judge Hamilton to show how far the proposed playgrounds and pitch will reach. To howls of derision, he draws two minute football pitches, and a tiny cricket pitch.

'A mouse could hit a six on that,' says Leo, who appears to be changing sides.

'And there's plenty of room for a hockey pitch in the middle,' adds the Judge with a placating laugh.

The audience gaze at him stonily.

Mrs Bond, having been nudged sharply in the ribs by Henrietta, wakes up suddenly, and says: 'Let's get up a partition.'

'Let's have a vote,' yells Old Dick.

Judge Hamilton then says quickly that it isn't the aim of the meeting to have a vote, and that the working party's proposals will be put to the Conservators, who run Putney and Wimbledon Commons, in the autumn.

'But how will the Conservators know the strength of the opposition unless we vote?' protests Henrietta.

Judge Hamilton shrugs.

'Then what was the point of our coming here?' demands Rachel indignantly.

'I don't really know,' says the Judge.

The meeting breaks up in disarray. Walk home with Rosie who says her art dealer has given her a Picasso drawing.

Tuesday, August 20th

Having written a piece for *The Sunday Times*, describing the protest meeting, I have become the temporary heroine of the dog walkers, and particularly Old Dick, who talks to me over the netting every time I pass, and offers me bunches of roses, or whatever is blooming in the ranger's garden. Today he offers me a huge marrow. Ask if I can collect it on the way back.

I am just admiring a clump of toadflax by the football pitch, with its lovely orange and yellow snapdragon flowers, when I see Judge Hamilton striding across the Common, no doubt to re-examine Putney's lack of natural beauties. I should have kept the marrow for protection. Bolt to safety into the Flower Garden, where the pipeline has been laid and covered over with earth. Notice dandelions are already growing over it. Nothing is indestructible. Pondering on mortality, I encounter an old lady in a pork pie hat and an orange wig, with a face as wrinkled as a dried-up river bed.

She tells me she was once a newspaper columnist: admired, controversial and widely read. Now in old age, she is bored, friendless and alone. Wonder, with a shiver, if this will be my fate.

Saturday, October 5th

So busy finishing a book that I haven't kept my diary for weeks. Out on the Common, the bracken ranges from hot red setter red to pale gold to labrador yellow. Chestnut leaves are much more systematic. They go brown round the outside first, then gradually the rust creeps inwards.

Everything looks glorious. I am delighted to hear from Old Dick that Judge Hamilton's plans to turn the Common into a sports arena have been scrapped.

In the afternoon, I walk with Emily. We cover the Lady with little gold oval-shaped acacia leaves. The Fairies' Swimming Pool is overflowing. Fill it with sycamore keys.

Friday, October 25th

Go out in vile temper. The children's Nanny, who replaced my Irish housekeeper a year ago, announced yesterday that today she was going for an interview for another job – in Leicester of all places. Today, to add injury to injury, she commandeered the services of the gardener (who only comes for two hours a week anyway) to drive her to Paddington, leaving me with a *Sunday Times* piece to finish, and two children to amuse. Find myself shouting a great deal.

Take the children out on the Common and shout some more. We take the path between the tennis courts and Barnes Graveyard, and I feel very ashamed when I read a tombstone, engraved with the words:

> Jane Selwyn, died 1889 – her children shall rise up
> and call her blessed. Her husband, also he praiseth her.

Very much doubt if the stone masons will chisel such a flattering epitaph on my tombstone and make a big effort to be nice.

Eventually cheered up, first by the beauty of the day. A soft west wind is turning all the leaves inside out. Leaves, on the ground, curl up like brandy snaps. Rain has stripped away the down from the thistles. Conkers litter the ground like Paynes Poppets.

Then Felix picks up a very spiky conker husk, and says: 'You're going to find a big prick in your bed, tonight, Mummy.'

Returning home, however, I work up new rage against incumbent Nanny for leaving me in the lurch. I'll give her several pieces of my mind for annexing the gardener.

Later she returns with a bunch of freesias, saying it was a bloody job and she doesn't want it at all. Feel so relieved, I decide not to mention annexing of gardener.

Monday, October 28th

Notice poplars keep their top leaves longest – as though their nails were painted with gold – but limes lose their top leaves first. A bare lime is an unruly ugly tree, spiky like Fuzzypeg or Struwwelpeter. The poplar, on the other hand, stripped, dancing and pale silver in the half light, is a thing of frenzied, naked, decadent beauty. Pondering on beauty, I bump into Rosie, who looks a bit sheepish. I ask after her art dealer. She says he's fine, but she does wish he wouldn't fold up their clothes every time he climbs into bed. It's getting on her nerves.

Thursday, October 31st

Deeply irritated to get telephone call from Rosie's art dealer. Poor Rosie has 'flu, and can't have lunch with him, could I possibly pop down to the shops and take her some roses and some grapes, and give her his love? Wonder crossly why he can't ring Interflora, and why everyone thinks writers don't work. Discover grapes are £2 a pound, and roses a good deal more. Wonder even more unworthily if I'll ever get my money back.

Go round to Rosie's and bang on the door. She answers it, reeking of scent, obviously just about to go out, and flushed not with 'flu but embarrassment. Sourly I give her grapes, roses and the art dealer's love. She looks sheepish, but also bursting with the desire to impart information. Then she admits she has gone off the art dealer – it's *so* boring and predictable to have someone who always rings and arrives on time. She has fallen madly in love with a doctor. Married? I ask. Yes, sighs Rosie, but utter bliss.

I suppose now the Picasso drawing will become the victim of a broken home.

Sunday, December 1st

Have just finished a great jag of writing. Endless rain for a fortnight has turned the Common into the Great Lakes. It is very beautiful. Misty grey skies reflected in sheets of water. Raindrops gleam on the flat clover leaves. Halfway down the path by the tennis courts, one of my favourite trees, a huge muscular chestnut, soars bronze and drenched as though it has been hewn by Michelangelo.

On the other side of the Graveyard, I meet an old lady called Mrs Woodward. She is eighty but still most attractive. She has a charming cairn bitch, who is being hotly pursued by a wonderfully vulgar mongrel with a smooth brindle coat, greyhound ears, and a curly tail. He has a jaunty battle-scarred face, and the outwardly relaxed air of the competent sexual operator.

Mrs Woodward says in her youth, those kinds of mongrels were called 'butcher's dogs' because they always followed the butcher's van. I said at home we'd always called them tight-skinned-curly-tails.

Her one terror in life, Mrs Woodward says, is that her little cairn will outlive her and be alone.

Tuesday, December 10th

Maidstone escapes yet again. Discover him fornicating joyfully on the Big Common with the brindle butcher's dog. Rachel, as disapproving as ever, tells me the butcher's dog lives in one of the council flats on the Ranelagh Estate beyond the bowling green. He is called Rex, known locally as 'Sexy Rexy', and always out making a nuisance of himself.

Thursday, December 12th

I don't know who is more in love: Rosie with her married doctor, or Maidstone with Sexy Rexy. Have the feeling that both liaisons will end in tears.

Today I go on *Desert Island Discs* with Roy Plomley. He is an enchanting man, like a little elf, and an inspired listener. We have lunch first, and discover we both live in Putney. I drink wine, he doesn't. Afterwards the programme goes splendidly, and we get fearful giggles, mentioning Putney as often as we possibly can, in the hope that we can push the value of houses up.

Wednesday, December 25th

Our Happy Christmas is not helped by Maidstone escaping through the left-hand fence, because Leo and I are cooking Christmas lunch, and have not yet had time to take him for a walk. He stays out for four hours – longer than ever before. We are all desperate. At two in the afternoon, we decide to go ahead and open our presents, but it is all hopeless. Every present opened – a doll for Emily, a space ship for Felix, a silk scarf for me – has a card with 'Love from Maidstone' inside it. Emily, Felix and I are all crying when the telephone rings. I pounce on it. It is from a call box, and misfires twice. Finally a voice asks:

'Have you lost a 'uge grey spaniel?'

'Oh yes,' I squawk, making frantic thumbs up signs to Leo and the children.

'Where is he?'

'In Roehampton,' says the voice.

'That's three miles away,' I think in horror.

''E don't seem to want to come home,' the voice goes on. ''E's 'ad a turkey dinner, and he ate everything except the sprouts.'

Leo sets off grimly to collect Maidstone, and says we shall have to put up a new fence on the left side.

1975

Wednesday, January 1st

Fearful hangover after New Year's Eve party. Not in the most together mood to take Maidstone for a walk. Meet Rosie, and remark how pretty she's looking.

'That's because I'm still wearing last night's make-up,' she says.

The Common is ridiculously muddy, like the Glutton's Circle in Dante's Inferno. As we squelch through the damp leaves and the puddles, I ask after her married doctor. She replies that her New Year's resolution is to give him up because he is so unreliable. He never rings or turns up on time. I say my New Year's resolution is to lose weight and control Maidstone better.

Maidstone meanwhile has streaked across the Big Common and is infuriating an old lady by barking noisily at her Yorkshire terrier. Whenever I get near him, he bounces away, grinning like Tommy Brock. By the time I catch him, I am pouring with sweat and feel I am fulfilling the first part of my New Year's resolution, if not the latter.

Saturday, January 4th

It must be the mildest winter for years. Crocuses and forsythia are out in the garden. The elder is putting out tiny olive-green leaves. Little green cow parsleys and docks are already pushing their way through the dead leaves along the Brook, and the trees have a spring-like blur softening their branches. The oaks, on the other hand, are still clinging onto last year's pale brown leaves. Is it this – rather than its vast girth – that makes the oak tree a symbol of strength and tenacity?

Sexy Rexy, the brindle butcher's dog, accompanies us on our walk. I adore him but I wish he wouldn't always choose the moment Rachel passes to leap on Maidstone. At least, so engaged, Maidstone doesn't pound on Bridie.

See patch of young green nettles, and vow to come out tomorrow with a pair of stout gloves and pick them to make nettle spinach, as my mother did in the war. I vow to do this every year. I wish everything would slow down. I like spring to come gradually, blossom by blossom, so you can savour it. Rosie's married doctor obviously thinks it's spring too. I see him emerging from a taxi outside her house, entirely hidden by a vast bunch of flowers.

Friday, January 10th

The weather is still ludicrously mild. Stalks and twigs litter the ground like the charred matchsticks round the gas fire in a slut's flat. Birds are singing, everything is mating and budding. Suddenly remembering that a writer should listen as well as look, I shut my eyes, hearing the dull roar of the traffic, the caw of rooks, the 'tack tack tack' warning note of the blackbirds, sounding against the counterpoint of Maidstone's great bass-baritone bark after the squirrels. When I open my eyes, Maidstone has vanished. I call and call, I scale the Common, but he is nowhere to be seen.

Spend fruitless day trying to work when not looking for Maidstone. At 4.30 Barnes Police Station rings; they have Maidstone and he is 'whining somefink horrible': will I go and collect him?

I order a minicab, and the driver turns up with a very clean car, and becomes very tight-lipped when I say that we have to collect a dog. At the police station, I am handed a piece of paper, which says:

'For Rest of dog: 12p.'

Think for a horrible moment I am about to be handed Maidstone's truncated paws and head, but suddenly hear low moans

49

from bowels of police station. Realise to my relief that 'Rest' is short for 'restitution' and pay my 12p. Maidstone is brought out, and goes into noisy ecstasy, as though finding me had been the only thought in his mind all day. He is covered in mud. The station officer says he can see he's my dog. The minicab driver is even more tight-lipped when Maidstone lolls all over him on the way home.

Thursday, January 16th

The pipeline is laid at last. Perhaps now the Common can get back to normal. One of the most disgraceful abuses of rate-payers' money is that, having spent thousands of pounds building a bridge over Beverley Brook, so that the people of Putney can walk along the path skirting Barn Elms playing field down to the Thames, the authorities have promptly closed and boarded up the bridge – in case dogs get loose on the playing fields. Bloody silly – do they honestly think Maidstone is going to take up hockey or football?

Friday, January 17th

I speak too soon. Maidstone crosses Beverley Brook like Leander and, dripping black mud, joins in a hockey match, to the delighted shrieks of the girls, and the apoplectic whistling of the games mistress.

Sexy Rexy and I hide behind a white poplar until Maidstone catches up with us.

Have long talk in the evening with Leo. He feels Maidstone is probably lonely and might settle down if we got another dog.

Tuesday, January 28th

Go to All Scents School (as Felix calls it) to drop him off. Notice a charming little brown mongrel on a lead. He has a smooth coat and huge black-ringed worried eyes and is very like Sexy Rexy. When I bend down to stroke him he wags his tail like mad and jumps up.

'What a sweet dog,' I say.

'I can't bear to look at him,' says the owner. 'He's going to Battersea Dogs' Home this afternoon.'

When I express my horror, she explains that the little mongrel was found hanging by wire from a tree when he was a puppy. A gang of louts had tried to stage an execution. After that he came to live with her. He is neurotically dependent on her now, howls the house down whenever she goes out to work, and all the neighbours are complaining. 'I know it's nice for kiddies to be brought up with animals,' she goes on, 'but he's too much.'

'I might have him,' I say. 'I'll just have to ask my husband first.'

Leo is incensed when I ring up:

'Why, when you have five cats, a depressed goldfish, and one setter who is totally out of control, do you want to add to your problems?' he says.

There follows a long, long pause.

Then he says: 'I shall be extremely annoyed if that dog isn't waiting for me at home when I get back this evening. He is to be called Fortnum.'

In the afternoon, Fortnum arrives plus a basket, an orange and blue knitted blanket and two rag dolls.

'He'll howl for hours when I go,' says his mistress. 'If you can't cope, ring me up, and I'll collect him and take him to the Dogs' Home.'

In fact, Fortnum whines for thirty seconds, then settles in at once and spends the rest of the afternoon rampaging up and down the stairs with Maidstone.

The children are enchanted by him, and Leo returning from the office says: 'Good God! That dog looks just like my first wife.'

I am thrilled to have our own butcher's dog.

Wednesday, January 29th

We are a two-dog family. Set out for Common in extreme trepidation. I had hoped to emulate Diana of the Uplands, the beautiful blonde in the painting in perfect control of four borzois on leads, but feel I look more like a superannuated maypole. My hair keeps falling over my eyes, and because I am holding two leads I cannot brush it back. Feel doggy and unglamorous, and imagine motorists crawling along Lower Richmond Road thinking: 'When women reach a certain age, they resort to dogs rather than men.'

On the credit side, Fortnum is extremely good. What a blissful novelty it is to have a dog that comes when he's called! In fact, he gets so worried when he can't see both Maidstone and me at the same time, he rushes off, and rounds Maidstone up, which rather inhibits the squirrel hunting.

On the way home, I run slap into Rachel, who demands why I am walking someone else's dog. Is it a stray I have picked up on the Common? Reply proudly that it is our latest acquisition. Rachel is not amused. Why get another dog, when I can't control one, she snorts, and why a mongrel? Why not? I say, and stalk off. Waste the rest of the morning thinking up brilliant replies.

Saturday, February 8th

Lovely walk with 'the dogs' (how I enjoy writing that!). Find clump of snowdrops to the west of Barnes Graveyard. The ground is still carpeted with last year's leaves, soft as Andrex after the recent rain. Daffodils, chickweed, and red dead-nettle are all coming out. Fortnum is a little duck, we all dote on him, he's so good. He is learning to lift his leg and keeps practising on trees when he thinks no one is looking.

Tuesday, February 11th

Bump into Dorothy, a fellow dog walker, with Thomas, her ancient collie – they are a stately pair. Thomas refuses to romp with Fortnum and Maidstone. He is like Childe Harold:

> 'I stood
> Among them, but not of them; in a shroud
> Of thoughts which were not their thoughts.'

Thomas, Dorothy always says, has 'inner resources'. Today she has binoculars for bird-watching hanging from her neck, and points out the green woodpecker in a chestnut tree. I pretend to see it but do not. One cannot go on saying 'Where, where?' for ever.

Maidstone is devoted to Dorothy because she gives him Spillers Shapes from her coat pocket, and has often brought him home with the crook of her walking-stick round his collar.

Saturday, February 15th

On Oedipus Corner, fat golden celandines with their watercress leaves, are pushing through the carpet of plane leaves. The osiers

on the corner of the football pitch are putting out fluffy silver buds, like a poor man's pussy willow.

Wednesday, February 19th

Heavenly afternoon on Common. Hawthorn and blackthorn are already beginning to come out. Last year the blackthorn didn't bloom until March 28th and the hawthorn was a month later. Ivy along Barnes Graveyard wall is putting out new acid-green leaves, the old ones are veined like a good steak. Crocuses are losing their blackbird's beak shape, and are opening up like trumpets. Some are the most glorious Lenten purple with fizzy orange sherbert stamens. Others are aubergine, striped with white. What gaudy, glamorous flowers they are!

The snowdrops are nearly over. With their white lop-eared petals hanging over a green underskirt trimmed with white, they are the perfect model for a Christopher Wray lamp.

On my way home I meet Cedric, our local telly star, looking very handsome. Wish I'd bothered to put on make-up before coming out. Stand with my back to the sun. He tells me he went to dinner at the Palace last night, met Tom Stoppard and Eamonn Andrews there, and had long talks with the Queen Mother, and Princess Anne, who were both extremely friendly.

What was nice, he went on, was the feeling that everyone was so grand you didn't have to ask them back.

Saturday, February 22nd

Very tiresome house guest staying. Emily and I escape to the Common, and are enjoying ourselves singing nursery rhymes and blowing dandelion clocks, when house guest comes pounding after us saying: 'Why didn't you wait for me, and why is Leo so irritable these days? Is your marriage going through a bad patch?'

Cannot explain Leo's irritability is entirely due to tiresome house guest, and mutter about pressure of work.

Emily, livid at being deprived of my undivided attention, gets understandably whinier and whinier.

'Why are your children so spoilt?' asks house guest.

Wednesday, March 5th

On the boundary of Barnes and Putney Common the blackthorn is still out, and, to the north-west of Barnes Graveyard, a lovely clump of rosemary is putting out the most exquisite flowers – tiny smoky-blue snapdragons, delicately striped with purple. What a perfect combination for a Harvie and Hudson shirt. The grass on the edge of the Eternal Triangle is being mown for the first time. Fortnum inhales deeply and rolls ecstatically in the grass mowings, then finds an old tramp's coat, and tows it round the Graveyard. On the way back, I break off a spray of blackthorn; the petals are already falling. Feeling how transient life is, I go home and put moisturiser on my neck for the first time.

Worried because Maidstone is so listless, and beginning to limp a lot. Perhaps it is too much romping with Fortnum.

Friday, March 14th

Maidstone no better, and shrieks if I touch his left back leg. I take him to see our vet, Mr Findlay, known locally as Dr Findlay, because he is Scottish, and because the rival vet a few streets away is called Dr Cameron.

'What I like about Dr Findlay,' says an old lady clutching a Peke in the waiting room, 'is that he remembers all the dogs' Christian names.'

Sure enough, as we go into the surgery, Dr Findlay says:

'Hullo Maidstone, you've grown into a lovely setter.'

Resist temptation to say it would have been hard for him to grow into a Peke. The smile is wiped off my face, when Dr Findlay looks at Maidstone, and says he's ninety-nine per cent certain he's got hip displacia. Some vets recommend putting a dog down at once, Dr Findlay goes on, but he doesn't believe in that, as there are lots of ways to relieve the pain.

I gaze at him uncomprehendingly. Then ask if hip displacia could have anything to do with his rough-housing with Fortnum.

Dr Findlay says this may have exacerbated the condition but that it's a breeding defect in which the hip-bone is deformed, and won't fix into the socket. He takes Maidstone off for an X-ray, gives him an injection and some painkillers, and says he'll let me know the result of the X-ray tomorrow. I cry all the way home, where

Fortnum is hysterically pleased to see us. Retreat to my study, where I cry all afternoon and fail to write my piece for the paper.

Later we have to go out to dinner. Our hostess, who has a consummate lack of tact, says she knows all about displaced hips.

'The wicked thing,' she goes on, 'is when people try and keep their dogs alive. One sees them in the park, shuffling along on their front legs, their pathetic back legs supported on wheels.'

Unable to stop crying all evening.

Saturday, March 15th

Wake at ten with blinding migraine. Darling Leo has taken the children to the office. Steel myself to ring up the vet, who says Maidstone's definitely got hip displacia on one side, but it's not acute yet, and to go and see him next week when the pills have had time to work.

Take both dogs on Common, and sob all the way round as I remember how gloriously naughty and wild Maidstone had once been and notice how closely he trails me now, terrified of being buffeted by other dogs. To cheer us up, Fortnum discovers a red bra in Barnes Graveyard, and runs round the Squirrel Wood with it.

Go home and give Maidstone his painkiller, not an easy task. He spits it out when it is wrapped in salami, or buried in a piece of cheese, and only accepts it in a piece of steak. I also discover last night's pill embedded in his neck.

Monday, March 17th

Wake feeling suicidal about Maidstone. I suppose he's my third child.

Friday, March 21st

Blizzard and slight fall of snow. Oh the poor unprotected flowers! The Common looks black and white, like a scraperboard picture. London children, unaccustomed to snow, run screaming down to All Scents School trying to catch the flakes on their tongues. The little girl who lives opposite comes out in a fur hood and socks as white as the pavements, and makes a snowball out of the snow on the bonnet of her father's eternally clean car.

Out on the Big Common, the wind is like a saw, the sleek green buds of the sycamore have shot out leaves like frilled fans – I bet they wished they'd stayed inside. The green parachutes of the chestnuts hang limp and miserable like dresses in a sale.

I tug at a loose piece of bark on a plane tree. It comes away. Underneath I find two ladybirds and a spider. Feel like a murderer. Before I can replace the wall of their house, Fortnum picks up the piece of bark, and bounds off merrily. I examine an acacia I see in Barnes Graveyard. The ribbed trunk is like a bar of Cadbury's Flake; the twigs have no buds, there is no suggestion it will ever flower again. It is as uncompromising as the fig tree, whose branches hang like lank, grey hair over Putney Hospital wall.

Sunday, March 30th

Easter – usual choc-in. Emily comes for a walk and says 'Flappy Oyster' to everyone she meets. Rosie took her to the zoo yesterday. Emily tells me she saw lots of animals: 'Giraffes, lions, gorillas and Germans.' (Can she mean gerbils?)

Friday, April 4th

Maidstone's hip is very bad. I pray it is caused by the continued wet weather. He is very frail, and not his usual bouncing self at all. He is even reluctant to go out for walks, and, after being bitten by an Alsatian on the first Common today, insists on going straight home.

Thursday, April 17th

Magical day. Speedwells out on the Hillocks, opening their blue eyes wide to the sun. The sycamore fans are turning into little bronze parachutes. The great elms along the Brook are dotted with green leaves, and papery green heart-shaped fruits. The ash is coming out at last, flowers like dark crimson broccoli forcing their way out of the black sooty-hoof buds. Barnes Graveyard is filled with bluebells.

Sunday, April 20th

Lovely walk with Felix and Emily. The fourth house along Lower Common South has a new roof, pale coral in lovely contrast to a dazzling white cherry in the garden. Firs are the trees of Christmas, white cherries are the trees of Easter. Nothing illustrates so perfectly the flaunting, hauntingly beautiful evanescence of the spring.

On the tennis courts, overweight players with pale legs pant their way through the first game of the season.

By the Eternal Triangle, we meet a naughty red setter, enjoying the sunshine, and showing no desire to go back to his house in Briar Walk. We take him home. With typical setter dumbness and enthusiasm, he looks eager and sniffs in excited recognition at every house we pass on the way.

Monday, April 21st

Meet Cedric, our local television star, looking bronzed, having just returned from filming in Egypt. He tells me the pyramids are four times higher than the great plane trees around the First Common.

'Really?' I say, then, as an elderly English setter lopes purposefully after a rotund female bulldog, 'Oh look! There's Maidstone's double.'

'Really?' says Cedric.

Feel we are not really on net today.

Friday, April 25th

We all forget Maidstone's birthday. Just as well, perhaps, we don't know little Fortnum's date of birth, and it would be unfair to celebrate one without the other. Happily the warmer dryer weather has brought dramatic improvements to Maidstone's hip.

Heavenly day; spring has galloped forward apace. Seven days of hot sun have brought out the limes round the churchyard. The little brown chestnut candles tremble, waiting to be lit; the planes have now put out pale khaki leaves shaped like angels' wings. The grass is lush and shiny and catches the white light like a Persian cat's fur.

Much to the delight of Ken, the Putney Common ranger, the football pitch, which belongs to rival Richmond council, has been mown too early. As a result, two huge muddy grooves have been dug out from one end of the perfect green to the other.

Meet Henrietta on the way home. Feel deeply irritated because she has acquired a horse box for Phineas, and parked it outside our house for six weeks

Wednesday, April 30th

Beverley Brooks is all white and bridal, choked with new cow parsley. A man on the opposite bank is examining my five beloved elms. To my horror, he tells me they are all dying of Dutch elm disease, and will soon have to come down. On closer examination, I see several of the branches are dead and not putting out green leaves any more. Feel desperately upset, and ask him how long he thinks they'll last.

He shrugs his shoulders, and says perhaps a year, perhaps more, but in the end all the elms along the Brook will have to come down.

Thursday, May 1st

The Fair has started arriving. Cars are already parked on the Fair Triangle, which divides the first Common and the Big Common. Notice they are mostly BMW's and Mercedes, although the Fair people say business is terrible. Unfortunately, the Fair affects Felix exactly in the same way bitches on heat affect Maidstone.

Saturday, May 3rd

Take both the children to the Fair. Emily goes on the little train roundabout and, whirling by in her fur coat with her brilliant blue eyes, and delicately flushed cheeks, she reminds me of Anna Karenina. Later, she wins a mug with Piccadilly Circus on it, a popcorn bracelet and a poster of the Mona Lisa wearing too much lipstick. Felix wins a set of Lucozade-coloured Bambis and a china Alsatian at darts, which he says will look nice in the drawing room. He also wins five goldfish. I wish fairs would make goldfish more difficult to win; they probably hate cleaning them out as much as I do. See Cedric, our local telly star, intently watching the terrified, hysterically giggling faces of the people whirling around on one of the more fearsome roundabouts. Everyone else is intently watching Cedric.

All the Fair people ask after Maidstone, remembering the time last year when he lost his virginity to one of the old fairground bitches.

'We always feel he enjoys the Fair more than the children,' they say.

As we are leaving, I look up and see Henrietta going round on the big wheel, eating an apple, and sitting next to one of her children, who is paler than usual and with its hand clamped over its eyes. Next minute an apple core lands on my head. Wonder if it's deliberate, but feel that Henrietta is far too Bloomsbury to have played cricket at school.

Saturday, May 24th

The Fair is still here, bankrupting everyone and bringing what Mrs Bond calls 'vine-dals' to the area. The vine-dals have pulled up saplings, broken off tulips, trampled all over people's gardens, and, worst of all, peed on Rachel's privet hedge. The retired Brigadier, who lives in the same road as Rachel, suggests wiring the hedge up to give the young shavers a shock.

Wish the vine-dals would turn their attention to Henrietta's horse box, which is still parked outside our house. Try to tell myself that it's perfectly all right for her to put her wretched horse box there; it's not in anyone's way, but do not feel convinced.

Jolly dinner party at home that evening. Rosie turns up with her married doctor. They are so bats about each other, I feel terribly glad I don't know the doctor's wife. He brings a bottle of gin, which I tuck into. About midnight, everything becomes crystal clear and I know what I must do. Cackling with laughter, I pick up my new Dior lipstick, which is very dark crimson and bought to be fashionable, but which I shall never wear because it doesn't suit me. Then I rush into the street with it and write fearful obscenities all over Henrietta's horse box.

Sunday, May 25th

Wake next morning with frightful hangover. Jump out of my skin as I remember to my horror what I did last night. Henrietta will be incensed. She might think it's vine-dals; however, on the other hand she knows my writing, if not my lipstick. Put on Leo's dressing gown – rush out with Vim and a bucket of water, and frantically scrub off obscenities as the bells toll down the road for early service. Just rubbing the 'F' off the last obscenity, as the vicar passes on the way to church.

Trying to get back into the house, I find I am locked out. No one can hear me. Leo, fed up with droppers-in, has ripped out the door bell wire. Even when I go round the back and throw up stones, he won't come downstairs, because I am wearing his dressing gown. In the end, he lets me in, holding a flannel as a figleaf. He is *very very* cross with me.

Sunday, June 1st

The Fair is gone, leaving no trace behind, apart from a few cars stuck in the mud on the Fair Triangle, and (in our case) a full tank of dying goldfish. By some miracle, Henrietta appears not to have found out about the obscenities.

Monday, June 2nd

Heavenly day. Birds' voices singing joyously out of the new green anonymity of the leaves. Hawthorn blossom already turning brown, although its sweet soapy smell still hangs on the air. A glorious clump of cow parsley to the east of Barnes Graveyard is now as tall as me, a great white lacey mass with the sun on it, a table laid for the butterflies. Beyond, the acacia is at last putting out little acid-yellow feathers. And on the plane trees, new little scarlet bobbles hang beside last year's old bobbles, which look like tiny curled up hedgehogs. From the undergrowth of Putney Graveyard comes the strangulated clockwork whirr of the resident pheasant.

Friday, June 6th

Lilac and laburnum are over. The Common is being mown. This means my shoes are always full of grass mowings, which means grass seeds all over the carpet when I get home. The elder flowers hang like lace doilies over the matt green leaves. Today is referendum day for the Common Market. All the passion and patriotism seem to have evaporated as the day approached, and England sank into her usual apathy. Someone has put a 'Yes to Europe' sticker on a tombstone. Audrey, a fellow dog walker, is deeply shocked because I laugh. I suppose the poor thing is too recently widowed to appreciate jokes about death.

Saturday, June 7th

I'm glad we appear to be into Europe. Rachel is livid. Why should we want to associate with all those foreigners? she says. The clump of cow parsley near Barnes Graveyard is Jeremy Fisher green now.

Sunday, June 8th

Very, very hot. You can hear the buzz of insects, the soporific pat of tennis balls. A man in an ill-cut shiny suit stands motionless with his nose to the tennis wire, hands deeply in his pockets, watching a pretty girl serving in a very short tennis dress.

In the long grass, which is drying in tawny swathes on the Yarrow Meadow, homosexuals without gardens raise pale freckled shoulders to the sun and eye one another speculatively.

Friday, June 13th

Emily's fourth birthday. When we sang 'Happy Birthday', Maidstone lay on the floor and thumped his tail in time. Emily comes for a walk with me, and says she is going to call her new gollywog Sally. I suppose so many women these days wear striped trousers and bow ties that she can be forgiven the mistake.

Meet Mrs Bond. Her fat mongrel, Scamp, accepts Maidstone's advances philosophically.

Mrs Bond says she's fed up with her daughter who leaves a rim of hairs round the bath every time she delapidates her legs and armpits.

Saturday, July 5th

Go for another walk with Emily. Maidstone disappears into Putney Hospital. He is chased round the wards by a yapping Fortnum, me, a delightedly shrieking Emily and about fifty furious officials in white coats. The dying and people on drips rise up in horror to have a look. We corner Maidstone in the kidney department. Feel I could cope with him better if he ever showed an ounce of contrition.

Sunday, July 6th

It is very warm today with a tearing wind. My five elms creak rheumatically, which can't be doing them any good. Pink and white Himalayan balsam flowers are coming out along the Brook, with their thin necks and strange heavy orchid insect faces. Also find spiky teasel with its little purple flowers. On the Flower Garden, the flat hogweed flowerheads are polka-dotted with ladybirds.

Tuesday, July 29th

Get up very early: heartbreakingly beautiful morning – the sun at ten degrees is a glittering disc. The trees are dark bottle green now against the yellow grass. The small pink striped flowers of the convolvulus that creeps along the ground are shut up like parasols. Blackberries are still harsh and rude, but like Lycidas, people have already come to pluck them. It is a bit creepy so early in the morning. Quite pleased to scuttle past the pink ramparts of the willow herb lining the Flower Garden onto the Big Common where one can be seen from the Lower Richmond Road.

Suddenly I jump out of my skin as a man pounds past in pink

satin shorts. Maidstone watches him with his mouth open, Fortnum gives chase for the hell of it.

'I'm training for the Olympics,' screams the runner. 'If one of those dogs takes a bite out of me I'll sue you.'

Saturday, August 9th

This has been the worst nine days of my life. Felix has been in hospital very very ill with meningitis. I went in with him and slept, or rather didn't sleep, in the next-door room. Even now when they claim he is out of danger, I cannot quite believe it. How do parents who have chronically ill children ever survive? Today, I have come back from hospital for the first time to see Emily and take her for a walk. The weather has been impossibly hot for the past fortnight, but last night it rained heavily, and the Common, refreshed, appears green and radiant, like a girl in love who has just received a long-delayed telephone call from a feckless boyfriend. On closer examination, however, I find the nettles are yellowing, the sorrels rusting, willow herb is growing whiskery, and the thistles are a mass of kapok.

Emily says: 'If Felix dies, will he go to heaven?'

I say: 'Of course he will, but he *won't* die.'

Emily bursts into noisy sobs: 'Then I'll never see him again, because I'm so naughty, I know I'll go to hell.'

I try to comfort her, saying that Felix is fine, and hell doesn't exist anyway. Emily says she doesn't believe in heaven either, because she's been up in an aeroplane and she didn't see it.

Going back home, I discover that the twelve-bottle special offer of wine sent by *The Sunday Times* for me to drink and write about has been consumed by Leo and the Nanny while they were worrying about Felix. I am therefore forced to ring up the paper and, stammering my apologies and standing on one leg, ask for a second crate.

Monday, August 11th

Felix definitely out of danger. Not so sure about me. Out on the Common with blinding hangover, after having consumed with some chums the second instalment of the twelve bottles sent by *The Sunday Times*.

On reflection, they were quite disgusting.

Friday, August 15th

Felix coming home today. I am so excited that I am not the least put out when *The Sunday Times* ring up and say they cannot possibly publish my piece about their special wine offer because it is far too derogatory. Later the editor rings up, and says he cannot understand my attitude, as he always serves the special offer wine at his dinner parties.

Arriving at the hospital to collect Felix, I find Pandora, a delicious and talented local author, has turned up to visit him. She is wearing boots and breeches after a ride in Richmond Park and has brought a bottle of elderberry wine, made from berries picked on the Common. Together we finish the bottle: it is excellent, and certainly ought to be put on special offer by *The Sunday Times*. A boot-faced matron later discharges the three of us from hospital for making too much noise and disturbing the other patients.

Wednesday, August 20th

Felix well enough to walk on the Common with me and Emily. Maidstone behaving atrociously and careering across main roads.

Felix [*sternly*]: 'If you let my dog get run over you'll be in trouble.'

Emily [*philosophically*]: 'No she won't, the dog will be in trouble.'

Friday, October 17th

Haven't written my diary for weeks. I've been *so* busy finishing a book. Notice white campion still out along the Brook. In the Squirrel Wood, the trees are thinning so you can see thick white rays of the sun drifting down through the gaps. A pile of leaves lies waiting to be burned by the tennis courts. To arrest the process, Maidstone and Fortnum lift their legs on it.

Worried by a rather sinister development in Fortnum's character. His devotion to Maidstone has started manifesting itself in extreme possessiveness. He now sees off any male dog friends who stop to pass the time of day. Today for example, Sexy Rexy, the butcher's dog from the council estate, came bouncing up, and he and Maidstone greeted each other with every show of delight. The next moment Fortnum emerged like a bullet from behind a haw-thorn tree, and fell on Sexy Rexy. A nasty fight ensued, with Sexy Rexy getting the worst of it, retreating at a brisk trot, and breaking into a gallop when he reached the Flower Garden. Feel very sad; Sexy Rexy was very much a Common-enhancer and I shall miss his company.

Saturday, October 18th

I have started walking earlier in the morning to avoid dog fights, which means I sadly miss Rosie but happily see less of Rachel and Henrietta.

The acacia on the north-east of the Graveyard is still bluey-green, but tinfoil shavings of leaves on the ground below show it is moulting too. Squirrels scatter as we walk through the Squirrel Wood. Each year I look forward to a view to the north of the Flower Garden, where above the pale blond grasses, and the amethyst Michaelmas daisies, my five lovely golding elms rise like the entwined masts of ships in a harbour. Is there any chance they will last for another autumn? On the Fair Triangle, where the trees are always ahead, a maple is blazing crimson and the sycamores are brilliant amber.

Monday, October 20th

Felix is conker crazy. He has collected nearly 200 now, and has a special stick for bringing them down. He and his pals spend all day hurling these sticks into the chestnuts along Lower Common South. If another child moves onto their patch, they express all the outrage of gentlemen coming out of their clubs in St James's Street, and being pipped at the post for a taxi.

Saturday, November 1st

Worried about Fortnum's increased belligerence. He is starting to pick fights with any male dog he meets (regardless of whether it's a mate of Maidstone's) except Rosie's Peke Michelin. Even worse, he is egging Maidstone on to join in. Together they make a formidable duo. Understandably there are unpleasant anti-Cooper mutterings from owners of male dogs. Today, symbolic of their mood, there has been a hard frost. The grass is still white and sparkling when I walk with Emily in the afternoon. Notice sycamores, stripped of their leaves are a frenzy of bent twigs, as though they've received electric shock treatment.

Sunday, November 2nd

Walk with Felix. Birds sing sweetly in the liquid rain-soaked air. Middle-aged men in track suits play vigorous tennis. Always notice particularly vigorous male four who play every week, one of them is very bald with spectacles. Have been told they are a foursome of doctors from Weybridge, which seems highly improbable, as surely they could find somewhere nearer to play? Am I imagining it, or do they play more vigorously as I pass?

The chestnut avenue flanking Putney Cemetery is stripped of leaves and rain-black – 'Bare ruined choirs where late the sweet birds sang.'

Just admiring golden light flickering through a thinning sycamore, when Felix says: 'Matthew Roberts can't climb ropes because his willy is too big.'

Thursday, November 6th

Grass full of rockets and squibs after Guy Fawkes Day. Leaves damp and brilliantly coloured after rain. Everything dripping. On the south side of Barnes Graveyard, the poplar which is surrounded by small squat oak trees, has lost all its leaves. It shivers in the icy wind like a stripper dancing orgiastically for a group of stolid Northern businessmen. Notice that sycamore and oak leaves turn grey when they fall, poplar leaves turn black, elm leaves turn from yellow to mahogany. The fallen sycamore leaves, however, are brightened by cherry-red stalks. Leaves are caught up in the gorse bushes, the holly, the nettle beds and in the wire fence around the tennis courts. At this time of year, says our gardener, he dreams of leaves.

Monday, November 10th

Particularly beautiful thundery grey day. Boiling cauldron of sun breaks through the clouds. Emily and I rustle round the Common. Entertain her with story of how my grandfather was going home one autumn evening at twilight when an old woman shuffled past. It was only after she'd passed him that he realised she made no rustling sound in the leaves; whipping round, he discovered she had completely vanished – there was no sign of her in the long straight road behind him. Emily makes me tell the story over and over again. Bitterly reproach myself – I'm sure it will give her nightmares.

Friday, November 14th

Ravishing moody day. All the red and gold is on the ground now, except for the oaks and the sycamores. Each tree has its pool of colour underneath – like a spotlight.

Barnes Graveyard is being swept up by Richmond council workers, a group of unionised sourpusses, who grumble continually about dog turds, saying dogs shouldn't be allowed.

Mrs Woodward, the saintly eighty-one-year-old, who is still beautiful and who owns a little cairn, completely defuses their wrath by sitting them all down on a vault, handing round toffees and telling them what pleasure a dog gives to old people. On my way back twenty minutes later, they are all still chatting to her.

Saturday, November 15th

Golden elm leaves are clogging the dark water of Beverley Brook. They are so beautiful. Understand exactly why Jupiter managed to seduce Danaë when he turned into a shower of gold. It is quite ridiculous that the bridge across the Brook is still closed to the public.

Monday, December 1st

Henrietta is in a high state of bossiness. She and some other local worthies have started a Society for the Preservation of Rural Putney, which she already refers to pompously as the SPRP. They are holding their first meeting in the augustly named 'Function Room', of the Spencer Arms by the bus stop.

Henrietta buttonholes me in the street, and asks if I'll say a few words at the beginning telling people what a good idea the Society is, and encouraging them to join. Wetly say yes.

Friday, December 15th

Waste a whole day writing 'few words', to which Leo makes several last-minute alterations. Arrive to find the Function Room packed. Make absolute cock-up of speech, because I'm horribly nervous and can't decipher Leo's writing, and because the whole spiel is punctuated by a fat woman in the front row who's been drinking and keeps very perceptively crying 'Roobish.'

Cedric chairs the meeting. Despite all his expertise in handling current affairs programmes on television and keeping rival politicians from each other's throats, he cannot prevent the meeting degenerating into a frightful squawking match between the vicar, who wants to build modern flats in the churchyard, and the local trendies who go into complete hysterics at the thought of the vicar wrecking the environment. Agree passionately with the trendies that flats really would spoil the churchyard and the look of the Common. But also feel very sorry for the vicar, who is very good-looking, despite a tendency to wear white polo-necked jerseys (I suppose it's the nearest casual thing he can get to a dog collar). He desperarately needs the money to run All Saints' Church, and understandably gets fed up with dogs-in-the-manger like me who

69

seldom go to church, but scream like hell if a hair of the churchyard is touched.

Saturday, December 6th

Dreadful day on the Common. Fortnum fights with everything including a Yorkshire terrier, a greyhound who has to have four stitches, a King Charles spaniel and finally a border terrier. Next moment, a fat castrated golden retriever comes round the corner, Maidstone leaps on him, and starts fornicating briskly, to the outraged screams of the retriever's owner, who lays about Maidstone with her condensed umbrella. Her screams redouble when Maidstone takes no notice. At this juncture, Fortnum drops the border terrier and gathering up an old French letter rushes up to Maidstone yelling encouragement.

Suddenly a woman with an iron-grey bun rises out of the sycamore saplings, fierce as ten furies, terrible as hell: 'I know you, Jilly,' she bellows. 'Everyone on the Common is fed up with you. You and your dogs are a menace. I am Mrs Norman Potter.'

I drag Maidstone off, and pull him, protesting bitterly, all the way back to the Lower Richmond Road, whereupon the lead breaks, and Maidstone hurtles back into the fray. When I get back, Mrs Norman Potter, whom I don't remember ever meeting, is talking about lodging a complaint, and having Maidstone muzzled. I'm sure Fortnum and I will join the vicar – on the local blacklist.

Thursday, December 25th

Fortnum celebrates the birth of our Lord by not having a single fight. Going for a cold but lovely walk with the children, we get onto the subject of God.

'God doesn't make things very well,' grumbles Felix.

'Of course he does, darling,' I say airily, 'look at the beautiful frosty leaves and the trees, and all the flowers in summer.'

'Well he didn't make me very well,' says Felix, 'I can't draw, I can't sing, I can't write or read very well, and I can't run fast.'

'But you make me very very happy,' I say.

1976

Thursday, January 1st

Helicopter buzzing overhead on Common; resist temptation to wave. What a stupid vain fantasy that they might have spotted me and be circling to have a better look! They wouldn't like me anyway with a New Year hangover.

Pass anguished weekend father, obviously groaning with hangover, trying to amuse small boy already blue with cold, by taking him for a walk. 'Only ten o'clock,' one can see the father thinking desperately, 'and how the hell am I going to entertain the little cherub for the rest of the day?' On the way home, the father is carrying both child and bicycle – at least the bicycle isn't bawling its head off.

By the bus shelter, a 22 bus (no doubt also groaning with hangover) has skidded off the road into a plane tree, and is having great difficulty reversing out of the mud. Felix, who's been building a camp in the churchyard, takes his spade over and offers to dig them out. He points out a rather nice matching bra, pants and suspender belt hanging from plane tree.

Thursday, January 8th

A piece written by me appeared in the paper last Sunday, describing Fortnum as the Jaws of Putney, and chronicling the traumas of walking him on the Common. Say I am suffering from Old Bagoraphobia, and Mrs Norman Potter is the leading bag – although I change her name. As a result I am ostracised by practically everyone on the Common, which is lonely, but more restful.

Saturday, January 10th

The politics of the Society for the Preservation of Rural Putney are getting worse and worse. Leo spends his time at meetings at Cedric's house, which are always well attended because everyone likes to drop the fact that they've been there. During the only meeting I attend as well, Henrietta marches up to Leo, and says: 'Why have you been going round Putney saying I'm an interfering bitch?'

'Because you are,' replies Leo calmly.

I hide behind a pillar topped by a large arrangement of dried flowers for the next twenty minutes, but on re-emerging find Leo and Henrietta chatting cheerfully and with great animation. Seems unfair that men can get away with this kind of insult, but if I make the mildest crack, I am ostracised by everyone on the Common.

Sunday, January 11th

Elections for the establishment of a Rural Putney Preservation Committee are coming up. Heather Harris, a frightful social climber, corners me in the church porch and asks me if I will canvas for her husband, Raymond, to become a member of the committee. He has such an urge to do good in the community, she says.

Forbear to reply that the last time I saw Raymond Harris he was French-kissing Rosie outside Barclays Bank in broad daylight.

Tuesday, January 13th

Go for a walk on the Common: the day is very mild and full of bird song. Fortnum has mini-spat with a Norfolk terrier. 'Is that the famous Jaws of Putney?' says the owner, grabbing the terrier and retreating into the bushes.

Saturday, January 17th

Out very early on Common to avoid dog fights. Cold morning, sun very wisely not bothered to get up yet. The voling season is at its height and Maidstone keeps getting side-tracked. At least when he's plugged into a vole hole, he's not likely to be fighting, but it does mean I never know when he's going to unplug and come pounding over the hill to Fortnum's aid like the US Cavalry.

My five elms look all right in winter, when all the other trees are bare and their sickness is not apparent. Just admiring bare trees reflected in the lovely curve of the Brook, when a white woolly hat comes bobbing over the hill. Friend or foe? Oh dear, very much foe. It is Mrs Norman Potter, striding out with her border terrier, crying: 'Leave, leave, leave!' Irrationally think that if she says 'Leave' a bit faster, it will turn into 'Flea'. I reverse briskly and crouch behind a hawthorn bush with Fortnum on a lead. Alas, perfidious Maidstone hurtles past, face spattered with earth from voling, and jumps joyously on Mrs Potter's border terrier.

Forced to emerge from hiding and catch Maidstone. Whereupon Mrs Potter opens fire, urging me to take both dogs to training classes.

'I am not cruel when I shout "Leave", Jilly. I'll be glad to give you the address in Mortlake of the dog training classes. You have no idea of the joys of having a perfectly trained dog.'

And on and on she goes, her voice rising and rising hysterically, until I say: 'Please go away.'

So she flounces off in a flurry of 'If that's all the thanks I get...'

According to Leo, who knows her husband, the thing that really upset her about the Jaws piece was when I described her as 'a lady with an iron-grey bun,' which makes her sound seventy when she's only about forty-two.

Go round the corner, fortunately with both dogs still on the lead, slap into an old lady, with a Yorkshire terrier, who'd been the recipient of one of Fortnum's attacks in December.

'That's them,' she screams to the empty air. 'Them's the dogs that gave my Sammy fibroids.'

'Them's not,' I say quite reasonably.

'Yes, them is,' she screams back. 'They frightened my Sammy so bad, he came out in fibroids.'

Not a very satisfactory walk.

And as if this wasn't enough, Raymond Harris drops in for a three-hour drink in the evening to bully me into pressing his suit as a committee member. His suit, which is blue, looks far too well pressed already.

Friday, January 23rd

Bitterly cold day. Slight fall of snow – like caster sugar on top of a sponge cake.

In Barnes Graveyard, they are burning a cedar blown down by a recent storm. Fortunately it missed any tombstones. It makes a glorious blaze and smell. Huge red flames make the surrounding air hazy and indistinct, and as the sparks fly upwards, the stone angels seem to be rubbing their eyes. A saw is whirring away, cutting up logs which are all burnt on the fire. The blaze is still going next day: it seems a bit prodigal when O A Ps could have used the logs. One so often sees them with canvas bags gathering twigs and branches for firewood.

Sunday, January 25th

Heavenly frosty morning – every blade of grass etched with white. Playing fields a sheet of silvery green, against the silver grey of the goal posts. Leaves crackle under the feet like cornflakes. On days like this I always think of T.S. Eliot:

> Now the hedgerow is blanched for an hour with
> Transitory blossom,

as hogweed and yarrow, crystallised with frost, appear to flower once more

Meet Alice and Henry and their Irish setter, Leo, his red coat ravishing against the bleached blond grass. Leo used to be a great pal of Maidstone's, before Fortnum came on the scene; now Fortnum won't allow him within fifty yards of Maidstone. I adore Fortnum, but he has divided both Maidstone and me from so many of the dogs and people we love.

Tuesday, January 27th

Monochrome day, rattle of sleet on the leaves. It is the first time

74

I've seen Ken, the Common ranger, wearing a cap as he strides round the Common, with his spiked stick, picking up litter.

Sleet settles on the path, but disappears pepper and salt into the grass. Fortnum slides, utterly camouflaged, through the brown leaves. The rattle of the woodpecker by Barnes Graveyard sounds like chattering teeth. Find I have lost Maidstone, retracing my steps I find him voling frenziedly by the tennis courts, watched eagerly by a robin, in anticipation of worms.

Tuesday, February 10th

Raymond Harris is elected to the Committee. See him walking, for the first time ever, on the Common. He has his hands behind his back like the Duke of Edinburgh, Prince Consort of all he surveys. The *Evening Standard* reports the election, with a large picture of Raymond. Heather Harris, says Rosie, is in a state of orgasm, and has bought at least 200 copies to send out to aunts in New Zealand.

For the next four months, Fortnum's and Maidstone's fighting became so bad that I avoided the Common, and walked along the towpath beside the Thames, in order to give the old bags a chance to cool down. Scenically I find the towpath very dull. It is lined mostly with white poplars. According to Greek myth, the white poplar was black, until Hercules wore a garland of it during his fight with

75

Cerberus, the three-headed dog who guarded the Underworld. Hercules' sweat from the struggle bleached it white. Along the towpath we keep meeting renegade dogs and owners, who've been also banished from the Common for fighting. It's a bit like Devil's Island. Perhaps Fortnum should wear a collar of white poplar to ensure victory over all contenders.

Wednesday, June 16th

Walk down to the off-licence with the dogs. Heavenly sunny day. Horrified to discover the vicar, presumably getting his revenge on the trendies for quashing his plans to build flats in the churchyard, has chosen the worst time of the year to pollard the limes round the church. Shorn of their burgeoning green glory, they stand, hideous truncated hydras. What a disastrous blow for Putney's tourist industry. Only a few years ago, *Harpers and Queen* gave the churchyard a four-star rating as one of *the* outdoor copulation areas in London. With no green privacy the lovers will now all defect to Barnes Common. Feel very sorry for all the birds who were nesting there. The lime tree bower is no longer their prison.

Meet Mrs Bond. She says she can just see the vicar in purple. As far away as posssible she adds.

To irritate me even further, I get home to find a circular from the Society for the Preservation of Rural Putney shoved through our letter box. It informs me that the Society are delighted to announce that they have been able to get a conservation order slapped on all the big Victorian houses in Lower Common South, and the first three houses on the east side of Egliston Road. Notice that the order stops just before our house, but conserves the pebbledash erection next door, known locally as Land Mine Villas because it was bombed and rebuilt during the war. Fail to see why this house and not ours, which is a solid Victorian pile, should be conserved. Deeply suspicious that Henrietta is behind this.

Going into the garden, I find my neighbour, who lives in the middle flat of Land Mine Villas, in a state of high glee. Any minute, he says, he expects the Compulsory Purchase people will be annexing my garden to build on. He meanwhile is intending to charge the public 50p a throw to see over his gladioli. I laugh heartily at his jests, but my heart blackens against Henrietta. Wonder if she could have heard rumours about my covering her horse box with graffiti.

Friday, June 18th

Weather very very dry. Make first tentative sortie on the Common for months. Everyone very friendly. They all assume I've been away – probably inside. Everywhere is very dry from lack of rain. Horseradish is in flower in the centre of the Big Common and over the Hillocks above Beverley Brook. It is very beautiful, like cow parsley, but smells unromantically of Sunday lunch.

One distinct improvement since I've been away is that they've at last opened the bridge across Beverley Brook, and fenced off the Barn Elms playing fields, so you can either turn right and walk down the footpath to the Thames, or turn left and walk along the north side of Beverley Brook. Even more amazing, they have built a second little footbridge upstream, so you can cross over back onto the south side of the Brook and walk up by the football pitch. All this may well have been achieved by Henrietta's persistent lobbying. Feel very slightly less cross with her for not conserving my house.

Although the Brook today is black, stinking and nearly dried up, Maidstone insists on having an extended dip, and emerges filthy and festooned with goosegrass, like an Ophelia who's been given

the kiss of life. Old Dick, who is sitting outside the ranger's hut, says he is very pleased to see me again and picks me a lovely bunch of flowers.

Tuesday, June 22nd

Still terribly hot. The paths are cracking, the grass is turning brown from lack of rain. The acacias have shed their white cascades and little yellow leaves are already dotting the green. The dog daisies are over and scattering petals. The black poplar in the Squirrel Wood is moulting white fluffy drifts everywhere, tarring and feathering nearby hawthorns and silver birches. The chestnuts already have tiny conkers.

I have christened the newly accessible triangle of grass beyond the new footbridge over Beverley Brook. It is to be called Lurker's Paradise, because it is the perfect place to lurk when Fortnum's canine enemies are travelling round the Common. Notice canine enemies also lurk there waiting for us to pass.

Today a man is painting a picture on Lurker's Paradise; everyone stops to admire it. What a good way of attracting attention. It is so hot today that Fortnum, who normally hates water, has a dip in the Brook, then dries himself carefully on the tall blond grasses, south of the new bridge.

Friday, July 2nd

The drought is getting critical. The Common is completely dried out. The chestnuts are dropping leaves as they would in autumn. Only the little pollarded limes round the church are still green and fresh and beautiful, like slender young girls holding up towels to cover their breasts.

Bump into the vicar, and apologise for being beastly about his pollarding in the paper, and say I never realised the trees would grow so quickly.

'Ah,' says the vicar, turning the other cheek, 'You should look before you leap into print.'

Sunday, July 4th

We have all been forbidden to use the hose or the sprinkler in the garden, which means I tear back and forth all morning with buckets and watering cans when I should be working. As a result, our lawn is an oasis of unpatriotic green. I feel guilty when I look at other people's dried-out plots, but our garden is looking so beautiful. The mulberry tree looks as if it might take off any minute and walk towards us in the unreal, hazy trembling heat.

On the Common, I meet an enchanting woman called Mrs Murdoch who drives down from Chelsea every day to walk her two golden retrievers.

'The other night,' she says, 'I couldn't sleep because it was so hot, so I went outside with my cat Fergus, and sat in the garden. Suddenly we were both drenched with water from a next-door-neighbour illicitly sprinkling. Fergus flounced inside. I was grateful for the impromptu shower.'

Saturday, July 10th

Today the Society for the Preservation of Rural Putney is holding its first fête. Leo, who has been ticked off by Henrietta for being apathetic about running the bookstall, wakes up, then pulls the bedclothes over his head, groaning: 'The fêtes are against me.'

Go out to find All Saints' churchyard, in which the fête is being held, is a hive of activity. Henrietta grabs me and says: 'Don't forget you're drawing at 4.30.'

Round the corner I go slap into Raymond Harris, who asks why I haven't got the fête poster up in my window. I escape to the Common. The air is heavy with the sweet peppery smell of privet in flower. Après-Wimbledon enthusiasts are still bashing away on the tennis courts, galvanised out of the usual patball, elastic bands holding back their long sweaty hair. Fortnum has not found any balls this year along the wire fence by the tennis courts. Is this due to inflation, and people keeping track of their balls, or because the drought has discouraged the growth of the normally concealing long grass?

In the afternoon, the fête takes place, engendering a great spirit of togetherness and self-congratulation. A pig whose weight has to be guessed escapes during the afternoon and no doubt loses a lot of weight in a glorious joy-ride up and down the gardens of Lower Common South. Aramis Campbell-Jones, a splendid yellow labrador, lifts his leg three times unnoticed over the bowl in which

79

children are bobbing for apples. Felix and Emily get frightfully excited because they hear there is a 'nearly nude' stall. Henrietta annoys at least five ladies including me by holding up dresses we nobly sacrificed to the 'Nearly New Stall', and screeching:'Who on earth would be seen dead in that?'

She may well be seen dead in something else if she goes on like this.

Rachel sits looking martyred because no one wants to pin the tail on the donkey. Raymond Harris is much in evidence pinching bottoms and distributing largesse as a new committee member. Judge Hamilton, of the rival Putney Improvement Society, who caused such a furore with plans for cricket and football pitches two years ago, rolls up and organises races for the children. All the children defect in the middle of the egg and spoon race to watch Cedric, auctioning novelties at vastly inflated prices by the church door. Felix bids for and acquires a toaster that doesn't work.

Afterwards, I am overjoyed to learn that Leo, despite being a rank outsider and ticked off for being apathetic, has made £116 on the bookstall, miles more than anyone else.

One member of the committee resigns furiously because the Committee tick him off afterwards for not making enough money on the bottle stall.

Sunday, July 11th

I shall always remember this summer for the wail and jangle of fire-engines, and the cries of 'Concorde' as everyone spills out of their houses to watch the great white deathshead bird flying over. What a beautiful thing it is!

The weather is too hot to wear anything but cotton! Sweat runs in rivulets between breasts and under arms. Thank God the fashion is for long skirts, so my fat waist and swelling ankles are not apparent. Out on the Common, the thistles are turning to fluff. Emily calls the thistle heads 'fairies' shaving brushes' and rubs them against her cheek. Hawthorn and elder both have berries now, the only greenness along the bank comes from the mugwort. The drought has been the *coup de grâce* for my lovely elms. One can almost see the beetle munching away inside them like a Disney crocodile. The Eternal Triangle is carpeted with chestnut leaves, piles of them lying everywhere in the scorched grass. The silver birches are burnt to a cinder.

Walking home, I pass Henrietta, who suddenly shouts: 'Goddess!' in amused tones and goes off into fits of laughter.

Monday, July 12th

Leaving the house, I find two small boys counting the bees in the lavender.

'One, two, free, four, foive, six, seven, eight, noine bees,' they chorus.

Little bands of scarlet poppies, sow thistles, and hawkweed are the only flowers still growing. Even the oaks are turning. You feel it can't rain, however much it wants to, like going to the loo after an operation. There are huge cracks in the ground everywhere. The smell of smoke from numerous fires is very strong. There is no water for the birds, they fall on my illicit sprinkling every morning, making me feel less guilty. Crossing the Flower Garden I bump into Rachel who also snorts scathingly about silly people describing other silly people as 'Goddesses' and passes on.

Tuesday, July 13th

It rains for five minutes. How one has missed the sparkle of dew this year. Crossing the first Common, I meet Rosie who giggles and says, 'My goodness, my Goddess.' Ask her what the hell she's talking about; she says haven't I seen the *Wandsworth Borough News* this week? Evidently old Dick has written a letter, which they printed, extolling the beauties of Putney Common. Amazingly he lists one of them as me; describing me as 'the Goddess of the Common, passing every day in her long flowing dresses, carrying her writing materials.' Feel very touched and embarrassed at the same time! No wonder Rachel and Henrietta are irritated.

Wednesday, July 14th

Another example of my chronic wetness, is that in a weak moment, when I stayed with a friend called Virginia in Hampshire last winter, I agreed that it would be a good idea if she gave a concert in All Saints' churchyard in the summer. In a weaker moment, I said I would give a party for her afterwards. End up having to ask lots of locals to come and swell the audience, and (as it's far too hot for anyone to want to go to a concert) bribing them with the offer of supper afterwards. Feel I must also feed Virginia's choir, who are coming up from Hampshire in a hired bus – which means eighty people for supper. I normally freak out at cooking a dinner party for six.

In the morning, Virginia telephones from Hampshire and demands that I go and check if there's a suitable organ in the church. I do so sulkily as I'm in the middle of working, then ring her back and say it's not a very good organ, which sounds like a vicar with brewer's droop.

Cook lethargically, then go down to the shops. Meet Mrs Bond who says she's having trouble with her daughter-in-law who won't let her walk the baby.

'Of course,' Mrs Bond goes on, 'she's thirty-one, they often get funny at that age.'

Go home to find the telephone ringing. It's Virginia to say the conductor has a slipped disc, but a brilliant new conductor, who doesn't know the music, is coming instead, which doesn't sound very promising.

Go out on Common, find red admirals getting drunk on the lavender, and a rather sinister plague of ladybirds on the burdock, like a bus traffic jam in Oxford Street. Perhaps there are so many fires around, they have stopped paying attention if anyone says: 'Ladybird, Ladybird, fly away home.'

Return home to find pâté smelling off, the lentils rising like the peasants' revolt, the ratatouille tasting of sieved combinations – adding a chicken stock cube does not help. As I skin chickens for the Chicken Estragon, I realise I haven't eaten since last night. Guzzle too much chicken skin and feel sick.

Because I was the one who was silly enough to ask Virginia, Leo returns at 6.30, in his 'not my show' mood, and removes a few go-carts from the garden. Despite the fact that there are many more performers than audience, the concert is a success. I keep thinking the organist is making mistakes, but Leo says it's modern music. They end with 'Noyes Flodde', some of which we could do with on the Common. All the choir come humming back to supper, and eat so much there is nothing left for anyone else.

'Hurry up,' says a fat baritone to an even fatter tenor, 'or you won't get a third helping.'

They go off on their bus, singing into the night.

On balance, I think I really detest amateur musicians.

As she's leaving, Henrietta takes me aside and says she hopes I won't take it personally, but she really feels I should get better caterers next time. Feel very un-Goddessly indeed.

Thursday, July 15th

Cheer up, because I find that the teazels which were dug up last year on the south side of the Brook have now reappeared on the north side. Rather like a smart couple, Sir Peter and Lady Teazel, they have moved to a smarter address.

Wednesday, August 4th

Very peaceful on the dog front because everyone is away and the Common is deserted. Less peaceful on the child front. Both children come for a walk. Emily insists on wearing a party dress, my laddered tights and gumboots, and wants to talk about careers.

'I've decided to be a jockey or a tennis player when I grow up,' she informs me. 'Which do you think would be the most fascinating?'

'Neither,' says Felix.

Both children proceed to argue noisily, ending up with Felix thumping Emily.

'If you don't behave,' I cravenly threaten Felix, 'the moment we get home I shall ring up Daddy.'

'Who's he?' asks Felix.

Both children collapse in giggles.

Fortunately a diversion is provided by the blackberries on the Flower Garden. The drought has triggered off a bumper crop, dark, and ripe and sweetened by so much sun. The hogweed, on the other hand, which normally soars to six feet, is pale grey and has hardly struggled to more than two feet.

Go out in the evening. There is a touch of autumn in the air. The dahlias have shaggy white tops, but are brown underneath, like West Highland terriers who've been drinking out of peaty water.

83

Apples and pears are thudding. Delphiniums are coming up for a second innings.

Tuesday, August 10th

The Common is desperately sad. The crows, waddling from side to side like old Lancashire ladies over the cobbles, follow me along the path after dog-biscuit crumbs. The mugwort is losing its silver, horseradish is yellowing, thistledown drifting. The plane tree bobbles are as big as golf balls. The nettle tunnel which used to reach four feet and almost close over the top is a pathetic eighteen inches, and no threat to Emily's bare legs.

The little birch and plane saplings planted this year have all died from lack of water. They didn't stand a chance. The Fairies' Swimming Pool is dried out; the Lady goes unwashed. The roses are shrivelling. The box in Barnes Graveyard is turning brown. Going through the Flower Garden I pass a red kite caught up in a hawthorn tree, and a tramp frenziedly guzzling blackberries. Voling for the dogs is twice as hard work since the ground is so hard. They sneeze all the time from the dust. You cannot even drive a swingball pole into the lawn at home.

By contrast one enchantment is the incredible light around six o'clock in the evening, when the sun slants through the gaps between the houses in Egliston Road, catching the acid-green apples, and the weeping ash against a petrol-blue sky. What an example of the affluent society that no one bothers to pick their apples.

Thursday, August 12th

Grouse shooting begins. Heavy hot day. Malevolent crows still following the biscuit trail. I expect they're fed up because the dying elms will soon come crashing down like Ronan Point, and they'll be homeless.

Pondering this tragedy, I am disturbed by demented barking. Maidstone has a cat up a willow tree on the edge of Beverley Brook near Rocks Lane. Fortnum shoots up a nearby tree like a squirrel, and jumps eight feet down. I brandish a huge log and bellow at Maidstone, who takes no notice, rushing about with black muddy tart's legs covered in burrs.

An Irish groundsman turns up with a scythe, like Father Time. We walk in and out of the willows together pushing apart the leafy twigs like beaded curtains. I have no fears of getting raped – because the Irish don't somehow. Eventually, we extract Maidstone, now wearing a bobbly goosegrass veil and looking exactly like a deb's mum.

Saturday, August 21st

The drought is getting desperate. Wales has had its water cut off for seventeen hours a day. Feel very guilty about watering the garden even with buckets. The flower beds are still OK but the lawn is ash blond. According to the papers it is all to do with there being no spots on the sun. Never thought acne would get such a good press.

The Common is heartbreaking, the once lush grass shrunk to spiky strawlike clumps. Patches of mallow are reduced to creeping roots and a few yellow leaves. Even the ivy is dying on the planes. The ground is thick with leaves, yet, as with the blackberries, there has been a massive crop of acorns, two-tone green, like sleeping pills.

The bog on the south-west corner of Barnes Graveyard is filled with amphibious bistort – a strange snaky plant with flowers, that looks as though tiny pink beads have been struck on the end of a wand. Nearby, gorse burnt by numerous fires writhes black and sinister, shorn of its prickles. There is no green grass for the dogs to eat when they feel sick.

Sunday, August 22nd

Go out in the evening. Notice beautiful haloes of thistledown against the setting sun. The Eternal Triangle is stripped by the thinning shadows of the chestnuts. Barnes Graveyard, burnt to a cinder, is completely black and white, like an anti-apartheid cartoon in *The Guardian*. The wild rose bushes on the Flower Garden are filled with hips. So, for that matter, are all my dresses. Must lose some weight.

Wednesday, August 25th

It rains this morning. We all rush out and get absolutely soaked – like Sadie Thomson in *Rain*. The dogs are ecstatic. In the afternoon it also rains – the dogs get soaked, all the colours are heightened in the garden. Out on the Commons, the leaves rain down in sympathy.

Sunday, September 5th

Felix's birthday. What with opening of presents, I walk the dogs too late. The Common swarms with potential fighters.

Escape towards Barnes Graveyard, and have discussion with Felix about spending his birthday money, and whether a Nazi uniform with a German helmet is a good buy. When will he wear it, I query – rather like a see-through shirt.

Felix moves onto the subject of tits. Do they just pop out, like blown-up balloons, when you're fourteen, and will I promise to wear Grecian 2000 when I'm eighty?

Saturday, September 11th

Go and visit Old Dick who is now in Putney Hospital with

thrombosis. Brush my hair beforehand in a feeble attempt to look more like a goddess. But Dick, who has a new object for his admiration, goes into a stream of alleluias about the wonders of the medical profession adding in a loud voice, every time a nurse passes, how wonderful they are. He is a bit of a paean in the neck today.

Sunday, September 12th

Go to the country with Fortnum and Maidstone. Fortnum catches a hen, rushes about with a squawking ginger moustache, and has a polo mallet chucked at him by an understandably enraged farmer, who calms down when I bung him a fiver.

Monday, September 20th

Small boys are already chucking up conker sticks, which often get lodged in the trees and descend unexpectedly. One is likely to get brained at any minute.

A new friend is Crispin, a budding artist, who is still at art school. He is tall and very thin, and wears huge owl-like spectacles. Today he tells me at great length how funny Stanley Baxter was last night. I laugh unconvincingly, conscious of being very deficient in sense of humour. Must try to listen more, but it is so difficult when I'm desperately trying to concentrate on Maidstone and Fortnum.

As we pass Oedipus Corner, a terrified lady with a Labrador on a lead peeps round the nettle tunnel, and says: 'Are you a large dog?'

Tuesday, September 28th

Very very depressed. Maidstone has discovered an attractive spot on the corner by Beverley Brook below the Ranelagh Estate. It is fenced off by wire netting, so I am unable to follow him in there. He grins and bounces away every time I call him.

As a result, I spend hours and hours on nearby bench with Fortnum on my knee, trying to write pieces for the paper and waiting for Maidstone to emerge.

Rachel and Henrietta catch me sitting waiting for Maidstone in a downpour and bossily persuade me to book him into a dog detention school for a month. Later Henrietta brings round the address, and stands over me while I ring the headmaster. He sounds hell. Darling Leo comes home, finds me in tears, and says that there's absolutely no point in Maidstone going to prep school unless I intend going out on the Common wearing a police hat. It's me, not Maidstone, he goes on, who should go to prep school. He then rings up the dog school headmaster and cancels the booking.

Thursday, September 30th

Fraught time avoiding male dogs, and Rachel and Henrietta who are going to be absolutely livid. Don't know of whom I am more frightened. Maidstone behaves well today except for wallowing in muddy Brook. Workmen arrive to instal new kitchen units. Seeing Maidstone returning from Common, one of the workmen suggests that I instal a dog washer.

Thursday, October 7th

Still dodging Rachel and Henrietta. After heavy rain, the clouds have bustled off leaving a stunningly beautiful morning. The seasons are at sixes and sevens. Brilliant new emerald-green grass is appearing now, pearly drops silver the acacia. Puddles are everywhere on the rock-hard ground; the leaves are sweeping off the trees, edging the tennis courts with russet. The holly berries are coral, and the hawthorn berries a glorious crimson. Insects crowd the ivy flowers which have an acrid limey smell. Every day I come home with huge white mushrooms with pink pleated underskirts.

Wednesday, October 13th

Glorious misty morning. The blackberries are putting forth pale green leaves. Fortnum has a new yellow ball which is indistinguishable from yellow leaves carpeting the Common. Maidstone is busy bitching. Strange that I don't mind my dog being promiscuous with other dogs, as long as I know I am his favourite among human beings.

Pondering on this anomaly, I go slap into Rachel, and brace myself for lecture on Maidstone's absence from prep school. Fortunately she is so fed up with looking after her dotty father-in-law who is now living with them, that I have half an hour grumble about that instead. Perhaps she should dispatch him to prep school instead of Maidstone.

Sunday, December 5th

Walk with Emily, and discuss joined-up writing. She is very encouraged by the information that I have never been able to achieve it. She goes on to tell me in great detail how Daniel was sick in class.

'And Miss Burnside said, "Get back, get back children" and put chairs round it.'

Tuesday, December 14th

Today it is cloudy and mist is thick on the Common. It is like a Hammer film. A piece of frozen corrugated iron flaps by the first bridge. Crows caw in the bare elms. Everything is blanketed in silence, and one expects Dracula's carriage to rumble round the corner at any minute. Meet Rachel's father-in-law for the first time. Have been told he is a senile old menace full of animal cunning. He turns out to be an adorable rosy-cheeked old man, who clings to the arm of Rachel's husband Alastair, and says how lucky he is to be taken in by Rachel and not put in a home. I am just wondering what Rachel's been grumbling about, when the old man says he's met me before, and how are my four children?

Reply that they're all fine. Decide he's probably maddening to live with.

1977

—

Sunday, January 2nd

Maidstone still cat-crazy. Freeze with horror beside the Brook, as I see large black cat walking towards Fortnum and Maidstone – egged on noisily by a crow who hates cats. Fortunately Fortnum and Maidstone see a good-looking Labrador bitch coming in other direction and of the two evils choose the prettier, and charge off, giving the cat the chance to escape. Later both dogs gobble up all the bread a little old lady is scattering for the birds before I can stop them.

Monday, January 10th

Blackest of days. Maidstone and Fortnum catch and kill a stray cat down by the Brook.

All the people in the council houses come out and quite rightly shout at me, and say that they are going to call the police. Maidstone rushes proudly home with his booty. I rush sobbing home with Fortnum. Just as I am passing All Saints' Church, I feel a heavy hand on my shoulder. Spinning round I see a fearsome individual with blackened fingernails, not unlike the convict in *Great Expectations*.

'Do you own a large spaniel wiv a spotty face?' he asks in sepulchral tones.

'Yes,' I bleat.

'Called Midestone?'

'Yes.'

'And 'e's just killed a cat near the 'orspital?'

'Yes,' I cringe away. The cat is probably the favourite pet of his daughter, or the prop of his old mother's declining years.

'Well, Miss,' he goes on, 'Your Midestone's done me a very good turn, I've been hired as a cat catcher to round up the stray cats hangin' around the 'orspital. Your Midestone's saved me a lot of bother.'

But it is the most ghastly thing to happen. Poor poor little cat. I cry all day and at night dream hideously of rats.

Tuesday, January 11th

Walk in fear and trembling, keeping Maidstone on a lead most of the way round. He pants a lot, strains at his lead and drinks noisily out of puddles. Slightly comforted by beauty of the day. The trees are a rich smoky rain-darkened brown. The birds are singing their heads off. Sun after rain seems to be the climate they like best – a spirit of thanksgiving perhaps. Oaks still full of red leaves are the only touch of colour. The ivy along Putney Cemetery has dark purple berries.

Wednesday, January 12th

Very hard frost. A big red sun is rising turning the hospital smoky pink and all the frozen trees a soft russet. Jack Frost has been very thorough, not a blade missed. The tall grasses glitter like white-hot sparklers; even the wire netting cutting off the Ranelagh Estate looks like tracery at a church nave. Jack Frost must use colorant too: the little green cow parsley is as vivid as frozen peas.

Pass a jolly local man with an old mongrel called Jacko. He twirls his stick like a bandmaster, and calls out: 'I love this champagne air.'

The bowling green is an arctic sweep. My elms are bathed in orange as though they were caught in the spotlight of the last waltz.

The furry balls of the plane trees, coated with ice, look even more like Christmas tree decorations. On the path by the tennis courts the black ice on the puddles has been smashed like shattered windscreens. The ivy looks dank and subdued, as though its new hairstyle had dropped in the rain. There are still clumps of scarlet berries on the holly, but only at the top, where the Christmas saboteurs couldn't reach them. Oak trees frozen outside, still flame at the heart. A few hogweed stalks hold out tiny frozen fingers, like children numb with cold.

Fortnum holds up a frozen, clogged paw for me to remove the lumps of ice. I am touched when my dogs are suddenly vulnerable. Maidstone lopes off wolf-like, his frosted breath shifting in the sunshine.

Through January Maidstone was cat-crazy, and I spent most of my time walking him along the cat-free zone of the towpath beside the Thames.

Early in February, the BBC accepted a ten-minute play I'd written about the traumas of walking Maidstone on the Common. Diana Rigg is to play me – very flattering.

Friday, February 18th

Diana Rigg arrives at Egliston Road to make the film about dog walking; she comes in for a cup of coffee, and is extremely nice.

Am most impressed by her lack of fuss. When it is time to start shooting, she pulls on a woolly hat without even a glance in the mirror and sets out. But I suppose it's true to life – that's exactly the scruffy way I go out on the Common. Maidstone is played by an adorable woolly dog, who is actually a bitch and very well trained.

Ken the Common ranger is shaken out of his usual good humour because the BBC with typical contumely insist on filming on the Common without first getting permission from the Conservators. They now rush up and film a passing whippet lifting its leg. Ken tries to chase them off with the spiked stick with which he picks up litter. Terrified that any moment he will spear the director like a picador, I retreat wetly home.

Monday, February 21st

I am forty today. Not unduly worried. I have lunch with Michael

Parkinson and Douglas Hayward, the tailor, at Burkes, and we drink lots of champagne. I feel really rather glamorous, until I get home and weigh myself: ten stone! I must do something about my disgusting weight. A shower of rain just before I go out in the afternoon makes the earth smell sweet. See the first celandine and several yellow crocuses. Old nettle stalks tower over the young nettles.

Tuesday, February 22nd

Long golden catkins swing on the alders; the less forward ones are closed up and look as though they were dipped in red ink. Find a great clump of celandines clustering shinily along the Brook. Maidstone is embarrassed and not at all amused to be hotly pursued by a very fat Doberman – like all rakes he likes to do his own hunting.

Walk dogs again after splendid lunch with Lord Longford. He has an omelette and a glass of water, rather like Widmerpool. We discuss my writing a book on friendship for him. In the afternoon, I have to interview a spiritualist. Lord Longford terribly wants to come too. I love his sudden enthusiasms. Out on the Common late in the afternoon the starlings are making a frightful din along the Brook, and brawling and shuddering in the trees like a plague of locusts.

Interestingly, they don't go near the dead elms. Like men, I suppose, they shut their doors against a setting sun. Stone angel appears to wave in the Graveyard. In vino, I wave back.

Wednesday, February 23rd

Today it is the sort of soft gentle spring day that makes one head towards the plant shop. See lots of nettles by the Brook; vow yet again to bring out strong gloves and make nettle spinach. Brook very low, just a ribbon of reflection. Elders putting out little sage-green leaves.

On the way home I pass Old Dick now recovered from his stint in hospital and working in the garden round the ranger's hut. He has put up coloured bunting to protect his vegetables, which gives the place a festive air. He gives me a pot of daffodils and tells me he's in his eightieth year.

Thursday, February 24th

Lovely late afternoon walk after jolly lunch. The poplar on the corner of Putney Cemetery is saffron in the sunlight and filled with thrush song. The drained blue sky is criss-crossed with bright pink aeroplane trails.

My shadow in the setting sun is twenty feet long and admirably thin. Two ducks fly out of the Brook, circle perfectly round the five tall elms, wings going like propellers, then set off swiftly one behind the other, but in perfect time. Their gleaming emerald heads match the little green shoots which are thrusting everywhere through the counterpane of dead leaves. The goose grass is already covered in little green bobbles.

Tuesday, March 1st

Maidstone's behaviour on the decline. He corners a cat in the hospital grounds, and, witnessed by lots of horrified nurses and almoners, is about to disembowel it, when I just manage to pull him off by the tail.

Most of the stray cats fed by the hospital are living under the lank grey locks of the fig trees by the bowling green. Maidstone and Fortnum hang round there continually slavering and barking. I am at my wits' end.

Friday, March 4th

Exquisite day. Galloping dark blue clouds being blown across heavier white and grey clouds; the sun keeps appearing fleetingly, like a hostess coming into a second drawing-room, highlighting golden willows, coral roofs, and gilding brown tops of trees, and darting back again.

Must face fact that my five tall elms are dead, and their death will be more obvious when all the surrounding trees put out their leaves. There are little red shoots on the rose bushes in the graveyard, and the almond is out in the gardens along the Common – almost unbearably beautiful, that fragile pink against the soft blue sky. Old Dick presents me with a pot of hyacinths. I give him one of my romantic novels, because he says his wife is a great reader.

Saturday, March 19th

Home from a trip to Singapore. Children bliss. Dogs hell. Maidstone's latest trick is to climb up the fire escape of the hospital after cats, and stand on the flat roof outside the operating theatre, barking at operations.

Too lazy to go down to the towpath to watch the Boat Race, so look at it on television. It was nice seeing all the familiar local landmarks. Oxford win gloriously. In fact they were so far ahead that the commentators were reduced to remarking on pubs along the river. As a symbol of despair, one could not better the slumped, defeated Cambridge crew at the end of the race.

Monday, April 4th

Maidstone on hospital roof again. A kind nurse from Casualty holds an hysterically screaming Fortnum while I climb up the fire escape to collect him. I find him on a third-floor flat roof barking at a huge up-ended bare bottom framed by the window, while a lot of men in green masks and back-to-front overalls shake their scalpels at me. Then Maidstone bounds off up another fire escape onto the flat roof of the hospital. I shall never forget his spotty face leering down at me, with the black patch over his eye, like Nelson on top of his column. In the end I drag him back along a little ledge, endangering both our lives.

Thursday, April 7th

A letter of protest arrives from the hospital saying that Mrs Cooper's dog has been seen ascending the fire escape, and injuring one of the so-called hospital cats, and would she please realise that such canine invasions are unacceptable to us?

'In connection with the cats on the hospital premises,' the letter goes on, 'I would like to point out that these are unofficially kept by us to eradicate various pests that are bound to occur from time to time.'

Leo says it's a pity they can't eradicate Maidstone, and writes back apologising, but saying the letter of protest seems at variance with the congratulations in January of the cat catcher.

As a result of Maidstone's appalling behaviour, for the last few days

*I have been exploring fresh woods: Wimbledon Common, which is
beautiful, but an hour-long trek through the suburbs to get there; or
Barnes Common, which is laced with treacherous roads; or the
towpath. How I crave Barnes Graveyard, and my blackthorn and
the gentle walks of yore. Finally Maidstone is booked into prep
school in Middlesex. He is to stay there four weeks and it will cost
£95 and no visits allowed. Feel utterly miserable about it. Perhaps I
ought to order him Cash's name tapes and a cricket shirt. After all
he's nearly thirty-five in dog years. I have horrible visions of a lanky
middle-aged man in shorts cramped into a tiny desk wrestling
hopelessly with the rudiments of Dog Latin.*

Tuesday, April 12th

Take Maidstone to prep school. What a nightmare! The minicab
driver booked to take us down turned up thinking it was Felix who
was being sent away. The training school is horrible. Four little hen
coops, to take four dogs at a time.

The dog trainer, who is a bossy-boots, says Maidstone is much
too fat, and is wearing the wrong collar. He insists on having the
£95 up front, as two previous dog owners have died in the middle of
the training, he says, without paying their bills.

He gives me a list of all the things Maidstone will be able to do at
the end of the course, including Sit, Come to Hand, Retrieve and
Speak. At this rate Maidstone will be demanding his breakfast in
the morning, and being the life and soul at dinner parties.

Go home feeling suicidal, and take Fortnum for a walk. The
Brook has been dredged. The willows are like green ghosts, the
ashes have crimson flowers lovely against the silver trunks. Sadly,
because there are hardly any elms left alive, there are no pale green
hearts with their cherry-pink centres littering the path along the
Brook like confetti.

I am slightly cheered up to see that some vandal has painted huge
green four-letter words all round the plinths of the more august
female statues in Barnes Graveyard. This causes much chuntering
among the dog walkers, particularly Rachel.

In the evening we watch the Diana Rigg play about me and
Maidstone. I enjoy it. It is gentle and the Common looks very pretty
on film. Lie awake thinking of Maidstone in his little hen coop.

Wednesday, April 13th

Chuntering over the four-letter words round the plinths of the more august female statues is exceeded only by the chuntering over my play. Rachel and Henrietta are both livid because each is sure she's the bossy-boots character. Tempted to say to both, 'Of course you aren't: you're *far* bossier than that.'

Thursday, April 14th

Dark thundery blue sky, and brilliant sunlight on the apple blossom and the white cherry trees do not remotely lift my spirits. Fortnum and I are both missing Maidstone like hell.

In the evening I telephone the dog trainer to ask how he's getting on. The trainer says he's most unhappy: not eating a thing, howling, and slopping along behind the other dogs.

'Don't worry,' he says as he rings off, 'some dogs don't eat for ten days.'

Tempted to drive straight down and bring him home, then remember catricide is a serious business.

Friday, April 15th

Fortnum and I meanwhile walk peacefully on the Common and are able to admire the burgeoning of the spring. Job's comforters are working overtime on the subject of Maidstone and divide into two camps, the indignant who say: 'Poor little doggie, you'll break his spirit,' and the knowing, who claim: 'It won't make any difference, he's far too old.'

Rachel, who is still smarting about the play, keeps her distance.

Wednesday, April 20th

Ring up again about Maidstone. Trainer says he is eating at last.

'Nice dog,' he goes on. 'Pleased to see me in the morning. Loves the fillies too. But he's coming on very slowly. Very hard to penetrate.'

Forbear to say that Maidstone has been penetrating too many bitches for too long. Go out on Common in foul temper because incumbent Nanny refuses to work on Saturday in three weeks' time. Make speeches firing her all round the Common, then notice brilliant yellow sunlight over Cedric's house and pouring rain in

Egliston Road, with a thundery blue-black sky overhead. Then stretched across it is the most glorious rainbow. The reds and greens are particularly vivid over my next-door-neighbour's white cherry which is blanched to an almost Christlike whiteness. Fortnum and I watch it opened-mouthed until it fades.

Monday, April 25th

Gentle grey morning, cow parsley on the wane. Little alders by the Brook showing their leaves. Just a few elm saplings still alive. First bluebells out in Barnes Graveyard. I always think how miraculous Matthew Arnold is:

> Dark bluebells drench'd with dews of summer eves
> And purple orchises with spotted leaves

Find chickweed, shepherd's purse and Jack-by-the-hedge, which smells of garlic if you press the flower heads. Fortnum sniffs like a Bisto kid and rolls joyously in grass mowings.

Saturday, May 7th

Oh I love May! Dandelions spring up everywhere. Cow parsley just beginning to foam. Little saffron oak leaves coming out. Sycamore covered in acid-green hanging flowers. Little speedwell all over the Hillocks, a lovely faded denim blue. The gardens along the Common are filled with bluebells, lilies of the valley, wallflowers, and dark purple velvet irises. The lawns are littered with daisies with brilliant crimson tips – rather like cigarette butts smoked by a tart with a very thin mouth. A black crow hangs morosely on the football pitch fence like a DDT parrot. Both Putney and Barnes church bells are practising for the Jubilee celebrations.

Hawthorn blossom and chestnut candles nearly out – it is a race between them. The musty, soapy smell of the hawthorns is beginning to tinge the air. The lilac is out – lovely against the bluebells – and the nettles are covered with white droppings from birds' nest above.

Today we collect Maidstone. I have a sleepless night. Fortnum has been thoroughly spoilt while he's been away, lunching in restaurants, going to parties and the Booksellers' Conference in Harrogate, and behaving like an angel. With Maidstone's return, will chaos come again?

Drive down to collect him, shaking like an aspen leaf.

'Why the hell d'you keep brushing your hair, and putting on perfume just to look nice for a dog?' asks the minicab driver.

We all have to stay in the car while Maidstone does a demonstration.

'They've broken his spirit,' I moan, as he sits still as a statue, while the trainer walks round the field and bashes a dustbin over his head. Then he jumps over the trainer's lifted leg, and barks three times to order. He looks absolutely defeated and miserable.

I shall never forget the incredulous joy on his face when he sees me. He bounds forward moaning in ecstasy and puts his speckled arms around my neck for about thirty seconds like a lover. He is terribly thin, and filthy from living inside, but quickly regains his high spirits on the way home. It is only then that I realise that he hasn't been off the lead for a month.

When we get home he rampages round the garden, then breaks into the fridge, and eats, among other things, a whole packet of sausages, a totally frozen shepherd's pie, and a plate of raw mince.

In the afternoon, I decide to go out on the Common, and demonstrate his perfect behaviour. I leave Fortnum behind. After a few kicks Maidstone walks to heel on the first Common, sits at the two main roads, and sits when I take off his lead and walk away from him. Oh the joy of a perfectly trained dog, I say, looking around for admiring fellow dog walkers to witness this transformation.

But oh hubris, hubris, the next minute Maidstone takes a sharp right, and hurtles towards the hospital, ignoring my hysterical bellows of: 'Sit! Down! Speak! Come to Hand!'

Fortunately he is going so fast, he overshoots the hospital and I finally manage to corner him after a frenzied chase, knee high in dark red wallflowers in some alms cottage garden. Try to tell myself it is just first day excitement, but feel deeply gloomy.

Tuesday, May 17th

Maidstone is dead. The training school had no effect on him, he was more cat-crazy than ever. He was in a raging mood all day. Then I took him and Fortnum out at lunchtime, we went down the Fair Triangle towards the Yarrow Meadow. On the border of Barnes and Putney he vanished into the grey poplar copse. Suddenly there was a terrible growling and barking. I rushed in with Fortnum on a lead, and found Maidstone tearing a grey cat apart. Having killed it, he picked it up and set off for home. When Fortnum and I got back, he wasn't there, but turned up twenty minutes later, with shifty eyes and an earth-brown nose.

There was no point in beating him, as I decided he'd got to be put down. That was the moment of abdication. I rang up Dr Findlay and took him straight round. He began to pull backwards when we were 300 yards from the vet's. There was a dead pigeon in the gutter. In the surgery, the wireless was playing pop music, and there was a poster of a large cat with the caption: 'Your cat is too fat'. Doctor Findlay came in and turned off the pop music. He was so kind, and, saying of course mongrels were always a risk because one couldn't predict their behaviour, was about to take Fortnum away.

'No,' I sobbed, 'It's not him, it's Maidstone.'

Dr Findlay was very surprised, and said was I sure?

I felt awful not staying with Maidstone, but I funked it. I felt Fortnum needed me anyway. Let us honour if we can the vertical dog.

Maidstone whimpered a bit in the surgery, but I think that was only because he didn't like being shut away from me. Then the doorbell and the telephone rang, and I clutched Fortnum's trembling body. Afterwards the nurse held Fortnum and I went and saw Maidstone – he was still warm, and he looked so beautiful and at peace.

Fortnum and I set out for home, the children's Nanny met us on the way; she'd seen the E–K directory open by the telephone, and deduced I'd gone to Dr Findlay's. She was very sweet, and in floods like me.

When I got home, I went upstairs, and letter by letter, like a child learning to walk, I finished my piece. Leo was angelic when I rang him, and just said: 'Oh my poor child.' The children were very upset. After all, Emily's first words had been: 'Puppy get out on the Common.' Their reactions were predictable.

Felix was furious and said: 'Why did you kill my dog?'

Emily kept saying: 'Felix, you musn't be unkind to Mummy.'

Leo came home with buckets of tranquillisers and sleeping pills. I spent all night crying, and misquoting Belloc:

> Of this bad world, the loveliest and the best,
> Has growled and said goodnight and gone to rest.

Wednesday, May 18th

I can't stop thinking about Maidstone. It was all my fault. Each man kills the things he loves, and I did it with a kiss by being too lenient.

Thursday, May 19th

Still shell-shocked. I miss so many things about Maidstone. The quizzical way he'd look at you with his head on one side. The way he wiped his face on the mulberry tree after meals, round and round like the nursery rhyme. The way he thumped his tail but didn't get up when you came into the room, and his silly sleepy face grinning at me if I got up in the night to go to the loo. Whatever the hour, he always insisted on accompanying me.

Outside it is still quite cold – two-sweater weather. My five elms – those sky-touching beauties – were felled the same day as Maidstone. In a way their thundering crash was symbolic. They were cut down like him because they were dangerous and a liability. Their boles are pitted with holes from the wretched beetle. I remember them in their yellow glory in the autumn and how their pale pink flowers were always a first herald of spring.

I'm so sorry for the birds that nest there – it's like compulsory purchase; but somehow I don't feel things very much since Maidstone died.

The Brook looks different now that the elms are gone, like one of those slow-moving meandering Wiltshire rivers, flanked with osiers.

Wednesday, May 25th

Life goes on, it is peaceful but so dull without Maidstone. I can't work. Fortnum still looks for him everywhere.

Thursday, May 26th

On the Big Common, lots of beautiful youths, stripped to the waist, are out on mowers sprucing up the grass for the Jubilee, and being hotly eyed by myself and sunbathing homosexuals.

One youth keeps his dog – a white mongrel bitch, heavily on heat – on his knee as he mows and is followed by scores of amorous dogs.

Saturday, May 28th

Common at its most seductive. Hot with a slight wind, that makes the grass all white and shining. The bluebells offer an exquisite contrast to the young bronze oaks. The white chestnut flowers are out, so are the red chestnuts, which hang sideways from the snaky branches like Christmas tree candles that won't stay upright. The cow parsley, frothing and lacey, softens every ride.

The hawthorn cascades everywhere in white stalactites. On the Flower garden I find yellow horseshoe vetch, and bird's-foot trefoil – the two plants are very alike but the horseshoe vetch has more leaves, and is just yellow.

The poor crows are disconsolate now the elms have been felled. Along the Brook, the nettles and the thistles are breast high and form a green protective rampart for the wild cats that live along the bank.

No one notices the humble shepherd's purse, which makes a pretty red path down to the first bridge. It is the same red as the wavy hair grass which grows in great profusion on the Common, which in turn is like the rusty sheen on Maidstone's coat. Everywhere I go, I am reminded of him.

Sunday, May 29th

Heavy thunderstorms in the night. Fortnum absolutely terrified, which is a lovely excuse to get him into bed with me. Common exquisite next morning: gentle blue hazy sky, the cow parsley standing up like newly starched lace, the hawthorn rusting slightly but still smelling like fresh soap, the nettles giving off a heady hot blackcurrant scent. The buttercups gleam as though they'd got a new coat of gloss paint. Mare's-tails surge through the grass in the Flower Garden like little Christmas trees. All the greens are levelling out.

The male holly is putting out little crimson metallic leaves at the end of each branch while the female holly is a mass of white flowers. If you stand still you can hear the vetch pods popping.

Saturday, June 4th. Jubilee weekend

We spend all morning draping red, white and blue streamers across the house and garden. Then we hang a huge Union Jack from the balcony. We are the only people in the road to decorate our house. I think it's bloody wet of everyone else.

Out on the Common, the chestnuts are snowing rose and cream petals. White dog daisies are out in the churchyard. I listen to the hiss of wind in the newly thickened June poplars.

Sunday, June 5th

Crêpe streamers run in the rain, our lovely flag is stolen from the balcony – such is the spirit of togetherness that the Queen tells us this Jubilee year should engender.

Thursday, June 9th

Very nervous about opening Putney Arts Festival, which is being held in the church for the third year running. Declaim speech, written by Leo, round the Common.

Later have to make speech to large, very close crowd, and do not master microphone, which goes in a succession of whoops and whispers. Mr Cooper, who runs the local football club, replies and is very funny.

Church looks lovely inside. We buy Jubilee mugs and glasses, and a lovely green and blue picture. Fortnum follows me into the church, and is forcibly ejected by a couple of shocked Festival stalwarts. I can't think why dogs shouldn't be allowed to worship as much as people. Several people come back home, and we all drink too much and then dance to *My Fair Lady* and *The Pajama Game*.

Then Crispin, the budding artist, arrives; he's been to a fancy dress street party with Felix and Emily, and is wearing a dinner jacket, and one green sock and a sandal. None of us can guess him. He is supposed to be Spot the Deliberate Mistake.

Someone else turned up at the party in an Australian bush hat hung with Tampaxes dipped in ink – he was supposed to be Picasso's blue period.

Saturday, June 11th

Everyone getting into a panic over the Jubilee celebrations on the Common. No one can make up their minds where the portable lavatories are going to be situated. They started off by the bowling green; then the bowlers objected that it lowered the tone, so they were moved up in front of the nurses' home. Then Old Dick, from the ranger's hut, who's still wildly pro-nurse since his stay in Putney Hospital, got terribly upset about the little nurses having to put up with the stench. So the loos have now been moved up near the ranger's hut, which he likes even less.

There are also great chunterings from Colecroft Road, which

must be the best kept street in Putney, because some Marxist is refusing to tidy up his front garden for their street party.

Tuesday, June 14th

Beautiful soft rain-soaked day. The long lush grasses have grown up to touch the drooping, dark emerald branches of the oak trees in the Squirrel Wood so one is blanketed in greenness. It is midgy still today. Barnes Graveyard is filled with huge dog daisies, old faded roses in soft pinks and cyclamens, foxgloves and ragwort. The wild rose bush on the Flower Garden growing out of its seas of grass is so lovely with its little coral buds, and pale pink flowers. Their sweet delicate scent is strong today. Along Putney Cemetery, the elders are still scattered with pink confetti, shed by the chestnut trees, which are already showing little conkers the size of gooseberries – oh, the hustling, queue-barging relentlessness of Nature!

A fat pigeon with a white collar sits on a tombstone like a vicar taking a funeral. The cedar near the cricketers' 'Ut is putting out tiny pale green fingers.

Wednesday, June 22nd

Gradually the lovely long locks of the Common are being shorn for the Jubilee. Meet sweet woman who has a mongrel house guest: he is called Rover, and is a very slow walker. She feels such an idiot having to bellow 'Rover' all around the Common.

The Common itself now has a ring, made of palings, with four tiers of green seats round it, and millions of posts everywhere for dogs to lift their legs on. Fortnum is in his seventh heaven – all this and grass mowings to roll in too. The 'toilets', to Old Dick's delight, have been relocated back to the bowling green, but will soon no doubt be complained about again and moved under the Cemetery wall, resulting in lots of ghosts all holding their noses. As I walk along the Brook, a duck comes out of the water to pay homage to the stumps of my five elms. A blackbird is singing; it is very melancholy.

Dorothy, with Thomas the collie, says the evicted crows are getting very dangerous: they call each other up, and bomb her when she brings bread for the other birds.

Thursday, June 23rd

Glorious heatwave. Bronzed workmen stripped to the waist unload jumps for the horse show. Some of them wear gloves to protect their hands, which looks very camp. This is a terrible season for flashers; all the workmen have driven them into hiding.

Felix goes to cubs on the Common and rather enjoys it, but doesn't like all the pow wows about team spirit. He tells me he's going to Buckingham Palace to be investigated.

Saturday, June 25th

Our first Putney Common Show – a great success enjoyed by all. One of the star attractions is a game called Push Ball, in which opposing teams have to push a vast six-foot ball over each other's lines. When we arrive, the Spencer Arms is playing Queen Mary's Hospital Roehampton, and cries of 'Come on Spencer,' 'Come on Queen Mary' give it a quaintly sixteenth-century ring.

The ball is obviously very heavy because it is knocking players over like skittles. Putney Divorced and Separated Club, who obviously had a heavy night, were absolutely trounced by a team from the Putney Police. One of their players collapsed, and, according to a wag, had to be fed beer intravenously.

Other events include Musical Steam Rollers, and steam engines doing a post horn gallop; a gymkhana in which Lady Godiva fell off in the Fancy Dress competition; and a 'Mayor' as Emily said, 'with metal on,' who wandered round in search of people to be gracious to. The air was filled with the wailing of little children who'd failed to hold onto their gas balloons.

'Can we watch the tight writer men?' said Emily, meaning three brilliant acrobats, one of whom pushed another in a pram across a high wire, while another hung on underneath.

Touched by how many people came up to me and said how sorry they were about Maidstone.

Sunday, June 26th

Up early on Common, to find eager gardeners collecting manure with buckets and spades.

We go to Berkhamsted for lunch. Meet very nice couple who look at Fortnum, who is wearing his Jubilee bow, and say: 'That dog

106

looks just like our Shelley.' Shelley turns out to be a brindle smooth-haired mongrel, slightly larger than Fortnum and heavily on heat. Fortnum loses his virginity by the fish pond, Jubilee ribbon flying. I'm not sure Her Majesty would be amused.

Saturday, July 2nd

As a result of the mower breaking down, the Common by the Brook is exquisitely beautiful. First there lies a white sheet of drying hay, then the tall green grasses beyond, then a dark bank of trees, and above them, broken only by a few strawberry-pink houses in Rocks Lane, is a dove-grey sky. The pigeons are singing: 'How are you, how are you?' The willows are silver in the morning light, and without the elms the landscape is gentler and less sad. The long grass is flattened everywhere by the bodies of lovers. The bracken is darkening and about eight inches high, but still with chubby brown fronds uncurling.

The trees on the Common are full of stray kites – Battersea Kites Home. The bells are singing joyously – odd early on Saturday morning. The elder is still out.

I am constantly reminded of silly little things about Maidstone: the goofy way he used to peer into the coal hole every time he came back from a walk, and how every Monday after Leo had gone to work he would rush upstairs and unmake all the made beds.

Sunday, July 3rd

Our own glorious street party is a colossal success and engenders a great feeling of togetherness among the neighbourhood.

Leo and the children are out first sweeping the street at 7 am. I don't make it until eight, by which time a jolly band of organisers are putting up bunting. I rather feebly drape some streamers on a cherry tree. A minute later Henrietta bustles up and says they look untidy and takes them down again.

The sky is that untroubled dove grey that signifies blistering heat to come. The huge planes round the first Common are already decked out in red, white and blue cumberbunds and cast indigo shadows on the white grass.

In the security of a blocked-off street, the children are enjoying a tremendous bike-in; the lordly are showing off their skateboard skill. Emily and her friends gambol in the newly shorn grass, burying each other with shrieks of delight. I put on a ravishing new pale green dress. Emily looks horrified and says, 'Allbody can see your tits, Mummy,' so I change into a more decorous pink one.

Everyone brings food. Cedric's beautiful wife keeps saying, 'Have one of my curried balls.'

A newcomer to the area, and very much in evidence at the party, is Frances the feminist. A one-parent family, with several children by different lovers ('God knows how she attracted a lover in the first place,' says Rosie), she is writing a book on the Women's Movement. Frances is also a vegetarian and – even worse in most dog walkers' eyes – she insists on her poor boxer bitch, Germaine, being a vegetarian too. If disadvantaged feminist vegetarians weren't fashionable, as Rosie also points out, everyone would ostracise her.

Today Frances irritates everyone by producing disgusting lentil and carrot cake which no one wants to eat, and then rushing round guzzling everyone else's food. Like all other disadvantaged lefties, she also feels she has a perfect right to drain any capitalist's cellar dry, and is soon stuck into everyone's drink.

Three o'clock: Out on the burning Common, Cedric is organising races with the same benevolent despotism he displays on television.

'You're well over five,' he says reprovingly to a long-legged youth crouching beside a small blonde sister, about to embark on the under-five crawl.

'I'm only her coach,' comes the reply.

'I want to run in a fat race,' sobs a small boy.

Groups form and re-form. The local bobby who has swayed at eighty degrees at most street partes this summer, keeps his distance and says our party is quieter than most. Mothers are hitching up their skirts for the mothers' race. The fathers load up their cameras. Henrietta wins easily, with Frances the feminist second. I am easily last.

The fathers' race is more eventful.

'Why did the Daddies all fall over?' enquires a small child.

'Because they were drunk,' comes the reply.

Egliston Road win the ladies' tug-of-war from Lower Common South, but only after the most frightful cheating. We have six fathers, at least fifteen children, and sundry dogs pulling surreptitiously on our end.

The sun is going down, the fun becomes fast and furious. Rosie is being chatted up by Henrietta's husband. Germaine, the vegetarian boxer dog, has been fed scraps by everyone and is being sick in the churchyard.

Finally, as darkness falls, we all dance, going round in huge circles. Children, dogs, and adults, all chanting: 'Pinka, Pinka, Pinka, Lydia Pinka, Pinka, Pinka.'

Leo and the children, who were the first on the street, are last off at eleven o'clock. As I fall asleep I hear Leo saying, 'Neither of you need to go to school tomorrow, I will be personally responsible for ringing up your form mistresses.'

Monday, July 4th

It seems only seconds later that I am being woken by blinding sunshine and shrill protesting voices, being howled down by Leo saying, 'Life is never fair – if I can get up and go to work, you can bloody well go to school.'

Later in the day, Rosie and I take our dogs and our hangovers for a gentle totter round the Common. Rosie is rather smitten by Henrietta's husband, Ned.

'No,' I say firmly. 'Leave him alone. Henrietta would make mincemeat of you.'

Monday, August 1st

Common lovely and empty – everyone away. Walk in the afternoon with Felix, who tries to persuade me to take him into the Spencer Arms for a drink. I say I can't till he's eighteen.

'If I screw my face up,' he says, 'I could easily pass for an eighteen-year-old dwarf.'

In the evening Emily returns from a tour of Hampton Court Palace.

'There were lots of naked ladies on the ceiling,' she says, 'but it wasn't rude.'

Wednesday, August 3rd

Walk with Felix. The Common is covered in butterflies and less

attractively with wodges of dog fur. House-proud dog owners have a revolting habit of bringing out brushes and combs and grooming their dogs on benches. They can't even justify this action by saying the birds can use the fur to make their nests, because nothing is nesting at the moment.

Oh dear, yellow leaves are already flecking the willow, and the sycamore keys are turning coral. Why, when I'm lusting after handsome players on the tennis courts, do I always trip over tree roots, and do they always serve double faults?

Find yellow lady's bedstraw and, even rarer, star of Bethlehem on the Flower Garden. Evidently the Virgin Mary lay on a bed of lady's bedstraw in the Inn at Bethlehem, because the donkeys had eaten all the other fodder in the stable. Legend also has it that if you lie on a bed of it you'll have an easy childbirth. The star of Bethlehem is an enchanting flower, white and shaped like a star. The leaves have a white stripe up the centre, and the white petals have a green stripe up the back. We are lucky to see it, as the plant is supposed to close up at midday.

Felix says he wants to stay up and see the midnight movie, because it has a black parrot in it that talks. It turns out to be Boris Karloff in *The Raven*.

Thursday, August 25th

Darling Fortnum has become a father. Shelley, the bitch he lost his virginity to in Berkhampsted, has produced five puppies: four bitches and one dog. We are to have a bitch puppy; she is to be called Mabel, after Leo's grandmother.

Monday, September 5th

Felix gets a metal detector for his ninth birthday, and is hell bent on discovering buried treasure on the Common.

Thursday, September 15th

Meet sweet man walking his bike across the Common. He is going to collect a new pair of spectacles. He says his son is going to Eton if possible.

'Of course he'll make it,' I say.

'But I may not,' says the father.

Meet nice fattie with a springer spaniel, who says he used to go pot-holing, but the holes became too small.

Saturday, October 1st

Leo and I go down to the river with Felix who assures us it's low tide, and ideal for metal (or 'me-al', as he calls it) detecting. We are greeted by the highest tide ever, a terrific wind is overturning all the boats, and hearties in yellow and orange oilskins are trying to right them. Leo and I have great fun watching them, and quote Lucretius to one another:

> Sweet it is, when on the great sea the winds
> are buffeting the waters, to gaze from the land on
> another's great struggles.

The sun is lovely on the turning plane trees. Felix and Max, his friend, are thrilled to unearth some rusty nails.

Sunday, October 2nd

Glorious morning. The chestnuts are turning now on the Eternal Triangle, with their orange gold beautiful against the pale blue of the slide and the faded rose madder of the roundabout.

They are filming in Barnes Graveyard, and have draped plastic ivy round the plinths beneath the august female statues and white-washed out all the four-letter words. Fortnum is suddenly astounded to see a pair of tight pink trousers rushing towards him, topped by copious green foliage. It turns out to be a male advertising minion bearing sheaves of plastic bracken.

Friday, October 7th

Our sixteenth wedding anniversary. Mild, colourless day, trees still very green, but leaves drifting away like football crowds at the beginning of the end of the match. The hogweed is a lovely tobacco brown, rain has washed away most of the feathers on the willow herb, the ground is littered with conker husks, like an army of armadillos. Occasionally there is a dull thud, as a trapped conker stick falls out of the trees.

Saturday, October 8th

Irritation with children's Nanny (who has without asking bought hideous and wildly expensive pair of black shoes for Felix) almost spoils exquisite morning. The dew has been particularly heavy and every cobweb and frond of wavy hair grass is glittering. Mist rises like smoke in the sun. Felix comes with me and engineers me onto the subject of sex.

'Does Daddy still like it?' he asks.

'Sometimes,' I say cautiously.

'Oh well,' says Felix brightly, 'I suppose Young Mr Grace does in *Are You Being Served?*'

As Young Mr Grace is at least ninety, feel this is a little unfair to Leo.

Sunday, October 9th

Have a lovely walk with Crispin, the budding artist, who is now at the Royal College of Art.

He has written a poem about a vicar:

> I preach to the laity.
> And the laity lay tea for me.

Monday, October 10th

The Common gets lighter and lighter as the leaves fall off. I have never felt such hot sun in mid-October. Several chestnuts on the Eternal Triangle are quite stripped now. The holly and yew branches are filled with fallen leaves from other trees, the ephemeral being caught up by the evergreen.

Insects move leisurely in the rays slanting through the thinning oak trees, like specks of dust caught in the light from a projector. Lavender and evening primroses still bloom on bravely in the Graveyard, waiting for the first frost.

Tuesday, October 11th

The feathered grass silvered by the dew, is glorious in the sunlight, like glass blown in Venice, and how softly it caresses my bare legs above my gumboots! A fat tit is sitting on the stump of a tree. The black markings round his neck make him look as though his highwayman's mask has slipped. He is seen off by two starlings, whose nastiness is redeemed only by the brilliance of their speckled plumage.

Friday, October 21st

The Indian summer continues: midges and insects dance in shafts of sunlight; birds sing drowsily; the cigar box smell from the poplars is stronger than ever. Michaelmas daisies are out on the Flower Garden. The brown sycamore keys hang in such thick clusters; one is reminded of Mrs Danvers. The squirrels, stupefied by the sun, are fooling about in the grass, instead of gathering nuts. There seem to be very few acorns this year.

Friday, October 28th

Daren't tell Leo I have lost first four chapters of *Imogen*, the romance I am writing at the moment. Get up very early to try and rewrite it. As a result I am horribly bad-tempered with the poor children. Felix and I go down to the river to me-al detect. God it's boring. I have to stand holding a trowel, or alternatively the me-al detector depending on what he's doing. After forty minutes, he finds an old saucepan handle and asks me if I think it's worf anything. Meanwhile I have to keep throwing balls for Fortnum. He scuttles over old rusty tins and broken glass, and keeps losing the grey ball against the pebbles, so I have to find it for him. And all the time the eights hiss past, being shouted at.

Warm Sunday, October 30th

Everyone is keeping fit. I pass footballers shouting at each other, and Dads on bicycles saying, 'Are you with me, Jison?', and husbands jogging down to the off-licence to put on the weight they've lost, and people walking home with the Sunday papers.

Saturday, November 5th

Take Emily for miraculous dappled walk round the cricket pitch. She swings on the roller and the sight screen, which is like a great climbing frame. I catch two falling leaves which means two happy days for her and put them in her pocket.

Emily just misses catching one and says: 'Bugger.'

I reprove her.

'I adore saying bugger,' says Emily.

Friday, November 11th

Beautiful morning; leaves dropping slowly. The slight frost gives them the consistency of Twiglets beneath my feet. Orange leaf ceiling has been replaced by cloudy grey sky ceiling. Ash leaves don't change colour, they fall off in little green bunches of eight or nine leaves at a time – the way some people age overnight.

Meet Rosie, who says she went out with a very small man last night, so she'd taken her shoes off in his flat, but alas left them behind because he leapt on her and she had to make a quick getaway.

We bump into Mrs Bond. She says how busy her week's been, 'But last night,' she goes on, 'Hubby and I had nothing on, and it was *so* nice.'

Saturday, November 12th

Go for a walk with the children. Felix is manic at having been asked to review a book for the *Evening Standard*. As he is being paid £5 for it, he is convinced he is on the path to colossal riches and plans to take up writing as a career. Such is his hubris, he suggests the *Wandsworth Borough News* run a piece saying: 'Local boy leaves school particularly early'.

Slap him down mildly by saying he will never forge a great career for himself in journalism if he uses words like 'particularly' in headlines. The children then discuss what they would do if they were rich: Emily says she'd like to go to Scotland and Nude York.

So busy writing my romantic novel, I have neglected my diary, and have not even recorded the momentous arrival of Mabel, Fortnum's daughter. She is absolutely enchanting. When we went down to Berkhamsted to choose our puppy, there were two left – both bitches. One was blonde, black-nosed and utterly ravishing; the other was very, very shy, brindle, with huge anxious Alsatian eyes, and just like Fortnum.

'That's the one,' I said.

I went over and talked to her, and she wagged her tail and cuddled up to me.

Now she has been with us a week, and I have totally lost my heart to her. Her wagging tail constantly wiggles her body like one of those pull-along toys. She is as loose, leggy and unco-ordinated as a little Bambi. If she is reproved, she dives for cover – under beds, sofas, tables, the B M W. She chews up combs, biros and the gussets of pants, gently nibbles at the heels of my shoes and boots when I've got them on, and hangs onto my skirt whenever I go downstairs. She has ears like the finger of a glove that's been pulled inside out, but sometimes they come over her forehead in two triangles. She is terrified of other dogs, and always hides between my gumboots if one approaches, not realising her backside is still exposed.

She is terribly impressed by Fortnum, and follows him around slavishly all the time, which irritates him to death. He cannot see the point of her at all, and she is the recipient of a lot of curled lip.

Friday, December 2nd

Still ridiculously busy. Poor Leo has flu, but insists on going to work. Felix has flu, and has a temperature of 101 degrees. Leo comes home and accuses Felix of fudging.

'Daddy doesn't think temperatures are the truth,' says Emily philosophically.

Saturday, December 17th

Sunday walk with both children. They have long discussion about how old I'll be when they're both seventy.

Emily says: 'You'll be over 100, Mummy, and paralysed, and you'll have lost all your legs and arms.'

Felix says: 'You might not, if you use Oil of Ulay.'

Felix then says he loves me more than anything in the world, then on reflection adds truthfully: 'Except television.'

I feel this is a *very* high compliment.

Tuesday, December 20th

Emily breaks up today. She is leaving for school as I am leaving for the Common, so we walk down the road together.

Emily says that it's very, very disappointing that she's lost one shoe on the bus, but it's better than two; and her form mistress Mrs Giffen will be absolutely delighted to have three packets of peanuts for a Christmas present, but two will do, so is it all right if she eats one now?

On the Common, I meet Crispin, the budding artist. His normally light brown hair is brilliant auburn. He says he used a Harmony rinse, which is supposed to stay in through at least six washes, so it should last him through the Christmas party season.

On the way back we bump into Frances the feminist, who is extolling the merits of turkeyless Christmas dinner. Crispin and I decide to send Germaine, the vegetarian boxer, a food parcel.

1978

—

Sunday, January 1st

Go out on the Common in a pretty unidentified scarf, which someone left behind as a result of drinking too much at our Christmas party. One of the most beautiful sights is petrol-blue January skies, and the sun spotlighting the white seagulls and changing the trees from amber to dark red to dusky grey-brown as it goes in and out.

On the way home, I bump into Rosie who says:

'That's my scarf.'

'Just wearing it back to you,' I mumble in embarrassment.

'I'll take it now,' says Rosie very sensibly.

Monday, January 3rd

Lovely windy day. Wear two jerseys and a coat – also left behind after party – and look like a tweed barrel. The wind pleats the water in the Brook and makes the dogs very snuffling and over-excited with their ears laid back. The seagulls don't have to fly; they're just blown about. The bracken is shrivelling; the blackberry cables on the Flower Garden are a dark crimson, still hung with green leaves. The blackthorn is a donkey-grey lifeless blur.

Vandals keep picking the bricks off the top of the old russet wall round Putney Cemetery.

Mabel is absolutely enchanting. I love her more every day. She is so soft, merry and pliable, and still wriggles her body when you call her, and her tail waggles all the time when she walks. Fortnum, having ignored her to begin with, now rather likes her. They roughhouse for hours, lie together in front of the fire, and on the Common she follows him everywhere. He bullies and nags her just as he used to bully Maidstone.

She is intensely greedy, plunging her head into my carrier bag after dog biscuits, like a horse with a nose bag, and often crossing both main roads, thus blindfolded, to the amusement of passing cars. She has already filled out and is beginning to get stuck in the cat door.

Sunday, January 8th

Go to the Function Room of the Spencer Arms for a meeting of the Society for the Preservation of Rural Putney, leaving the children with the dogs and a *Carry On* film.

Excitement is added to the meeting by the first glimpse of a newcomer to the area: a sculptor called David. He is very good-looking with a black beard and huge shoulders, presumably from chiselling away at hunks of stone. According to Rosie, who goes to art galleries and exhibitions, he is very successful and has an open marriage. Both she and Frances the feminist have high hopes of him.

A lovely row breaks out because David the sculptor comes up with a proposal to close the little road up the centre of the first Common, and turn it into a skateboard area for the local children. This causes bellows of rage from the people who live in the big houses round the west side of the Common, because it means all the traffic instead of hurtling up the centre of the Common, will be diverted past their houses.

By way of retaliation one of their leading lights suggests that the east side of the first Common should be close mown, so that youngsters can play football.

'Football!' screech all those with houses on the east side, hysterically, 'Not in front of *our houses*!'

'Why not in front of *your* houses?' howl the west side. 'Why do they always have to play in front of *our* houses?'

'The trouble with Putney,' snaps David the sculptor, 'is there are far too many middle-class people motivated by self-interest.'

Henrietta shoots him a frosty look.

'I'm not middle-class,' she says haughtily, 'I'm upper-class.'

Matters are not improved when Cedric, perhaps conscious of competition, keeps calling David the sculptor 'Donald' to irritate him. Then a resolution is passed to stop the building of a new cricket pitch on the big Common, and the usual grumbles follow about the damage done to the grass by the horse show.

'The grass looked like Lords before the Show,' says a fat woman who's getting rather drunk.

'Roobish,' howls a rude leftie.

Leo gets up and says we are all too silly for words and he's going home. I should like to follow him, but wilt under Henrietta's stern eye. Come home an hour later, and burn up the sprats. Leo says I should have deep-fried them. When I was first married, sprats were one of my specialities. In every way, I seem to be disintegrating.

Monday, January 9th

Everyone has gone crazy over jogging – making the Common very unpeaceful. One cannot go out without some stockbroker pounding past, puffing like a grampus. I am just crossing the Eternal Triangle this morning, when a car stops, and a large woman in her fifties gets out. She has swept-up hair and a huge bum and is wearing high heels, and suddenly sets off briskly jogging through the Squirrel Wood. She is like a Gilbert and Sullivan contralto. Feel if I do not stop lapsing on my diet, I may well reach her size. There will be too much of me on the Common by and by.

Tuesday, January 10th

Terrific fog and white frost; traffic crawling along Queen's Ride; headlights and huge branches like antlers loom out of the gloom. The Common looks exquisite: all the leaves starched underfoot and every twig like a fluffy Persil-washed pipe cleaner. The mugwort leaves are particularly beautiful, like Jack Frost's hands. The tall grasses, each with their rime of frosting, burn with a white heat of their own. Silver frozen gorse, with its cruel spikes, looks like an instrument of torture – knuckledusters, perhaps, or a crown of thorns. There are layers of black and white ice over the puddles. Mabel slides across them like Thumper.

The only sounds are the muffled roar of traffic, the dogs tearing through the leaves, and the whip, whip, whip of my corduroy thighs rubbing against each other. I MUST LOSE WEIGHT.

Friday, February 10th

Bitterly cold but sunny. The voling season has started, and I am towed across the Fair Triangle by both dogs on their stomachs, snorting frantically. The leaves are crisp and rustle a great deal, which adds to Mabel's excitement. As a result of recent gales, the paths are strewn with branches. With such *embarras de richesse*, why does Fortnum always decide he must have the branch that Mabel has just picked up?

Tuesday, February 14th

I receive no Valentine cards except from the dear children. The weather, however, is more suited to polar bears than lovers: raging blizzards all morning, snow stretched across the trees like pulled cotton wool. The blackthorn looks like a white hedgehog.

Beautiful cold evening – the clouds roll away leaving very bright, newly polished stars. Lights for Evensong shine through the rainbow-coloured Burne-Jones windows of All Saints' Church.

Wednesday, February 15th

Leo goes off to work, and is quietly reading *The Times* on the top of the 22 bus. As the bus moves off, he hears a commotion downstairs, people are clicking their tongues disapprovingly, and saying:

'There's a dog on the bus.'

'I know that dog. 'E's always abe-out.'

'Look at that dog, isn't he sweet?'

'Shame really.'

'Disgusting,' etc.

Leo cringes behind *The Times*. Fortnum is forcibly ejected outside the French Revolution.

Tuesday, February 28th

Snowdrops out by Barnes Graveyard. Lovely mild, furry day, the trees look blurred and springlike as though at last the buds were pushing through.

Go out at dusk. In the trees along the Brook, starlings are working themselves up into a frenzy, all clustered in one tree like a deb's drinks party in a top-floor flat in Sloane Square. Then, as though they're all bored and want to move on to another party, they fly off and reassemble noisily on the top of another tree.

Thursday, March 2nd

Lovely soft day. Purple and gold crocuses out on the Common. Felix walks with me. He is very worried because he can't afford a Mothering Sunday present, and 'borrows' a quid off me to buy one. February and March are lethal months for the children: Valentine's Day, my birthday, Mothering Sunday, Leo's birthday and then Easter.

Sunday, March 5th

Hazy day, pale blue sky. Fortnum has his first dip of the year in the Brook, so spring must really be on its way. Feel like death; it takes an eternity to walk round the Common. I have been asked to open Putney Hospital's Bring and Buy. Is it an olive branch after Maidstone butchering their cats? After much dickering, and because they want to get the poster printed, I agree to do it. Feel I am being very disloyal to Maidstone's memory.

Thursday, March 16th

I have now been in bed for eleven days with Red 'Flu – and in despair at missing the most tremulous and beautiful days of the spring. This morning a fox ran across the garden. He was young, very thin, yellow and mangy, and jumped over the wall at the bottom. He'd been ransacking the dustbins.

Friday, March 31st

Red 'Flu turned into pneumonia. Out for the first time, somewhat ill-advisedly. It is bitterly cold. The celandines huddle with petals closed among the dead leaves. The daffodils are coming out very cautiously, the birds have that sulky, aggrieved, petulant sound, as though nature should know better than to produce weather like this. Only the nettles, blackberry shoots and cow parsley are soldiering on cheerfully.

Tuesday, April 4th

Exquisite fall of snow makes it light as day at midnight. The daffodils, with their spiky leaves, look like white pineapples, the bamboo is bowed down to the ground. The orange sky is lit up by the whiteness, and the dazzle from the kitchen window. At the beginning, when the snow tumbled thickly down on the blossom and the spring flowers, it looked as though petals were raining from heaven. The autumn cherry was particularly beautiful, as though its white flowers were being topped up.

Wednesday, April 5th

Woken at six by children screaming with excitement. It was

Emily's first real snow. Manage to smile as children play snowballs all over my adolescent peonies in the front garden.

Alas, by the afternoon, only grey dwindling snowmen are left.

Sunday, April 9th

Keep-fit mania has hit Putney. Everyone is playing tennis or jogging. Gracing the tennis courts by All Saints' School is a marvellously beautiful Chinese girl. Instead of bicycling briskly across the Common to the off-licence, all the fathers now make excuses to take their children a very slow round-about route past the tennis courts, so that they can gaze at her.

'Timothy didn't get back with the tonics until 1.15,' said one furious wife.

Friday, April 21st

Delicious row brewing over the Society for the Preservation of Rural Putney's newsletter which has just been sent out. It kicks off with vigorous plans to replace the bus shelter, which is described as 'a public eyesore' with something green which blends tastefully in with the scenery and doesn't leak. Feel sad – I'm very fond of the

bus shelter. It is covered with very mild graffiti – 'Punk rules OK,' 'God Save the Queen,' and 'Fulham FC' – and certainly taught both my children to read. Before its demise, Leo suggests I should review it for the *Wandsworth Borough News*.

What, however, causes the most indignation, is the newsletter's proposal to tidy up the garden of the only house in Lower Common South owned by the council.

The garden isn't that bad anyway. I rather like dandelions and long grass. At least it's better than those cabbages in the front garden of the house further down, which smell when it rains.

Leo suggests the problem could be solved if the garden was declared a conservation area of outstanding natural beauty, and left to its own devices.

Saturday, April 29th

Open Putney Hospital Bring and Buy.

Put up a slight black by calling it a 'Jumble Sale' rather than a Bring and Buy. In fact the behaviour is distinctly jumble: before I've finished speaking, the ravening hordes barge through the door, and sweep away me, my microphone, and all the VIPs on the platform.

During the speech, I can't resist making a crack about Maidstone and the hospital cats. I expect the sky to open up, and a reproachful spotty face to appear, saying 'Et Tu Brute.' It is nearly a year since he died: darling Maidstone. Everyone is very nice to me, and the Bring and Buy makes £825.

Monday, May 8th

Spring can seldom have been more lovely. Days of torrential rain have dyed the Common a brilliant emerald but mowing for the horse show has striped it light lettuce green. The scent of new-mown grass is everywhere, the Common is covered with puddles, each with its own pair of mating ducks.

Wednesday, May 10th

Still very cold, cow parsley just frothing out of the lush squeezed grass. Pink campion and bluebells beginning. A handsome jogger trots purposefully by, overtaking me several times, as I shamble round communing with Nature. On the first lap, he talks about a writer called A. J. Tessimond, whom he is shocked I have never read. On the second lap, he tells me he comes from 'a ce-ounty family,' which I don't believe, because his vowel sounds are very suspect. He is nice but I wish he'd go away and leave me to my meditations.

Tuesday, May 11th

Watch snails crawling up the old stalks of the nettles above fierce young green nettles, to indulge in copulation and even troilism. I hope they don't fall off in ecstasy and get stung.

Friday, May 12th

Utterly bloody vandals have been at work in Barnes Graveyard, decapitating statues, and smashing tombstones. Two stone angels have also been ripped from their pedestals, and lie battered and wingless in the long grass.

Most tragic of all – from Emily's and my point of view – the vandals have smashed up the fallen tombstone of Maria Kathleen Ayoub and stolen the lovely bronze of her face, cast by her husband.

She was the 'Lady' whose face Emily and I used to wash with rain water, and tuck up with dry leaves to keep her warm in winter. 'R.I.P.', says one of the fragments ironically.

Saturday, May 13th

The Fair is here. Very touched they all ask after Maidstone, and say how sorry they are he died: 'He was a personality dog, Jilly.'

The Fair reduces children to fever of excitement, and their parents to the usual state of bankruptcy, and also attracts the usual horde of young thugs to the area.

Friday, May 19th

Heavenly day, wafting an exquisite commingled smell of lilac, wall-flowers, lilies of the valley and mown grass. Foaming bank of cow parsley along the Brook is lovely against acid-green knotweed and darker bank of nettles. The ashes are feathering. In the distance, archers and cricketers playing on Barn Elms.

Saturday, May 20th

On the way to the Common, I meet the retired Brigadier, who lives near Rachel. He is one of the few local indications that the age of chivalry is not dead. He raises his hat and, obviously encouraged by the springlike warmth of the day, suddenly tells me: 'Never go to bed with a woman in the morning, because you might see something better in the afternoon,' and then rushes off to catch a bus to Lord's.

Pondering this sentiment I wander down to Barnes Graveyard and stumble on the tombstone of J. P. Ewin, 'Who fell asleep in Jesus,' in 1917.

Sunday, May 21st

Out on the Common, very very nervous about bumping into Henrietta or yet another newcomer to the area called Horsey Miriam. This is because last week in *The Sunday Times* I took the mickey out of people in the suburbs who pretend to be following country pursuits and park horse boxes outside their own and other people's houses. It was partly a retrospective crack at Henrietta – who actually sold Phineas and the horse box last year – but also aimed at Horsey Miriam, who has moved into a large nearby house with a huge garden, in which she keeps ponies for her three children. Although she's never been on a horse in her life, she spends her time strutting around in jodhpurs telling everyone how to ride.

See both Henrietta and Horsey Miriam in the distance, but hover in Lurker's Paradise until they are gone, terrified that they will both take umbrage. Sternly tell myself one cannot be both popular and a writer

Monday, May 22nd

Walk on the Big Common and go slap into Horsey Miriam by the bowling green. The dear thing isn't cross, thank God; at least she is too anxious to tell me about her recent burglary to take umbrage. All the four colour televisions and her son's decks were stolen, she says – and the break-in took place at lunchtime. Their red setter, Sampson, was lying on her bed, and slept through the whole thing, so she's thinking of getting an 'outdoor Alsatian'.

Sampson looks suitably sheepish and wags his tail.

Miriam then notices someone has put wire netting across the path leading along the bowling green to the council flats.

She frowns and says, 'I don't like that closure, I must write to the Council.'

Will her words carry weight, I wonder?

We are joined by Mrs Bond. She says the 'closure' is to stop dogs going toilet on the grass in front of the flats. Her son lives next door to a farmer, she goes on, who gets 'very agnostic' if people walk across his fields.

The cow parsley is glorious, so is the pink campion. The oak apples are fat, puffy and cherry pink. The nettles after a sprinkle of rain smell wonderful.

Tuesday, May 23rd

For once, the hawthorn, the chestnut candles and the cow parsley are all out together, like a triple wedding. After so much cold weather, the birds can't believe their luck and are singing their heads off. The sweetest sight in the world is Mabel leaping like an impala in a succession of bounds to land on some imaginary vole.

Friday, May 26th

Appalled that I have forgotten the anniversary of Maidstone's death. Is all mourning like this: agony because of the loss, then almost as agonising remorse because one keeps forgetting?

While I am planting a monkey puzzle in the front garden in his memory, an old man stops and tells me he remembers, in his wild far-off youth, climbing a monkey puzzle for a bet – 'A great tall thing' – and being lacerated to pieces by the spikes.

Emily comes home from a tea party, admires the monkey puzzle, and says she's just been sick.

'Very sick?' I ask, pressing down earth.

'About two mouthfuls,' says Emily.

Sunday, May 28th

Walk with Rachel, who is having a very bad time at the moment. Her two layabout sons hang around the house refusing to get jobs; and she is still having to look after her dotty father-in-law who is getting dottier every day. All this makes her very difficult company, because whenever she puts me down, which is continually, I feel it is below the belt to snap back. Today, she had a go about my new monkey puzzle.

'I cannot stand them,' she says, 'and what's more, when my mother heard you'd put one in, she said she'd certainly strike you off her visiting list.'

Thursday, June 15th

Rings and seating for Putney Horse Show going up on Common. With all the elegant blue and yellow striped tents, it looks as though some eastern warrior – Tamburlaine perhaps – has pitched his camp for the night.

Friday, June 16th

Putney Show is a great success. The first day is windy and cold, the second blazingly hot. All the horsey fraternity and particularly Horsey Miriam are electrified by the presence of Princess Alexandra's daughter, Marina Ogilvy. She enters the Fancy Dress Competition dressed as the Lion, with her horse dressed up as the Unicorn. Five officials spend hours trying to get its horn to stay up.

I judge the Fancy Dress with the actor, Anthony Andrews, who lives in Wimbledon. He is very very handsome, blond and slim. His wife, Georgina, who is also slim with short dark hair, was a Simpson of Piccadilly before she married him. They both wear Daks check trouser suits, and look rather like Archie Rice in *The Entertainer*. Any minute one expects them to break into a soft shoe shuffle. He has just started a new series on television about Sappers called *Danger UXB*. To start off he is very post-rehearsal, bombed and aloof. Both he and his wife have that poker-faced horsey detachment, but after a bit they both unthaw and are extremely nice.

Horsey Miriam, who appears to have organised the whole show, sits about in tight breeches and boots looking elegant, and saying she feels exhausted, and gets her picture in the *Wandsworth Borough News* with her arm round a horse's neck.

During the show Leo and I have a drink with a local minicab driver, and a CID chum of his called Driscoll. Driscoll is rather good-looking and starts chatting up our incumbent Nanny. You can tell he is C I D because he gets her telephone number without having to ask, by looking at the number on Fortnum's name tag. Very smooth operating.

Tuesday, June 20th

Everyone revving up for our second street party. Factions dividing sharply into those who believe you can't repeat a good thing, and those who say how would great institutions like the Grand National or the Boat Race have got started, if people hadn't been brave enough to try them a second time?

Leo supports the former view, and says WE ARE NOT GOING. I and the children support the latter. Children alternate between feverish excitement and tearful rage with Leo. I say: 'Daddy will probably change his mind on the day,' and very feebly allow Felix to buy some tickets for the street party; then feel wildly disloyal to Leo.

Cedric, who obviously feels the same as Leo, is pushing off to some Opera Ball in the country and refuses to organise the races. This results in a blazing and very public row with Henrietta who is trying to organise the street party.

She tells him he's got *folie de grandeur*.

He calls her an effing suburban housewife.

It is all rather like Consequences, and keeps the whole area in a state of delighted chunter.

Wednesday, June 21st

Street party day dawns grey and very cold. Leo still refuses to go and is livid with me. Children also livid with me and in a state of mutiny, saying 'CAN WE TAKE OUR TABLE OUT NOW?' every five minutes. I feel like a tennis ball at the end of the men's doubles final at Wimbledon.

I walk the dogs, and find Henrietta inspecting the pitch like a test umpire. One of her five pale children stands on a bench and says, 'My mother will make a decision about the street party at 11.30.'

Raymond Harris, who enjoys the dancing later when he can get off with all the pretty girls, has already started putting out chairs on the Common.

'I don't care what anyone says,' he announces, 'as a committee member I'm going to have a street party.'

Bump into Cedric's beautiful wife. She says Cedric is very ill in bed: some dreadful tropical disease – he can hardly walk.

'He insisted on going to this Opera Ball,' she goes on, 'which consisted of 500 people in fancy dress.'

Cedric evidently went as Don Octavio in doublet and hose (to show off his good legs). On the way to the ball he kept having to get out of the car in his fancy dress to be sick – all the locals in the villages evidently looked at him in amazement.

I go back home to find Leo even crosser, even so I start sneaking chairs out one by one.

Although it is 11.30, Frances the feminist is still standing in the street in a very sexist thigh-length nightie, probably because she, like Cedric, has very good legs.

Meet David the sculptor, who gives me a big kiss, which tickles because of his beard, but is nice as he's very handsome. He says he's waved at me over the past few months, but I'm either short-sighted, or deep in thought.

'Thought-sighted,' I say.

I stop and have drinks at nearby table, at which several rather respectable women are sitting, including Rachel and the Brigadier's wife. Fortnum leaps onto my knee. We all discuss Princess Grace animatedly, suddenly I realise I am the only one talking, all the women have glazed expression on their faces, and Fortnum is flashing a large red cock at them. God! Dogs are embarrassing!

Up the road, find Cedric, miraculously recovered, tucking into green pepper and tinned peach salad, and addressing a laughing group. Say I am delighted he's better. He giggles.

His wife, looking faintly embarrassed, introduces me to a handsome blond American boy with Cambridge-blue eyes, who says he could be pulling against me in the tug-of-war.

He then says: 'What are you working on now?'

I say a book on the English class system.

He says class doesn't exist in America; then adds that he belongs to one of the leading families in Pennsylvania, which goes back seven generations.

Thursday, June 22nd

Walk dogs early in the afternoon, so I can watch Wimbledon. In the evening Leo and I go to a concert in the churchyard, not in the most harmonious of moods. I want to work, but am overruled by Leo who says we ought to support the local arts.

'You didn't support the street party,' I grumble.

'We are *not* talking about the street party,' says Leo heavily.

Music therefore does not have much chance to soothe the savage breast. I listen stonily to Bach, John Ireland and Benjamin Britten.

In the interval I talk to our Labour Member of Parliament, who is Minister of the Arts, and give him the impression – by talking about 'We' – that I shall be voting for him in the next election. Next minute, Judge Hamilton (very high Tory) joins us, to whom I have previously given the impression that I will vote Tory. Feel my hypocrisy straining at the seams, my two faces very red.

Wednesday, July 12th

Through the white tombstones above the acid-green box stand the evening primroses like a pale gold army.

Friday, August 11th

I have neglected my diary shamelessly lately. I'm so busy trying to finish the book I'm writing on the English class system. This is the worst year for burglar alarms I can ever remember. Everyone is away and the slightest breeze triggers them off. The incessant jangle is worse than New York. This is also the first year people have been sunbathing topless on the Common.

A particularly beautiful blonde lies topless near the bus shelter today. David the sculptor, who usually posts his letters at the top of our road, says he has instead gone to the pillar box beyond the bus shelter five times this morning.

Sunday, September 10th

Bed at 6.30 after the *Spectator* Ball. Woken at 8.15 by Henrietta who wants to borrow Felix's metal detector to find a diamond ring which fell off in Sloane Street garden last night because, unlike me, she's lost so much weight lately. Feel fantastically unco-ordinated.

My hangover is waiting to pounce. As I rush up and down stairs looking for batteries, Henrietta hangs about humming.

'New wallpaper' she says, peering into the loo, but making no comment, then turning to Fortnum and Mabel adds, 'Hasn't your cruel mistress taken you for a WALK yet?'

Whereupon moaning and squeaking from the dogs puts an end to any possibility of further sleep. Also feel deeply depressed because Henrietta's pale son Dominic is going to Felix's school this term, so Henrietta will be joining the school run and will no doubt bellyache like hell if we are a minute late.

Out on the Common the jays sound like Henrietta; they are so bad-tempered and squawking. I love the flash of their blue wings.

Monday, September 11th

Plant bulbs in all casserole dishes, so we shall have nothing to eat out of for months. On the Common thistledown drifts idly by; elderberries turn crimson; dew thickens on the cobwebs; sun rays slant through the thinning oak trees. Almost imperceptibly, inch by inch, the autumn begins; the trees are still very green, but leaves are clinging to the tennis wire, and settling on the holly. Ruby-red berries gleam on the woody nightshade. The chestnuts on the Triangle are tinged with orange, and through the roof of leaves you can see patches of blue sky.

With autumn, the plantains no longer slap against my gumboots; the sting of the nettles has lost its intensity. The house is filling up with bags of conkers. Blackberry pickers sway like masts in a harbour.

Monday, September 18th

Utterly bloody Monday morning. Woken at eight by Emily in high glee. As a practical joke Felix, she says, set the Nanny's alarm clock for six o'clock; it went off and the Nanny was 'utterly livid' but has now overslept. Emily goes on that she can't find her leotard as Felix wore it round to Thomas's on Saturday.

Say that I very much doubt Felix could have got into her leotard. Emily then says she can't find her cardigan or her recorder either, and will I do her hair in a pony tail? We are then interrupted by shouts and banging from downstairs. It is all the boys on Felix's school run including Henrietta's son, Dominic, saying *we* are taking and, because Nicky Waring is form prefect, we must get them to school by 8.30.

I am far too nervous to wake the Nanny, but not so Henrietta, who turns up five minutes later roaring:

'Where's Nanny, where's Nanny?'

'Still in bed,' I say, which is not tactful, as the Nanny emerges from her room, tight-lipped and says she's dressed, thank you, and no one passed the message on to *her* that *we* were taking.

Henrietta then sweeps the delighted little boys out of the house saying, 'This house is a shambles. Mrs Waring will have to take, or you're all going by bus.'

Go out on Common in vile temper. Meet Rachel, and admit I am spitting. She lowers her voice like Mrs Thatcher and says, 'Would you rather be alone?'

Refrain from saying yes, and launch into long moan about Henrietta and the school run, and the Nanny, and Felix setting off alarm clock. Finish off feeling guilty and ask how Rachel's mother is.

Rachel then tells me her mother will have to come and live with her as well as dotty father-in-law, and Dr Fielding has already rung up a nursing home in Wandsworth about admitting dotty father-in-law, as the strain of looking after both of them will be too much for Rachel. Now understand exactly why Dr Fielding treats me (and the rest of my family by implication) as a spoilt bitch.

Tuesday, September 19th

Very worried about money. We don't have any and the bank keep writing us rude letters. Also very conscious that my character is deteriorating in every way. Half the world is getting on my nerves, while I seem to get on the nerves of the other half.

Walk on the Common with Henrietta who makes me somehow feel guilty that she did not find her diamond ring with Felix's metal detector.

Somehow the conversation moves on to politics and John Braine.

'Neo-Fascist,' she says dismissively.

'He's lovely,' I snap crossly. 'I adore him.'

'There!' she says triumphantly. 'We're all insecure about something. You're insecure about your friends.'

On the Eternal Triangle, we bump into a local actor declaiming his lines, who says new Edward Bond play is perfectly marvellous. Subsequently discover he has long part in it. Note that actors like plays that give them a lot to say. Aren't I the same about newspapers which give me a lot of space?

Wednesday, September 20th

Walk dogs along Egliston Road, and fall over Henrietta and friend unloading crates of drink for a party that night to which we have not been asked. Hear their suppressed mirth as I go down the road. Intensely irritated, not at not being asked – why should anyone ask anyone to a party? – but that they should think I'd mind. (In fact – *do* mind.)

Saturday, September 23rd

Walk dogs with dear Rosie, who said it was a bloody party. Not enough drink and very chilly con carne.

Tuesday, October 3rd

Mabel on heat. Oh dear, oh dear. Forced to put her into kennels, as Fortnum, her father, is already leaping on her.

Wednesday, October 4th

Take Mabel to kennels.

Feel utterly, utterly miserable, never missed a boyfriend like this. What the hell will I do if the children ever go to boarding school? Feel ashamed that I may mind less, because you can at least explain to children that it won't last for ever.

Thursday, October 5th

Walk Fortnum, who is much less stroppy without a bitch to defend. Breathe in the heavenly after-shave cigar box smell of autumnal poplars. Also notice mushroom smell when you raise oak leaf mould.

Friday, October 6th

Missing Mabel desperately. Slightly distracted by distant cousin, Beatrice, and fairly new psychiatrist boyfriend, coming to lunch.

Perhaps egged on by all the current talk about the equality of the sexes, she had declared her love for him that morning and he had told her he was not ready to settle down. I can't say I blamed her for loving him; he was most attractive – the sort of man who makes you rush upstairs and put on make-up the moment he arrives.

After lunch we go for a walk on the Common. It is an angelic autumn afternoon: all the pale oranges and yellows softened against brown and grey grass, with the air gentle and a pale misty silver coin of a sun.

Beatrice keeps drifting close, trailing her hand near her boyfriend's to give him the chance to hold it, but he doesn't. I'd forgotten the utter torments of being twenty and in love.

Saturday, October 7th

Very depressed about Mabel. When I ring up the kennels they say she won't eat, and is terrified of being handled. Also absolutely fed up with joggers, pounding round the Common. I shall write a novel called *The Overcrowding of a Long Distance Runner*.

David the sculptor comes by on a bicycle – his concession to keeping fit. Given the eye by a passing beauty, he pushes his Beatle cap down over his eyes and smoulders at her. Looking back at him she trips over a paving stone. You can see him purring that he hasn't lost his power.

Saturday, October 14th

Mabel is back – her heat finished after ten days. Bloody rude woman at kennels says she may be pregnant, and that one shouldn't bring any more mongrels into the world when there aren't enough homes for breed dogs, and Mabel's father ought to be 'carstrated'. When we picked Mabel up, she seemed utterly bewildered and ran straight past me. Even when we get her home she is quite shell-shocked and hardly recognises anyone. She's as thin as a rake and moulting terribly. Even worse, the moment we arrive, Fortnum goes berserk and jumps on her. I give her a bath, dry her and then let her into the garden. She appears to have cystitis. Whereupon the incumbent Nanny goes very quiet and says, 'Wilhemina had that,' and then stops.

'What are you talking about?' I snap.

'Wilhemina died of cystitis,' she says.

Feel quite sick, wrap Mabel up in a hundred blankets, and put her in front of the fire. She refuses to eat, but at least Fortnum has stopped trying to jump on her, and licks her face gently instead.

Monday, October 16th

Take Mabel to vet. She has a temperature and cystitis. Vet says if she's pregnant she can have an injection to abort it. She seems more cheerful.

Tuesday, October 17th

So busy worrying about money, fail to avoid Frances the feminist and her vegetarian dog on the Common. She says, 'You are the most disorganised person I've ever met.' She then goes on to say how 'extra bright' her children are, what wonderful terms she is on with all three of her ex-lovers, and how the children aren't at all screwed up. When her last lover left, they evidently said, 'Isn't it lovely – we can now put the pillow in the centre of your bed again.'

Wednesday, November 1st

Go to Hallowe'en party with the children. Tremendously impressed at how hard the hostess has worked. Cardboard cut-outs of black witches, and hollowed-out pumpkins with candles inside hang from the ceiling. Feel guilty that I don't do more to entertain my children.

Apple bobbing is not a great success, as the children keep leaving their loose teeth in the apples. Discover Henrietta holding forth in the kitchen, I retreat to the drawing-room. Five minutes later, she follows me, saying bossily, 'Please will you do something about Felix, he's beating up all the little girls? Sorry,' she adds with a Chekhovian dying fall. I go outside to find not just Felix but *all* the boys beating up all the little girls.

Fortunately a diversion is provided by a ghoul arriving. It is Rosie in a white sheet with a skeleton mask stuck on the front. It is wonderfully spooky, and all the little girls have the vapours and scream with terror.

Later Rosie and I drink too much wine and I take her in her ghoul kit out on the Common. First we accost two middle-class, middle-aged women, who start to walk very fast away from us, then break into a high-heeled run. Then they hear me say, 'Really Rosie, you mustn't frighten people.'

So they creep cautiously back like little calves, and start to giggle and say, 'We really think you're rather wonderful. What a se-uper idea,' etc.

Then two punks come up, so Rosie jumps on them. They are quite unmoved, and say, 'You don't look well, dear, do you want us to call a doctor? There's a lot of 'flu about.'

Rosie and I get totally hysterical with giggles.

Friday, December 22nd

Feel utterly desolate. *The Sunday Times* is on strike, it appears, indefinitely. Also receive telephone call from bank manager; after which it finally sinks in we have no money to buy the children any Christmas presents. As I don't want to cry in front of them, I go out after dusk and sob on the Common. Bump into Rosie and her Peke, Michelin. She is so sympathetic. I pour out my troubles and then, having dumped, feel better and enough in control of myself to go home.

Three-quarters of an hour later, hear a dull thud on the hall carpet. It is an envelope from Rosie, containing £100 in notes. Unbelievably touched, particularly as I know she is desperately broke herself at the moment. Walk round to her house at once and return the money, but feel never could I be richer in friends.

Monday, December 25th

Christmas Day. Beautiful, mild and gentle, midges everywhere. Mabel swims in the Brook, and the little green cow parsley is putting forth shoots. The Common is all cleansed by the recent frosts and wears a brown ruff of trees against a sky the colour of Mary's robes.

Sunday, December 31st

Watch miraculous performances of *Die Fledermaus* on BBC 2. Decide one should never be ashamed of being a popular writer, or of the joy comedy can bring.

Go out into the garden at midnight under a russet sky; all the bells are ringing the New Year in. You can hear the happy chattering of parties all around. The autumn cherry is smothered in white blossom, ghostly in the half moonlight. There's a cat plate filled with rain-water on the table. Mabel does not like the New Year. A firework party in Lower Common South results in a lot of woofing. We can hear All Saints' bell tolling – appropriately, in fact: unbeknownst to any of us merrymakers, a car bomb had gone off in Albemarle Street a few moments before, killing two people. Make New Year resolution to be a better writer.

1979

Monday, January 1st

Heavy fall of snow, the sun comes out round the church, pale
amber through the bare spiky lime trees, casting a pale blond rinse
on the snow. Beverley Brook is the most beautiful I've ever seen it:
inky black between the white banks, with jet trees swathed in
white above. Sexy Rexy, the brown, smooth-haired mongrel, who
looks so like Fortnum and who used to be such a friend of
Maidstone's, is doing some practical barking, from the safety of the
path leading to the Ranelagh Estate and a hundred yards away
from Fortnum. Hundreds of footprints, from birds, dogs and
people have already spoilt the virginal white of the snow.

Lunchtime: go out in a blizzard, all the morning's footprints have
been wiped out and whitened over. Snow – the J-cloth. Fortnum
slips when he tries to lift his leg. As he looks hastily round to see if
anyone has witnessed his loss of dignity, I quickly study a blackbird. Mabel keeps taking snorting bites of snow. In Barnes
Graveyard, each grave sleeps under its thick eiderdown of snow,
and the evergreens are bent double with the weight, particularly
the cedar – I bet it's sighing for Lebanon.

Each branch has its coating of snow, making strange patterns –

particularly on the arthritic acacias and the rheumatic multi-twigged thorn bushes. The vertical branches of the Lombardy poplar, however, have already lost their witness. The tree looks like a paintbrush dipped in burnt umber against the stark white landscape.

During most of this year 'The Sunday Times' was on strike. In the spring, I was too busy finishing my book on class, getting Felix into a new school and worrying about money, to write much in my diary. As we could no longer afford a secretary and a Nanny we decided very reluctantly to replace them both with one girl. She is called Maxine, is from the country and is an absolute darling. I don't know how else we could have got through this time.

Friday, April 27th

Felix goes off to boarding school. He is ten and three-quarters. Most boys go at eight, or even seven. Will he find it more difficult to adjust? He looks so happy and excited in his new uniform. Disgrace myself by being the only member of the family to cry. After he leaves with Leo and shiny new dark blue trunk, I go for a cold, green walk with the dogs. Spring returns, but not my Felix.

Sunday, April 29th

Out on Common with Emily. Unable to appreciate beauty of spring because so furious with our bank manager for bouncing Felix's first term's school fees without reference. Emily has bought two balls like pale Jaffa oranges.

'They are very useful balls,' she tells me, 'as they don't hurt when they bounce.'

How very different from our dear bank manager.

Wednesday, May 2nd

Absolutely shattered by miserably homesick, tear-stained letter from Felix. He hates school, and wants to come home.

Meet Henrietta in Lurker's Paradise. Make the mistake of telling her Felix has sent a miserable letter home, and asking how long did it take her pale elder son, Henry, to settle down at his prep school?

'Oh, at least two years,' she says airily. 'But then Henry is *so* sensitive.'

Digest this information round the Common. Either she's implying Felix isn't sensitive, or I'm going to have to endure two years of miserable letters.

Bump into Rachel, who I know disapproves passionately of private education, and particularly boarding schools. Can't resist dumping on her that Felix is miserable.

Rachel says surely I saw the film *If* and should have known and didn't I read that piece in the paper about bullying in prep schools? Feel utterly suicidal.

Sunday May 6th

Spend a lot of time on the Common or hiding in the potting shed, to avoid creditors. Maxine, our new secretary, tells them I'm abroad. Mrs Thatcher has won the election. Having met her and rather liked her last year, I am pleased she has won. Leo is absolutely furious and spends the evening growling in a *Planet of the Apes* gorilla mask. Cheered up by happier letter from Felix; he has made 'quiet a lot of friends, including some boy who's seventh from the frone, and lives near the Dead Sea'. He hopes I'm not going to have a 'navoss brackdown'.

Monday, May 21st

The white chestnut candles are out. I love the different coloured flecks of candy pink, flame and yellow, and the stamens like lovely long eyelashes with orange tips.

Monday, May 28th

Very excited to find viper's bugloss on the north side of Beverley Brook. It is very pretty, like an Edward Lear plant, curling over at the top and hung with pink and purple bells – not unlike comfrey. Heartsease, which is purple and yellow, like miniature pansies, is blooming on the west of Barnes Graveyard. Have tried and failed to transport it to our garden. Feel this is rather unflattering when it flowers cheerfully on in the Graveyard until November or December.

Tuesday, May 29th

April shower weather continues. Puddles everywhere reflect thunder grey sky, brilliant green grass, young trees and the clashing cochinealed pink of the hawthorns. The cow parsley sways along the Brook, like foam breaking over a green wave.

Meet Rachel and Henrietta and lead them off to admire my discovery of the viper's bugloss. Henrietta says, crushingly, that it is not viper's bugloss at all but merely a variety of comfrey.

Thursday, May 31st

Caught in an electric storm on the Common. Never seen anything like it. Rain like machine-gun fire, incredible green light above bottle-green clouds, trees bowed down with rain, gutters overflowing. Get home drenched to find water pouring through the drawing-room ceiling, on account of blocked balcony drain.

Fortunately, our next-door-neighbour is at home. He jumps gallantly across from his balcony – rather like *Private Lives* – and dries off my balcony with an amazing suction contraption called a 'Jet Vac'.

I have never been wetter. Hope I might look rather like Sophia Loren, with my clothes sticking to my magnificent figure. Alas, when I look in a mirror afterwards, I find the remains of last night's mascara have streaked my face, and my figure is not swelling nearly so voluptuously as Sophia Loren's.

Saturday, June 2nd

Darling Felix comes home for half term; wait excitedly for his first reactions on seeing the Common again. He says it looks a tip and why hasn't it been cut? I suppose he's used to the shaven pitches of school.

Monday, June 4th

About to leave for launching party for Putney Common Arts Festival when I receive a telephone call from our new bank manager. If we are to extract ourselves from financial mess, he says, we must sell the house to realise some capital. Putney, despite Rachel and Henrietta, suddenly becomes very dear to me.

Go to party feeling shell-shocked. Watch new Conservative MP

145

for the area being stopped at the gate because he hasn't got a ticket.

'But I am your Member,' he tells a lot of Scouts on the gate. Scouts are totally unmoved and he has to wait five minutes until Scoutmaster arrives and establishes his identity.

Our Member, in fact, turns out to be rather nice, and jolly to talk to, a slightly Bertie Wooster exterior hiding an astute brain. His pretty dark wife, who is a barrister, straightens his tie and brushes a few flecks of scurf off his shoulders.

I chat to Roy Plomley, who lives on the other side of Putney. What a charmer he is! – and so sympathetic, I nearly dump on him about our financial crisis.

Everyone keeps coming out of the church and saying, in delighted tones: 'Such a shame it's so packed and one can't see the exhibits'; thereby relieving them of the onus of buying one.

The Brigadier stands beside his five oil paintings, as though he were taking the salute. Would love to buy one but our bank manager would not feel the same way.

Tuesday, June 5th

Felix goes back today. Shock of telephone call from bank manager has subsided and panic is beginning to take over. Have last cold walk with Felix who says he is being dreadfully bullied by his dormitory captain, whose father is very rich and has five cars. He shows me a black bruise on his arm, caused by some dreadful torture called 'dead arm', where they pummel away at you. Says they also flick him with wet towels. Feel quite sick and say I'm going to ring the Headmaster. Felix says don't do that, or they'll bully him even worse.

Return home and hollow out centre of Biggles novel, by cutting a square out of inside pages, so Felix can smuggle in sweets. Hope he doesn't forget and open up the book like Amelia Ann Stiggins' umbrella, so that all the sweets fall out. I brisk about like a jolly nurse trying to stop him crying. I now understand exactly why nurses adopt this hearty 'How are we today?' manner.

Thursday, June 14th

Bitterly cold; incessant rain. Putney Show may be cancelled. Both Fortnum and Mabel decide it is too cold to bathe today.

Mallow is out by the Brook, hideous with its pinky-mauve stripes. How much prettier is the purple goatsbeard called salsify, which has the palest drained heliotrope flowers with violet centres. The nettle tassels are turning pink; cow parsley leaves are turning crimson.

Last night's storm has brought down a large plane tree on the Big Common, and scattered tiny green conkers all over the paths. The snails usually crawl up last year's nettles to make love, but today it is too windy. Wonder if they have a snail coastguard who puts out a 'Dangerous for Copulation' sign. The acacia is in blossom; its white cascades shiver in the breeze like lambs' tails.

The Common is so lush the long grass can't carry the weight of water. The dogs make tunnels through or hurdle over it. On the Flower Garden the bryony is curling round the elder and falling in lovely cream drifts.

Friday, June 15th

Walk with Emily, who is delighted to be off school because she woke up with a bellyache. We pass a group of young and rather handsome men mowing the grass by the bridge. I walk through high thistles and nettles, rather than display my fat, purple hairy ankles. Their mower struggles through the undergrowth, followed by a smoking froth of green grass rather like blendered spinach.

Emily says 'Do you know adders? They live in cracks.'

Sunday, July 15th

The path on the north side of Beverley Brook is now christened the Pineapple Walk because it is covered in summer with pineapple weed, an unobtrusive plant that smells of pineapple when you squeeze it between your fingers.

Saturday, August 4th

Very warm. Common very empty. Lulled into a false sense of security and do not keep an eye on Fortnum and Mabel as they pass Cat Corner. Next minute they are baying furiously after a black cat which shoots up a slender rowan tree. I rush after them, yelling for them to lay off, which brings the entire Ranelagh Estate in curlers and braces out onto their balconies for a Grand Guignol perform-

ance. The cat, poor terrified idiot, jumps out of the tree, before I can reach it, and lands on Fortnum. The dogs lay into it; a second later it is dead. It is utterly horrible. Having dropped the leads, I can't find them. All the Ranelagh Estate erupts over my head; 'Oughta 'ave them brutes put to sleep'; 'That's the mate of that spotty-ficed one'; 'Keep them on a lead'; 'Eighty-six percent of dogs are out of control'; 'That's Mrs Bowen's Blackie they got, she'll have somefink to say when she gets home'; 'Put 'em to sleep' etc. etc.

Finally I find the leads, catch the dogs, beat them and shaking like an aspen, I go round and bang on Mrs Bowen's door. Fortunately, she is out but her husband is at home, 'On the sick,' he says.

I ask him if he can come and see if it is Blackie. So he and I return, to identify the corpse, with more catcalling, fishwiving and torrents of abuse descending on my head from the gallery. To their intense disappointment and my equally intense relief, it is not Blackie.

Go home, praying it's a wild cat; but that still doesn't make it any better. Mabel is bitterly ashamed. She presses her head against my thigh all the way home, then leaps into the air to kiss my face, pleading with me to forgive her.

Sunday, August 5th

Still feeling sick about the murdered cat. Both dogs firmly on the lead past the Ranelagh Estate; the air is full of thistledown. The rowan berries are a brilliant orange. I squeeze the mugwort flower, it smells medicinal and acrid, like athlete's liniment. The bindweed is blowing out its delicate white trumpets, so beautiful, to conceal the treachery of its ascent. Pink and white columbine stars the path with its sweet vanilla smell. The hogweed is very high; so are the nettles and the thistles. The willowherb, rose mauve with its cherry pink stems, rises out of the nettles like sun-flushed bathers in a high green sea.

Later, as I type in the garden, I am constantly distracted by the 'tink tink tink' cry of the blackbirds, trying to divert feline predators from their nests. Feel slightly less guilty about the dogs getting a cat – but not much. An eye for an eye is no justification.

Monday, August 6th

Fortnum is in love with an apparently spayed bitch called Mandy. Mandy's owner, a grandmother with auburn hair, is very nice about the romance but says it was very embarrassing as, last Sunday, Fortnum mounted Mandy in the churchyard (carrying on in time to the five minute bell, no doubt) and then got stuck. All the old ladies, hurrying to be in time for Matins, had to avert their eyes.

Tuesday, August 7th

Go for a walk at dusk to Barnes Graveyard to smell the evening primroses, having just read a passage in Eleanor Sinclair-Rhodes's *The Scented Garden*.

No evening scent [she writes] has the fascination of the delicate fragrance of the evening primrose, especially that of the commonest variety. These pale moons irradiate the twilight with their sweet elusive perfumes. Like the flowers themselves, their scents as night draws in become full of mystery and hold imagination captive.

Reach evening primroses, but disappointed to find scent rather voluptuous and unbathed, liked overworked courtesans.

Bump into my lovely friend Mrs Murdoch, who has two golden retrievers and walks with a marvellously straight back. She doesn't think the smell of the evening primroses is much cop either.

As it is getting dark, we walk home together and don't wait to see if the scent of the evening primroses improves as night draws in.

Wednesday, August 8th

Go out at lunchtime: find a small crowd with placards outside Putney Hospital, ringed by four times as many policemen. They are protesting against the proposed shut-down of the hospital and set off in a very orderly fashion along the Lower Richmond Road, intending to link up with other protest groups. Feel desperately sorry for them. As the unemployment figures rise and rise there seem to be marches everywhere. Is Jarrow going to be repeated?

With such a rainy summer, August this year is ravishing and not gone to seed as it usually is. The trees have had time to reach their full, dark green maturity: the blackberries are reddening, the bracken turning yellow; pale pink soapwort in the Flower Garden is charming against the gold of the ragwort.

Tuesday, August 21st

The planes this year have lost more bark than I have ever seen before. All along the paths, it is coming off in great sheets, crunching beneath my feet like popadums and leaving white corpse-like trunks behind. I hope they are not dying off like the elms, or the sycamores, west of the Flower Garden, which all seem to be slowly dying of 'sooty bark' – a disease in which the branches lose their bark and eventually drop off.

Mabel clambers eight feet up a tree after a squirrel. Fortnum, mouth watering, gazes up at another squirrel washing itself on an oak branch. Suddenly the squirrel stops washing and, reaching into a hole, starts pelting Fortnum with nuts. Fortnum retires abashed.

I cross the Big Common to the ranger's hut. Old Dick comes out and presents me with a beautiful bunch of roses. Tomorrow he says he will have a surprise for me.

The second Common, happily, hasn't been mown since the show and is now covered in sow thistle, clover and dandelion clocks. Also allowed to grow have been a rough yellow cow parsley, which I think must be wild parsnip, and an enchanting cornflower-blue daisy, which turns out to have the unromantic name of chicory. Evidently it closes at midday and doesn't open at all in bad weather. Sensible plant.

Wednesday, August 22nd

The hot weather has brought out the flashers, who have been kept away by the cold and rain. Meet Ken, the Common ranger, who says Putney is very quiet compared with Wimbledon. That morning a message had come over the walky-talky that a man was running round the Wimbledon Common horse exercise ring wearing only a hat and dark glasses. I say he would have looked much more decent if he'd been on a horse.

Progress on into Barnes Graveyard. Quite relieved to see policeman on a motor bike, patrolling flashers. He says flashing is only an offence when the member is erect. Surely that can't be so – what about streakers at Twickenham? Hope Fortnum doesn't get arrested.

Just as I am passing the ranger's hut, Old Dick scuttles out and hands me 'the surprise', which is wrapped in brown paper. He tells me not to open it until I get home. It turns out to be his autobiography, beautifully written in long hand in a blank-paged scrapbook. He has even gone to the trouble of ruling all the lines in pencil.

In the enclosed letter, he says he is certain – as the Goddess of the Common – that I will be able to get it published. Alas, no heavenly powers could achieve this: it is of absolutely no literary merit at all. Feel desperately depressed about the whole thing.

Friday, August 24th

Oh dear, oh dear, spend my time walking round the Yarrow Meadow and Barnes Station, because I daren't face Old Dick and tell him his book is unpublishable.

Saturday, August 25th

Sneak out at dusk and go slap into Old Dick.

'Well,' he says, no doubt expecting me to produce a publisher's contract.

I stammer that I enjoyed the book, but I think in the present economic climate it will be very difficult to get it published.

He looks at me astounded as though I have just turned down *Hamlet* or *The Iliad*. So I mutter that I will try it out on my publisher friends.

'Well if you enjoyed it,' he demands, 'surely other people will.'

Go home feeling gloomy and ungoddessly.

Saturday, September 1st

Still avoiding Old Dick. Leo says that there's no point in trying the book on anyone: just keep it a month, then say I've tried and give it back.

Sunday, September 2nd

Walking along north side of Beverley Brook the pineapple weed rattles against my feet. The lovely green willow south of the corner of the football field is collapsing, lying down on its elbows, and providing great sport for the dogs who run up and down the branches. The ivy has grown six feet up the plane trees facing the football pitch. The chestnuts are turning by the children's playground; the one second from the right of the slide always goes orange first.

Monday, September 17th

Go walking with Emily; a beautiful day. Old Dick shoots out of the hut and enquires after the fate of his book. Lie that it's still being read by one of our publisher friends. He gives Emily a packet of Polos. Progressing on, we decide that if Fortnum lifts his leg twenty-one times on the walk, my new book on the English class system will become a bestseller and we will get out of our financial mess. Fortnum wees eighteen times and we have to walk three times round the churchyard at the end of the walk before he achieves the required twenty-one.

Wednesday, September 26th

Outraged to find the children's playground by the Eternal
Triangle has been painted; the roundabout is grass green; the slide
bright red and the swings blue and yellow. All these primary
colours clash horribly with the autumn. The faded rose and
turquoises were so much prettier. One blessing is that the marigolds
on the putting green look less garish now the leaves are turning and
the grass yellowing.

Friday, September 28th

Autumn is full of red touches: red maple on the Common, red
leaves like moroccan leather on the sorrel, the peachy red hawthorn
leaves, the crimson of the dandelion leaves and the dark crimson of
the mugwort and soapwort stalks, all doing their bit. Bracken,
hideous at the moment, is brown and yellow. The blackberries on
the other hand are at their prettiest, with ruby red, yellow and coral
leaves. Every gust of wind brings a shower of leaves out of the
birch; the ground is covered with conkers and crunched acorns; the
autumnal smell of the poplars is very strong. According to the

Reader's Digest Field Guide to the Trees and Shrubs of Britain, it is only the balsam poplar by the bowling green which ought to smell and then only in the spring, but now all the poplars are giving off this heady voluptuous sweet tobacco smell.

Monday, October 1st

Walk with Rosie, who has a new boyfriend.

'Half of me's in love with him,' she says.

'Which half?' I ask. 'Bottom or top?'

(Rosie says she hasn't been to bed with him yet, so probably top half.)

Thistle still producing new pale amethyst flowers. Hawthorn berries darkening to the colour of garnets. Elder have lost their berries – just filigree stalks now. Roses and St John's wort still out in the Graveyard. The acorns are turning brown. Rings of toadstools everywhere – so relieved the dogs ignore them.

On the way home, Old Dick looks over the fence and asks about his manuscript. Stand on one leg and say these things take a long time.

Sunday, October 7th

Passing the ranger's hut on the way home, I jump nervously as Old Dick calls out to me; but he only wants to tell me the very sad news that Putney Hospital is to close. Have done nothing to help. Didn't even join the protest march in the summer, or write stern letters to the Minister of Health (Minister of Death more likely). Incongruously beautiful day – red berries on the holly glittering in the sunshine. Leaves drifting down onto a ground carpeted with orange and yellow.

Sunday, October 21st

Meet dear old man with tartan cap, who used to have two dogs: a sleek black mongrel bitch who never left his side, with whom Fortnum fornicated regularly, and a brown and black rough-coated street dog – a merry rogue, who was always whoring and fighting, wandering, charging across roads and bringing traffic to a standstill. Last week, ironically, the bitch was run over. The sun was in her eyes, she thought she saw her master across the road.

Never having run loose she had no traffic sense and charged across the road, hitting a lorry head on. She died in his arms by the side of the road. There were tears in his eyes this morning. The rogue brown and black street dog misses her, and now never leaves his master's side.

Monday, October 22nd

Surprised at the number of fathers going alone to church at All Saints'. Do men become religious so they can get a bit of peace and quiet away from their wives and children on Sunday morning? Old Dick asks again about his manuscript. Say it is with another publisher.

Tuesday, October 23rd

Go out on the Common. Fortnum meets one of his worst enemies, Buster, a beautiful collie. Usually Buster is walked by his master who is six foot, ringing-voiced and very capable of daunting Fortnum. Today, alas, Buster is with two little girls. Fortnum, who is no respecter of minors, wades in. The little girls run home in floods of tears. A great deal of Buster's hair is shed but no blood.

In the evening Buster's six-foot master bangs on my door. He is puce with rage. He says the little girls were very badly frightened, Fortnum is a menace, and if there is any more trouble, he will report me to the police for being a nuisance.

Saturday, October 27th

As a result of Fortnum's set-to with Buster, every time Buster walks past our house, he rushes up to the front door, jumps against the panes of glass and barks and barks. Fortnum and Mabel bark back dementedly in reply. I'm sure they're all going to go through the glass.

Sunday, October 28th

Very windy day. Our porch is full of leaves. Buster comes bouncing up in his usual noisy vein and, not seeing today's milk hidden by leaves, sends it flying and breaks the bottle.

Maxine and I chunter disapprovingly, and are just going out to get another bottle when Buster's master forestalls us. Opening the front door, we find another bottle, with a note saying: 'Sorry for my stupidity, Love, Buster.'

Thursday, November 1st

After the milk bottle incident, the ice is broken as well, thank God, between me and Buster's owner. Although our dogs bark like mad, they give each other a wide berth, and Buster's owner and I grin and shout pleasantries at each other across the Common.

Friday, November 2nd

The square of limes framing All Saints' have been stripped in a week. The churchyard is carpeted with gold. Walk with Rachel and Clarissa, a new addition to the Common, who has just moved to the area. A very handsome ex-headmistress with a direct manner, she is always impeccably dressed and made-up first thing in the morning. Junoesque, blonde and poker-faced, she reminds me of one of the more august female statues in Barnes Graveyard, suddenly come to life like Hermione in *The Winter's Tale*. I do hope no one graffitis her plinth.

Like Rachel, she approves of well-behaved dogs and has a well-trained cocker spaniel, called Hugo, with whom fortunately Fortnum doesn't fight, as Hugo is castrated and offers no sexual competition. Fortnum behaves impeccably today, probably because Clarissa is extolling the merits of castration, and says she will lend me a book on the subject.

Monday, November 5th

Last yellow leaves of the poplar, and the dark gold of the plane lit up by the afternoon sun. Go for last miserable very cold walk before taking Felix back after half term. Notice, once again, ash leaves fall late but in stems – seven or nine leaves at a time without changing colour. A sort of mass suicide, rather appropriate to our mood.

Felix insists on discussing where I want to be buried. He's going to buy me a solid gold coffin so the fleas and hedgehogs and foxes don't get me; and list all my books on the tombstone; and then build a chapel round in memory of me, so I won't get graffitied and dug up by vandals. He's also going to bury the dogs beside me. On such a morbid note we narrowly avoid a frightful fight on Barnes Common with a huge black dog.

Tuesday, November 6th

Common after rain – shining black tree trunks with drying grey patches against the orange leaves, lovely contrast of the turning bracken and the mole-grey feathers of the willowherb. Yesterday, the first frost brought the leaves off in shoals. So sad for the acacia to lose so many of its little egg-shaped leaves when they are still green. Ravishing dark brown trails of bindweed shrivelling on the mole-brown hogweed. All the world seems yellow and gold, and suddenly the most mundane things become beautiful: a redhead in yellow gumboots and a mac, walking a red setter across the first Common; the yellow AA van against the orange street lamps. A fleet of magpies wing out of the oaks like animated zebra crossings.

Emily runs down the path to meet me.

'Mummy, Mummy, something very wonderful and funny happened today. Lucy and I were both sick at the same time after macaroni cheese.'

Thursday, November 8th

Meet Chester, an English setter, who has a sweet-natured, handsome master whom Rosie and I both fancy like mad. A fortnight ago Chester's master tells me his mother-in-law gave him and his wife a lemon yellow sofa as a birthday present, much prized and worth a fortune, but which they both thought was rather ugly and promptly allowed Chester to appropriate. Alas, yesterday the mother-in-law arrived for supper. And before anyone could stop him, Chester sauntered in and measured his speckled length on the sofa. Whereupon Chester's master and mistress exclaimed in horror and pretended this was an unprecedented move on Chester's part, and tried to evict him.

It was like, said Chester's master, the flesh made lead. The eternally amiable Chester growled ominously and refused to budge. The mother-in-law departed – much affronted.

Very thrilled my book on class is Number Four on the bestseller list.

Feel very guilty about Old Dick's manuscript.

Friday, November 30th

Iron hard frost. The mulberry tree in the middle of our lawn is leafless in a day. Thrilled that *The Times* appears again after an absence of a year.

Meet Frances the feminist and her vegetarian dog; she says, 'I am a writer like you, but my drawback is that I'm an academic, and am not prepared to settle for anything second-rate.' Her book on sisterhood, however, is nearly finished, she says, and will make far more of a stir than my book on class. The English, she says, will read *anything* on class. Meanwhile, unobserved, her vegetarian dog is joyfully crackling the remains of a Kentucky Fried Chicken.

Saturday, December 1st

I finally screw up courage, and return Old Dick's manuscript with a letter from Leo in his role as publisher waffling on about the economic climate. Sadly, I do not think Old Dick will ever speak to me again.

Sunday, December 2nd

Another new arrival to the Common is splendidly stylish Scottish Molly. She is in her fifties, like Clarissa, but still very attractive in a tousled way. She is small, with a marvellous figure and a surprisingly deep voice. Her mane of red hair is only just beginning to fade and matches the oak leaves that still cling to their branches. She has spent most of her life living in very grand style in Aberdeenshire. But as a result of death duties is now living in a small cottage near the Hospital. She and Clarissa, the headmistress, are near enough in age and class to be rather wary of one another. I'm afraid Beverley Brook is no adequate substitute for a loch. Molly owns a charming, but very greedy, Dalmatian called Ophelia, who keeps scrabbling at my pocket after biscuits.

Today Ophelia tears the pocket of yet another coat. But I shouldn't grumble as this coat was left behind by a journalist made light-headed by too much of Leo's whisky. To placate me Scottish Molly says that at last year's Head of the River Race she heard a disgruntled woman saying, 'Well, at least I can say I saw Jilly Cooper and her two dogs.'

Discover I've come out on the Common without any Kleenex. Have to use scarf as handkerchief.

Saturday, December 15th

Icy wind and frost has whipped most of the leaves off trees. Stand on Common Road and look across to Maidstone's boundary. White bones of the silver birch with the very soft brown of the poplars behind them are beautiful above the lion-coloured grass, the donkey-brown yarrow and the rusting of the bracken.

A poplar tree on the Fair Triangle breaks in half. Ladies from Lower Common South – some rich and thrifty, some in straitened circumstances – rush up and gather firewood before the men with saws turn up.

Pull scarf out of pocket to put on head against icy wind and find it all crinkly from blowing nose on it yesterday.

The bracken in the sun is glorious – the stalks more ginger now that the greying leaves. It is bent over like muslims praying to Mecca. In the middle of the bracken is a large pink blanket.

Sunday, December 16th

A man in a woolly hat is altruistically mowing the grass in Putney Graveyard. The smell of new-mown grass suddenly brings back summer.

Monday, December 17th

Snow – bitterly cold. Along the Pineapple Walk, find an intrepid ragwort in flower. This has been an incredible strip-tease year for the plane trees. The ones by the three poplars have shed all their bark down to the ground. Evidently they do this to shake off layers of grease and dirt which clog up the pores and stop them absorbing sap. It is very pretty out to-day. Walk home with the snow and the apricot sunset.

As Leo is grumbling about dog shit in the garden, I walk dogs on the Common at midnight after watching Dracula film. Feel rather nervous, but find it's beautiful outside and very light. The snow is orange in the street lamp light, and gilded by the warm yellow lights in the drives of Lower Common South. There is the occa-

sional spat and crackle as clumps fall off the trees. Mabel and
Fortnum have a wonderful time, bouncing and snuffling.

Monday, December 24th

A mezzotint day. Going Christmas shopping down the Lower
Richmond Road, I see Shep, a local mongrel and one of Fortnum's
enemies, tied up outside the butcher's shop. Shep's mistress tells me
that she has taken in Sexy Rexy, as Rex's master fell under a train
while drunk, and for a week or so Rex has had no home. Shep is not
unlike both Rex and Fortnum, except that he has Spanish policeman's hat ears and a tail bent over almost to touch his spine.
Despite a wise, battle-scarred face from fighting, he looks very neat
and smart because of white socks and a snowy white shirt front. He
nods at me cautiously – recognising Fortnum's mistress.

Later I struggle back along Lower Richmond Road from the
shops, weighed down by fifteen carrier bags, face like a mandrill's
bottom with cold. Even the pink setting sun between the houses
over the grey poplars doesn't raise my spirits.

A kind boy in a hooded anorak, high as a kite, comes wheeling out of the Spencer Arms and runs after me. He seizes my carrier bags.

'Shame to see a lovely young girl having to carry so much,' he says. Then he looks round the front, and sees my tiny Christmas eyes and red-veined purple face, and says, 'Well shame, anyway,' and was I shopping for the family?

Walk dogs late on Christmas night. Very hard frost, but alas no snow; the grass is starched and glittering beneath my gumboots. Bells ringing out from Barnes, a carillon on the frosty orange air. See David the sculptor looking very glamorous in a fur coat, going to the post, of all unbelievable things – perhaps he's in love. Feel depressed and doubt if I'll ever be romantically in love again; that time has passed with all its aching joys and dizzy raptures. Must be tiredness, and a long draining year. But cheered up because the Common is looking so beautiful. All the Lower Common South houses lit up with gold light. Orion's sword points directly at Cedric's house, Cassiopeia is rising out of Putney Cemetery and the tail of the Great Bear falls into the doomed Putney Hospital. Go home and we pack the children's stockings. Emily has decided it would be expedient to believe in Father Christmas again.

Tuesday, December 25th

Heavenly frosty day. Walk dogs and meet Crispin, the budding artist. We discuss what Jews feel about Christmas. Crispin says a Jewish friend of his has a tiny Christmas tree in the back parlour, so that the Rabbi who lives opposite won't see it.

Feathered grass and hogweed are crystallised and beautiful. On the way home, I see Old Dick, presenting Frances the feminist with a bowl of hyacinths and feel sad that he barely nods at me. Fortnum, to make up for this, celebrates the day of our Lord by not having any fights. He and Mabel have two pounds of sausages specially cooked for Christmas lunch; Mabel has a squeaky cutlet, Fortnum a squeaky bun. Fortnum chews and squeaks both frantically until the squeaks fall out.

Wednesday, December 26th

Go for a walk with Rachel who has been quite nice to me this year. (Probably because I've been having a bad time.) She says Sexy

Rexy's mistress has died too and he's being looked after by his 'auntie' (Shep's mistress). He seems to spend a lot of time on the Common howling.

We meet Blossom, who is white and woolly with short legs and a sweet face and who, according to her owner, has a weak heart. Fortnum pursues her briskly, nose to bum.

A dog walker with two other woolly dogs, Sam and Wellington, has pinned a Christmas card to one of the acacia trees in Barnes Graveyard, saying 'A Happy Christmas to all Dog Walkers from Sam, Wellington and Jessie'.

Saturday, December 29 th

Fearful hangover. Leo, who is utterly fed up with me pouring out orange juice and coffee, and spilling milk and Alka Seltzer, dispatches me to the Common to get me out of his hair.

Going over the second bridge and looking back at the Ranelagh Estate, notice wonderful reflections of parallel trees. The planes by the three poplars catch the noon sunlight, filtering through the bare sycamore. It turns them a glorious saffron ochre – almost mustard – quite different from their usual whitish grey.

Sunday, December 30th

Meet Crispin, who says a new gay club called 'Heaven' has just opened in the West End. In the advertisements, it is described as 'Heaven – where the bad boys go'. Sounds like a good place for Fortnum.

1980

Wednesday, January 9th

Thank goodness, Fortnum waits until I've finished my *Sunday Times* piece and sent it off to have frightful fight with a black and white cocker spaniel on the first Common. Horrible owner in boiler suit launches into a stream of abuse.

'Bloody dog, keep 'im on a lead. Spoitful, that's what he is, spoitful. Let me get my 'ands on 'im and I'll kill 'im, and you're a bloody whore too,' he adds as an afterthought. Tempted to ask how he knows, but decide it is more judicious to beat a hasty retreat.

Thursday, January 10th

Still very cold. Large yellow Labrador plunges out of the bracken towards Fortnum. I grab him just in time.

'Is it a bitch?' I ask.

'It's all right,' says emergent lady in pull-on woolly hat. 'She's been seen to.'

Fortnum wades in, tail going like a vivace metronome. He does love Labrador bitches. A sort of Libido-Lab pact.

Friday, January 11th

Bitterly cold day, ground like iron. The willows swing like blond ghosts, lovely against the coral roof of Barn Elms Pavilion. Very conscious at this time of year of tree shapes: the planes look like some underwater weed splaying out their fingers. The branches and twigs of the pink chestnut hang snakily like Medusa. Most beautiful of all is the ash, gleaming silver, like a reversed catherine wheel.

Unaccountably, a scarlet G-string hangs high up from one of the plane trees along the football pitch. Has someone been doing a frenzied striptease?

Tuesday, January 15th

One of Fortnum's favourite girlfriends is a rangy black bitch with a tightly curled tail, called Skip. Today her owner, Beryl, slides up just beyond Lurker's Paradise and says may she ask me a personal question? I steel myself. Then she says can Skip mate with Fortnum when she has her next heat? Skip, she says, is the runt of the litter, and Fortnum looks a strong dog and is, she adds, a nice size. Absurdly delighted with this declaration. Fortnum looks sweet, puffs out his cheeks and licks Skip's ears. He's jolly pleased with himself.

Wednesday, January 16th

Meet Rachel and tell her about Fortnum's impending nuptials. She snorts with disapproval and says do I know what I'm doing? Say no, but I'm sure Fortnum does.

Monday, January 21st

I love rainy days, particularly when it's mild. The Common is emptied of all but the most dedicated dog walkers, and all the colours are intensified. My muscular chestnut tree by the tennis courts gleams like bronze, the blackthorn is really black and the sycamore has a metallic silvery gleam. The plane trees, soaked, are a marvellous sulphuric saffron with patches of emerald and brilliant crocus yellow.

Definition of masochism: Fortnum lifting his leg on a gorse bush.

Thursday, January 24th

Walk late again, and meet Rosie who tells me that last night Rachel's husband, Alastair, said to her in Rachel's hearing: 'It's so nice to meet upper-class people who smell like you do.'

Feel this might have been better phrased, but evidently he was referring to her scent.

Friday, January 25th

So sad to pass Putney Hospital, which is now closed. The snowman from the Christmas party looks wistfully out of a downstairs office window and inside you can still see streamers, crinkly coloured bells and Christmas cards strung across the wards.

Feel that Christmas decorations ought to be down by Twelfth Night and their continued presence may bring bad luck to the hospital and not allow it to reopen.

Joined by Syd, the seventy-year-old carpenter who walks round the Common three times as fast as I do. We discuss the sex shop on Putney Bridge. Evidently every time Fulham loses at home, disgruntled home-going crowds smash its windows. Syd the carpenter then asks me if I saw Adrian's aunt on television last night.

'Was she in a play?' I say, panting after him.

'No,' says Syd, 'a Pedigree Chum advertisement.'

Slightly mystified by this revelation until I remember that Adrian is the name of Syd's dog, a beautiful Munsterlander, dappled like a rocking horse.

'Adrian's aunt,' Syd goes on, 'was a Cruft's champion.'

Saturday, January 26th

Everyone is desperately worried about the Russians going into Afghanistan. We'll all feel much happier when 1984 is over. Meet Rosie during lunchtime walk, we are busy discussing Afghan crisis when we see Fortnum and Mabel behaving in a very Russian fashion and chasing a poor blond Afghan across the Common and down the path by the bowling green.

Rosie and I have both read Barbara Castle's memoirs – evidently she adored dogs, and was heartbroken when her spaniel died. On the strength of this, we both feel she might have made a good Prime Minister after all.

Friday, February 5th

Fortnum is mated with Skip. He takes her twice and, between takes, treats her with profound indifference. I always thought he was at least one of Nature's gentledogs.

Friday, March 7th

Skip is pregnant. Well done Fortnum. All the dog walkers disapprove. But I am *not* going to have a puppy.

Friday, March 21st

Go out to very jolly lunch for the Cartoonists of the Year Award. Feel rather fat, so I wear black trousers, and a loose silver shirt to cover the bulges. Maxine, my secretary, is in despair. 'Why do you never wear dresses?' she moans.

After jolly lunch, I do a programme for Thames Television on romantic love in the East End. I am just attempting to interview two barmaids against the hiss of the beer pump, when Eamonn Andrews sidles up. Very pleased to see him, as he is an old chum, but shattered when he shoves a large red book under my nose and says: '*This Is Your Life.*'

Now I understand at last why Maxine spent all morning trying to get me into a dress. The programme is lovely. I either cry or giggle through the whole thing. The only thing missing is Fortnum and Mabel. Very gratified that Cedric comes on the programme with his beautiful wife. They say very nicely that I am the scourge of the Common, running round looking innocent and taking down notes. Afterwards we all have a splendid, splendid party.

Dear Rosie stayed at our house all day looking after the dogs.

Monday, March 24th

Out on Common, happiness battling with an impending hangover. Bump into Rachel. Am silly enough to tell her that they did me on *This Is Your Life* last night. She bridles and is deeply squashing, and says she can't stand the programme or the nonentities they have on it. Feel hangover taking over fast from happiness. On the way home I meet our dear next-door-neighbour. Snubbed by Rachel, I do not tell her about *This Is Your Life*.

Tuesday, March 25th

Go out and bump into next-door-neighbour, who is very, very hurt that I didn't tell her about *This Is Your Life*. As a result, she missed the programme.

Decide you cannot win in life, particularly when it's Yours.

Meet Rosie, who says it was all lovely. And she cried throughout the entire programme, and hadn't the children looked adorable? One of my great sadnesses in fact, this year, is that I see so little of Rosie. She is working for her physics Finals, which she takes in May. Although I think she has a terrifically quick brain, I cannot imagine her passing them. She is so pretty and so pursued, and seems to take life so lightly. But I may be wrong because she's certainly working very hard at the moment.

It is much milder today. All the birds are fluting and bubbling as though they were gargling in dew. Along the beck, poor celandines hang down their heads inches above the dropped level of the water, as though they were little yellow birds with very thin necks trying to drink. I notice incredible durability of plane tree leaves still reddening the paths. Strips of plane bark, now lying around, have turned a rich burnt sienna like leather. The grass verge along the Eternal Triangle is mown for the first time.

Wednesday, March 26th

Attend meeting of the Society for the Preservation of Rural Putney in the Spencer Arms Function Room. A fête is planned once more in the churchyard, which will no doubt lead to much squabbling. Rosie, who has rather a yen for David the sculptor, turns up dressed to the nines only to discover he has resigned from the committee in disgust – he says they're all flower pot men. He says what drove him mad at every meeting was Henrietta coming up and saying in a low voice. 'How very good of you to come.'

Saturday, March 29th

Grand National day. Pale purple rosemary flowering in Barnes Graveyard. I find first heartsease, red dead-nettle, periwinkle, groundsel and a first daffodil in the Squirrel Wood.

Speculation is seething on the Common. Ken, the Common

ranger, is very secretive and won't let on, except that something very exciting is about to happen.

Go out at lunchtime, Ken tells me the excitement: the Duke of Edinburgh landed by helicopter at eleven o'clock. He was opening a Sports Centre on Barn Elms. Ken heard of it from the 'Ut cleaner, who heard it from her butcher, who heard it from the barman at the Barn Elms Club.

Scarlet tassels from the poplars litter the path from the bowling green down to the first bridge. Little bronze spikes of the horse-radish are already pushing through the grass.

Sunday, March 30th

Glorious sky-blue day. Walk to Barnes Station. Last year's bracken still clings onto the dotted green hawthorn bushes, like some doddery ancient lady hanging onto the arm of a handsome lover. On Common Lane, a blackthorn tree is already out and scattering confetti. The little elm copse on the corner of Rocks Lane and the Lower Richmond Road is putting out green leaves, but so many branches are already dead. They are like haemophiliac princes, doomed to die young.

Find first daffodil already smashed in the mud on the edge of the Squirrel Wood; further down on the left of the path, pass dead elm in the prickly embrace of a holly tree. Remember wistfully how once it scattered green hearts in the spring.

Monday, March 31st

Find glorious patch of coltsfoot in the centre of the Flower Garden. According to the *Reader's Digest Field Flower Guide*, even in the coldest February a single sunny day will bring them out in an explosion of sulphur yellow. Because the plant flowers before the leaves appear, country people often call it 'son-before-father'.

The white patches on the plane trunks have turned to ochre and are the texture of suede. Find first cow parsley in the hollow near Oedipus Corner.

Tuesday, April 1st

Nasty cold day. Notice all the celandines by Oedipus Corner are closed up like green crowns. Reminded of Wordsworth:

> There is a flower the lesser celandine,
> That shrinks like many more from cold and rain.

which sounds like many of the dog walkers who come out only when the weather's nice.

Wednesday, April 2nd

Radiant morning, walk dogs as the sun is rising. The shadow of the lime trees stretches to the centre of the first Common. Sparrows quarrel in the eaves of the church. Fortnum in the soft sunlight is transformed from brindle to reddy gold, like a creature in a fable.

Evening: notice bare sycamores round the first Common are shaped just like Mrs Thatcher's hair. The sky is full of shooting stars. Orion is disappearing over Putney Cemetery. Sad to see him go – he adds glamour to the sky.

Saturday, April 5th

Very very happy: Old Dick has forgiven me. Today I wave at

him and he gives me a bunch of daffodils. I shall never get back to goddess status – but at least it's a start

Monday, April 7th

Easter Monday: lovely warm day – lovers out, girls wearing T-shirts. Men study girls' chests; I study development of chestnuts. To begin with the bud looks like a pale green fluffy child's glove with no fingers; then a lean brown shoot forces its way out like a flame-shaped light bulb; then the leaves uncurl and turn backwards into parachutes. Inside is a little grape-like bunch of buds – the chestnut candle in embryo.

Humble elder is one of the first leaves out, but it is such an unobtrusive green, and lies so close to the lichened bark, that one hardly notices it.

Afternoon walk: Peter's Common, on the way to Barnes Railway Station, which appears so green in autumn because the oaks are late in turning, now looks more wintry than other parts of the Common, because the oaks are still clinging onto their red leaves, and the ground is still rusted by bracken remnants.

Sunday, April 8th

Slight frost. Clover leaves close up as though they are praying. Jays still crackling. Hear a bird singing exquisitely from a sycamore at Cat Corner near the first bridge. Am trying to identify it, when a woman in a camel-hair coat, with very dyed blonde hair, walks past me and suddenly cries out:

> Oh to be in England
> Now that April's there,
> And whoever wakes in England
> Sees, some morning, unaware....

'Can't remember the next bit, but that's the "wise thrush" over there,' she goes on pointing to the pulsating sycamore.

> ...he sings each song twice over,
> Lest you should think he never could recapture
> The first fine careless rapture...!

'That takes me back sixty years,' she continues. 'Can't remember how it goes on. Pity they don't teach poetry in schools today,' and she is off, high heels sinking into the wet grass.

I wander on, trying to think what comes after 'morning, unaware'. Suddenly I remember:

> ... unaware,
> That the lowest boughs and the brushwood sheaf,
> Round the elm-tree bole are in tiny leaf. ...

But not any more ... : Oh, my elm trees and my Maidstone long ago!

Wednesday, April 9th
Bump into Rachel, reassure her that I am definitely not going to have one of Skip's puppies.

Wednesday, April 23rd
Skip has five puppies.

During April and May I went on tour to Australia with Leo. During the three weeks, at a moment when I was feeling very down and homesick, Leo said we could have one of Skip's puppies, as long as we called it Barbara.

Barbara turned out to be blonde and utterly enchanting, but as naughty and rebellious as Mabel is good and biddable. Having to walk three dogs on the Common, I found it impossible to write my diary. Acutely aware that all the other dog walkers disapproved of my latest acquisition, I became very uptight. Fortnum picked up the vibes and took up serious fighting again.

Thursday, July 3rd
The Society for the Preservation of Rural Putney holds another fête in the churchyard.

Feel that the tremendous communal spirit, that motivated the Society a few years back, has dwindled. Certainly this fête is a smaller affair and has a smaller attendance but makes just as much money. Probably because so many local husbands prefer to fork out large cheques towards the Society than have their wives involved in the hassle of a fête.

I feel that the community spirit, the obsession with conservation and ecology which characterised the seventies, is giving way to a keeping-fit, narcissistic egoism of the eighties.

Friday, July 4th

Walk round by Barnes Station to avoid dog fights. Crossing Common Road, find the big lime tree in flower and wafting its delicate, exquisite scent.

School sports are being held on Peter's Common. Barbara can't resist joining in. Could she be the reincarnation of Maidstone? I find a great patch of Timothy grass: each blade is splendidly imperious, sticking straight up like a kitten's tail. The Yorkshire fog grass is also adorable with its crimson bell-pulls and milky green leaves, while wavy hair grass (which the Barnes Community newsletter insists is bent grass) spreads in a pink haze across the Yarrow Meadow.

On the way back across the Yarrow Meadow notice the charming white burnet roses which grow two feet high on the left of the sandy path going towards the Fair Triangle. They now have very dark crimson hips. Also find the first red blackberries and meet very nice woman with charming Dalmatian with a curly tail, which she tells me is known in showing parlance as a 'gay tail', and is very frowned on.

'He won first prize at a show yesterday,' she said. 'All the other competitors were livid and said how could he possibly win with a gay tail? I said, "Because he was wagging it so hard all the time, the judge didn't notice".'

Feel cheered up by this piece of information, because it's quite obvious Barbara is going to have an incorrigibly 'gay' tail.

Monday, July 7th

Rainy walk; few dogs about, so go in search of toadflax which, since the blazing hot summer of 1976, has never flowered on the edge of the football pitch. Enchanted to find a huge clump rising in an orange and yellow fortress on the north-east of the Flower Garden, snugly surrounded by ramparts of blackberries. Also find a clump of yellow loose-strife; in the old days, they tied bunches round the necks of draught-horses to make them more docile. Might try it on Fortnum.

Tuesday, July 8th

I do miss Rosie, but the moment she finished her finals she took off to France for a break and won't be back until August for the results. She is convinced she's done terribly badly. In her absence, I have a new friend called Tommy. He is twenty-nine, tall, dark and slim and very good-looking, with a black moustache. He says he comes from a working-class background, and is absolutely devoted to his parents and his brothers and sisters who live in the East End. He now works the telex in a bank in the city. He and his boyfriend have a great Dane and a saluki, and all live in a tiny flat off the Lower Richmond Road. They are understandably looking for a house with a garden in Putney. Tommy is simply one of the best adjusted and nicest people I've ever met. He is terribly kind, and sympathetic, but not remotely frightened of people like Rachel or Henrietta. If they snap at him, he promptly snaps back, but doesn't bear any grudge the next day.

Not only does he protect me from their sharp tongues, but this morning, I was walking Fortnum on a lead across the Common when two huge Rotweillers descended on me. Fortnum started to growl, so did the Rotweillers. They were poised for the kill, when Tommy just stepped between the contestants with his beautiful saluki on the lead, and told the Rotweillers to eff off. They looked at him in amazement, and then turned tail and rushed back to their owner.

As a result, I am Tommy's devoted slave for life. He also understands about Fortnum's difficult temperament, as Treacle, his great Dane, was also a problem puppy, and had about eight homes before Tommy took her on.

The other marvellous thing from my point of view as a writer is he is quite unhung up about being a homosexual, and talks about his various conquests and failures as freely as Rosie does.

Wednesday, July 9th

Clarissa, the blonde ex-headmistress who looks like an august female statue and who has the cocker spaniel called Hugo, is also becoming rather a chum. Today she gives me a four-leaf clover. Very touched. Could do with the luck. All around the Common the lime trees are like heavenly scented checkpoints: one on the south of the Flower Garden, peering over the Cemetery wall, lots on Common Lane, a square like a picture frame round All Saints' (but not so heavily scented) and a very strong-smelling one in Egliston Road. Their feathery yellow-flowered branches sweep the road in a primrose haze, which is so much prettier than the strident yellows and greens of laburnum.

Everyone very cross because some idiotic Richmond council worker with weedkiller has destroyed all the grass between the Eternal Triangle and Barnes Graveyard.

In the evening I go to Emily's Open Day. Deeply touched by her description of Christmas dinner:

'Mummy cooked the turkey, and bought it steadily to the table [sounds most unlikely], Daddy calved [sounds even more so] and Mummy made gravy from Bisto.'

Friday, July 11th

First sunny day for ages. On the first Common, house martins are swooping, diving, looping the loop and showing off their snow-white bellies. The Brook is very deep, all the rosebay willowherbs on the banks are paddling. Red admirals flex their wings joyfully in the privet flowers; sycamore keys are turning coral. Pink and purple balsam are coming out. They are exotic flowers with their strange orchid faces, like children with cheeks full of spinach they can't bear to swallow.

Further downstream, two ducks followed by a troop of ducklings ruffle the dark water, then all enjoy a wonderful splash, frantically flapping their wings. In Barnes Graveyard, the bees have the good taste to ignore the evening primroses, with their cloying, musty scent, and cluster round the white spiked flowers of the veronica, which smell like wild roses.

Monday, July 14th

Still very wet. Scent of pineapple rises from the Pineapple Walk along the north side of Beverley Brook. Usually one has to squeeze the little stubby yellow flowers of the pineapple weed between one's fingers to catch the smell, but this year treading them underfoot is enough. The campion is still out, but the teazels have finally disappeared, like a couple moved to the country. On the second Hillock below the patch of osiers, facing the football pitch, is a creeping brilliant cyclamen-pink plant, like a small sweet pea or gigantic vetch. After a lot of consultation it is identified by the rather unedifying name of 'everlasting pea'.

Walk with Scottish Molly and her scrabbling Dalmatian whom I haven't seen for ages. She is now settled into her tiny cottage and is full of gossip. She says Clarissa, the headmistress, is miffed because Vic, who has two Dobermans and works as a printer in Fleet Street, presented an everlasting pea to Molly yesterday, but not to Clarissa.

Tuesday, July 15th

Talk to Mrs Bond. She talks at length about modern youth and how corrupted they've been by all those 'aphrodesiracs'.

Wednesday, July 16th

Heatwave comes to the Common after weeks of rain. Dazzling blue skies, the holly is magic, palest green with shiny leaves.

Thursday, July 31st

With the continuing heatwave, the Brook has returned to its normal disgusting state. Plants that had floated happily on the high water now lie in a bewildered mass on top of a scum of old bicycles, Express Dairy crates, bottles, tins, tarpaulins and French letters. The Himalayan balsam is rather subdued this year; perhaps, originating in India, it prefers sun. But white bindweed is rioting everywhere. I always think of Keats's 'Silver snarling trumpets gan to chide'. Thistles are fluffing gently and willowherb is turning from amethyst to rose pink, but there is still not a real grey hair in the countryside.

Friday, August 1st

Everyone is away – Tommy and his boyfriend, Rosie, Henrietta, Clarissa.

Walk on Common with Rachel and Scottish Molly. Rachel's

attitude towards Molly is ambiguous. On the one hand she is impressed by Molly's patrician origins. On the other, anyone grand has pretensions and should be slapped down. Rachel today is livid with her husband, who was dead against her and the family going away to Devon for a week. Then, when Rachel had booked the tickets and organised the whole thing, she was understandably incensed at hearing him saying, in a lordly fashion, on the telephone, 'I'm just packing Rachel and the family off to Devon for a few days.'

Saturday, August 9th

Rachel back from holiday.

'How was it?' Scottish Molly and I ask.

'The scenery was lovely,' says Rachel, 'but the house was filthy. I mean they'd put a carpet sweeper over it, but no one had swept behind the settee or anything' (make mental note to Hoover under the bed tomorrow), 'and I had to take Vim to all the cups before we drank out of them.'

Molly then says, wistfully, that she wishes her husband, Biffo, could afford a little holiday.

'Well, we wouldn't have wanted him with us,' snaps Rachel.

Scottish Molly, understandably, is very hurt.

Monday, August 11th

See old Mrs Willis and her mongrel, Spot. Fortunately we are divided by Beverley Brook, so Fortnum doesn't fall on Spot. I explain that Fortnum is difficult because he was badly treated as a puppy.

Mrs Willis is most sympathetic: 'Who could 'urt 'em,' she says, 'when they're all so lovely, in't they?'

Very windy day makes me ponder about Tennyson.

'Willows whiten, aspens quiver,' is an excellent line. I can see it happening all along the Brook. But saying, 'The robin has a more crimson breast' in spring, when the colour is a sort of burnt orange without any blue in it, is rubbish.

It is time for a word now about our new puppy, Barbara, who is like the little girl with the curl, except she isn't horrid when she's bad – just very, very bad. She has no conscience and believes the whole world is designed for her entertainment. Once outside, she totally ignores me, and there's no certainty of catching her.

She also bullies poor Mabel unmercifully, hanging on her ankles, her stomach and her throat. Whenever Mabel is stalking a vole, Barbara shimmies up and spoils it. Used to rough-housing with Mabel, she also expects all other dogs on the Common to be equally submissive. Fortnum ignores her, but brings her into line when she goes too far. On the lead she's a menace, dancing round the Maypole and tying us all up, and biting through everyone else's leads. If I keep her waiting before leaving the house, I invariably come out and find three chains with the leather handles chewed off.

Poor Mabel has become very matronly and dispossessed. She is such a sweet, good-natured dog and I feel I've ruined her life. Every time she hides in her basket, Barbara dives after her and tries to push her out. I adore Barbara – we all do – but she has caused complications. Fortnum is far more stroppy on the Common – I have to watch him like a warder; and no diary writing because I can't manage my bag and three leads.

Tuesday, August 12th

Cobwebs already hanging from the gorse like sailors' hammocks. Meet Scottish Molly, who grumbles about her window cleaner. She came back from shopping and found him lying on her bed, reading her daughter's comics.

'Nice winders,' he said. 'Regency aren't they? I've got Regency winders at home and I've made all Regency furniture to go with them.'

Thursday, August 14th

Bump into Rosie, who is very brown, having just spent a month in France. She says she feels sick as the results of her physics Finals are due any day now.

Saturday, August 16th

Rosie rings with the thrilling news that she has got a First in physics. She comes round and we drink a bottle of champagne and she tells me the riveting but infuriating news that David the sculptor has been having a walk out with Frances the feminist.

Monday, August 25th

Two of my favourite dog walkers, Henry and Alice, are leaving and moving to the country. I haven't seen much of them recently but they once owned a beautiful red setter, who was a friend of Maidstone's before Fortnum arrived.

Decide to give a little leaving party for them on August 27th. Leo says I'm crazy, and no one will have anything in common. I reply that they'll have the Common in common. Leo does *not* laugh at my joke.

Wednesday, August 27th

Ghastly ramifications over proposed party for Henry and Alice. Rachel and Molly put colossal pressure on me to ask Syd the carpenter and Vic, the good-looking printer who gave Molly the everlasting pea. Protest that I don't know Syd and Vic well enough, and I don't know if they're friends of Henry and Alice.

Nor am I to ask Clarissa, the headmistress, insists Rachel, as Molly and she don't get on.

Feel intensely irritated. Take dogs out, and bump into the mother of Crispin, the budding artist. She is lovely and has blue hair like Mrs Slocombe, and insists on telling me at length about Crispin's exhibition.

Suddenly hear fearful growling from the nettles, and freeze with horror. Fortnum and Mabel have a large tabby up a tree. Leaving Barbara, thank God, on a lead with Mrs Crispin, I plunge into the nettles. Get terribly stung but manage to drag Fortnum out. Mabel follows five minutes later, in a state of terrible shakes and contrition, tail rammed, like a greyhound's, between her legs. Meet Clarissa, who is very sympathetic. So grateful, I ask her to the party. She says she might be able to pop in for a drink – may she bring her husband? Oh dear, I know Rachel will be livid; so will Molly.

Next minute, a man approaches with three lurchers. Fortnum fortunately is on a lead.

'Grab Baby,' commands Clarissa, 'or they'll eat her.'

I just catch Barbara in time.

Clarissa then tells me that recently the lurchers ate an old woman's cat, tore a Jack Russell to pieces and nearly killed Clarissa's dog, Hugo, and the owner just stands there saying 'Sorry'.

'He's a settled gypsy,' adds Clarissa.

Wonder if Clarissa isn't confusing me with gypsy, as lurchers' behaviour sounds very much like Fortnum and Mabel's.

Thursday, August 28th

Morning after party. In black gloom – nothing is worse than giving a party that doesn't work. Molly and her husband, Biffo, arrived first. She looked very nice, in a navy blue dress which went with her red hair, and navy blue stockings which showed off her marvellous legs – which one doesn't usually see on the Common because people tend to wear trousers and gumboots. I expected Biffo to be very formidable, but he was smaller than Molly and rather shy, but very amiable.

Then Rachel turned up wearing pale blue which matched her eyes and also looking very pretty. Rachel brought her husband. I said how glamorous their daughter was getting. So he said, in front of Rachel:

'Yes, isn't it a good thing she's inherited my upper-class looks?'

I'd have hit him if I'd been Rachel but she just laughed.

Then Clarissa arrived, which annoyed Molly and Rachel. She brought her husband who is very distinguished-looking, with a very slow, considered voice. He reminds one of a Jane Austen hero/vicar. They were followed by various dog walkers and their wives.

Then Henry and Alice arrived, a bit tearful about leaving, with Ken the Common ranger, looking incredibly smart in a pin-striped suit; followed by Tommy and his boyfriend, also looking very smart, in open-necked shirts, slashed to waist; followed by Vic the printer, whom I'd asked after all, who was reeking of aftershave. Finally Rosie rolled up, in a see-through shirt open to the navel, looking very sheeny and beautiful.

Everyone talked like mad, and we filled up and filled up their drinks, then people started to go next door and eat fish pie, and Leo kept saying:

'For God's sake, look after people, I can't do everything,' which always unnerves me.

Then Rachel had a row with her husband and went and sat on our unsafe bench in the garden. And all sorts of people declared eternal love, which had obviously been bubbling up for years on the Common, to people to whom they were not married.

Rosie, who'd been flirting with Vic the good-looking printer (to all the other lady dog-walkers' irritation), left early, and Vic proceeded to get drunk on Party Fours. Finally everyone left; except Vic who stayed talking about printing until four o'clock in the morning.

Go to bed, feeling the whole thing was a total waste of time. Oh God, these little things that cost so much and mean so little.

7.30 am: Leo, getting up, says party was a flop because you can't mix different classes, particularly when half the people had nothing in common except being unfortunate enough to be married to people who were boringly obsessed with their dogs.

Go out on Common in irritable mood, and bump into dear Molly. She says thank you very sweetly, and the food was marvellous, but quite understandably cannot find much else to praise. I say it was GHASTLY, and that I was fed up with Vic the printer staying until 4.30. Poor Molly said she's already been savaged by Rachel for asking Vic.

The only outcome of the party seems to be that Molly's husband, Biffo, is to give Rosie German lessons. Perhaps we'd better all start doing the goose-step. Rosie tells me she is going to take her PhD at Cambridge. She should enjoy that – plenty of men to choose from.

Saturday, August 30th

Rachel tells me desperately sad news that Sexy Rexy has been put down. How are the matey fallen? He evidently had gangrene of the ears so painfully that he couldn't bear to have his head stroked. One day his stable mate, Shep, pounced on him in play and tugged his ears. Rex turned on Shep, a terrible fight ensued.

'All in the lounge, with cocktail cabinets, china Alsatians and the G-plan flying,' says Rachel. Shep's eye was nearly gouged out, the vet had to sew it back. As a result, Sexy Rexy, who was only a long-term house guest, was put down.

I am convinced he was Fortnum's father. They shared so many characteristics: looks, loucheness, over-aberrant libido – and certainly both Barbara and Mabel inherited Rex's ears which were shaped like a Spanish policeman's hat. Now I suppose Fortnum is truly King of the Common.

Sunday, August 31st

Fortnum's scraps on the Common have become so excessive that Leo comes out with me today. All three dogs behave impeccably, and walk in Indian file behind him. Feel they might have been a bit naughtier, just to show Leo what I have to put up with.

I point sententiously to an ash tree south of Beverley Brook, and say that in Norse mythology the ash tree is where Heaven and Hell meet.

'Sounds like our house,' said Leo.

Monday, September 1st

Meet Rachel in the contented aftermath of a successful dinner party.

'We had Molly and Biffo to dinner last night,' she says.

Biffo is no longer 'that toffee-nosed blimp,' but 'rather an old sweetie'.

She gave them 'my lamb'. Molly, she goes on, is such a darling. Evidently the froideur over Molly asking Vic the printer to Henry and Alice's leaving party is now melted.

The scapegoat is now poor Rosie. She is no longer Molly's best friend, but the temptress, who never turned up for a German lesson with Biffo. Evidently the poor man had done lots of preparation and mugged up German syntax beforehand. It's nice of Molly to be so protective.

Rachel then says: 'It's probably a good thing Rosie is going to Cambridge, as she has obviously "sucked our little circle dry"' – which sounds most dubious.

Monday, September 8th

Go on the Common. Nightmarish time avoiding bouncing Afghan, predatory male golden retriever and another of Fortnum's enemies, a half-bred Labrador called Bobby. Retreat in confusion to the Yarrow Meadow. By the coach house go slap into a fierce Rotweiller called Carly. Thank God manage to get Fortnum on a lead in time. Barbara flirts with them all just to irritate him. Return home nervous wreck.

Tuesday, September 9th

Barbara particularly naughty at dinner. Leaps onto the table and nicks everyone's chop bones. After the children go to bed I say, 'Ought she to go, because I can't manage her?' Leo says: 'Yes,' very forcibly. Take dogs out on Common and cry and cry. Feel utterly suicidal. The dogs ignore me. Maidstone, for all his stolid amorality, was the one who always came up and comforted me. Feel hopeless, because although I adore Barbara, she has complicated life. Go home and have a bath, read the end of *The Incredible Journey* and cry some more.

Imagine Barbara finding her way back to Putney, like the bull terrier at the end of the book. She's so adorable I can't give her up. She comes and tries to dry me by licking me when I get out of the bath. I shall just have to write my diary in the evening.

Wednesday, September 10th

Sirocco wind in Putney, blowing furiously from the south-west, but warm and caressing. Leaves pour off the trees. I think the cold then the sudden warm has unhinged them (literally). Barbara rushes about catching them as they fall. Lots of happy days for her.

The lovely silvery willow on the Big Common, which used to be a blond ghost in winter and shaded the seat where the little nurses rested in their lunch hour in summer, is ripped in half. Surely it can't survive such a loss? Himalayan balsam beginning to look messy; the long grasses are separating and turning blond.

Thursday, September 11th

Go off to party in Surrey, carrying a large gin and tonic out to the car as one doesn't get much to drink there. Walk slap into the vicar coming back from Matins. At the party meet heavenly old woman wearing basket-weave shoes, who says it is impossible to keep up appearances these days.

'I shaved my shoes before I came out in them,' she goes on.

Friday, September 12th

Our kitchen is being ripped apart. Barbara has pink-eye and has given it to me and all the builders. We all look like a colony of white mice.

Monday, September 15th

Lovely day. Mist rising, blue haze on the trees. Leaves falling very leisurely through the thick atmosphere. Still very green. Rachel sidles up to me, and says Fortnum has been behaving very very badly recently and just followed a bitch across two main roads, to the extreme embarrassment of the bitch's owner, and I must keep him in in future. Yesterday, she goes on, he had a fight with Rebel, one of the local wandering mongrel studs.

I feel very low. Scottish Molly joins us, then Clarissa, who is followed by Rebel, the dog stud.

Stay behind to keep Fortnum away, and lose yet another lead. Rachel insists on staying behind as well, lends me her lead, and launches into another lecture about Fortnum's behaviour. Fortnum, she goes on, is upsetting everyone – why don't I always keep him on a long lead on the Common as he's obviously going to get worse as Barbara reaches puberty?

I slope off and sob by the bog south-west of the Graveyard and study triffid burr marigold. What a bloody ugly plant it is – yellow and brown and green. According to the flower book, when the seeds of triffid burr marigold develop, they have small barbed spines – like other people I could mention.

Wednesday, September 17th

Walk with Molly, who has made it up with Rosie but says she will have to go and visit her by the back roads instead of the quickest way past Rachel's house so that Rachel doesn't realise her defection.

Thursday, September 18th

Walk with Tommy who is very excited he has found a house in Putney, which he thinks will be big enough for his boyfriend, his great Dane and his saluki, and they think they will be able to get a mortgage.

Monday, October 6th

Heartsease still flowering on the grave of Emily Rixon, who died in 1925, and her husband William, who died in 1937 – twelve years later. Perhaps in lonely widowerhood he needed his heart eased.

Common dangerously swarming with cats, and Rachel. Barbara sees her first squirrel and leads the others in proudly. When Mabel sees a squirrel and tries to leap after it, Barbara gets deeply irritated and lies on top of her, to stop her jumping.

Tuesday, October 7th

Mist rising. The sycamore on the edge of the boundary and the Flower Garden is a beautiful sight, with the sun travelling across the gold leaves and the tobacco brown keys, and picking out stray blond patches of grass behind.

In the Squirrel Wood, Mabel raises her sooty muzzle to the trees, searching and searching with her huge, seemingly innocent eyes. She's like Lennie in *Of Mice and Men*.

Wednesday, October 8th

Rosie goes off to Cambridge. She is half-excited, half-sad, because she cannot take Michelin, her Peke, with her. I shall miss her very much.

Friday, October 10th

Barbara's first frost. Her mistress's frost with Rachel continues – the only weapon I have is to keep my distance.

The poplar smell is very strong. The grass is silver white, smouldering with mist, unthawed by a very low, round October sun.

Barbara is being very obstreperous, jigging up and down like Alexander in *Pigling Bland*. Mabel, thinking my back is turned, gives her a vicious growl and a curled lip, then licks her apologetically. Mabel is the conscience of all three dogs.

A new and terrifying phenomenon is the dogger: the jogger who runs with a dog and suddenly emerges, panting and beetroot-faced, out of the bushes. For whoever walks in England meets some jogger unaware.

The nightshade berries hang from the tennis court wires like huge ruby earrings. Mabel finds a squirrel but is daunted when it takes refuge inside a holly bush.

Saturday, October 11th

Common very funny. Every time Molly rings up Tommy she gets his boyfriend who, hearing her deep voice, thinks it's some upper-class pouffe after Tommy, and slams the telephone down.

Sunday, October 12th

Clarissa's cocker spaniel, Hugo, rolls in manure. Molly and I giggle. Nemesis Nemesis. On the afternoon walk, Barbara rolls in exactly the same patch.

Wednesday, October 15th

Poor Old Dick is not well. He has thrombosis and has been in hospital for a month but is now back home again. I take him some books and grapes at home, but don't stay, as he is frightened of the dogs.

Monday, October 20th

Walk dogs after gallivanting lunch. Meet Rachel and decide to give up sulking because of ravishing sunset. The sky is all apricot, rose and lavender, the sun moving slowly down towards the sycamores. The poplars are golden silvery blond against the sky as the rose deepens and deepens to a glowing luminous dark pinky coral.

The starlings are making a frightful din in a plane tree by Barn Elms. Rachel claps her hands and they all vanish in a black cloud across the playing fields.

Thursday, October 23rd

Lovely morning after grey damp cold yesterday. The beck is high and full of leaves; the trees are thinning out fast. Barbara has taken up rolling: fox's crap, dead hedgehog, goose droppings – everything goes. She folds up her front legs like a camel and squirms her shoulders along the ground, then bounces up terribly pleased with herself, as though she has smothered herself in Miss Dior. Evidently dogs roll to make themselves more important and more attractive to other dogs.

Barbara is placid, tremendously merry, affectionate, and totally lacking in guilt. She walks with a wiggle, and her tail looks as though it's just come out of rollers. She has a fox's face with sleepy slanting eyes, and one ear up and one ear down. She is always up to some kind of mischief. I truly think she is the reincarnation of Maidstone.

Friday, October 24th

The path down the right of Barnes Graveyard is brilliant red with leaves.

'We lost Hugo last autumn in Richmond Park,' says Clarissa.

'Oh dear,' I say.

'Because he was the same colour as the leaves,' says Clarrisa.

Today Clarissa suggests I take Fortnum to Mrs Woodhouse and offers to lend me a book on training dogs. Fortnum, out of sheer spite, lingers behind, voling in the middle of the horseradish, ignoring my shouts, and wagging his tail like mad. Clarissa and Rachel both bellow at him. He takes no notice, but when they bossily advance he sees them coming and scampers off puffing out his cheeks and looking important.

Saturday, October 25th

Emily comes on a walk, having been to stay with her friend Lucy.

'Lucy's granny is nice, but a chatterbox,' she said. 'And I'm not inviting Tamara to my party – she flicks peas everywhere.'

Meet Crispin, the budding artist, who tells me of a lovely misprint about a violinist who 'had a sensitive feeling for Beethoven's quarters'.

Friday, October 31st

Meet dear old lady and tiring ancient Yorkshire terrier bitch. She tells us in a corncrake voice that the bitch has been better since they removed an ovary the size of a cricket ball. Then we meet darling grey-haired woman who used to have a black spaniel, who died recently. She says she is so bored now she's retired and can't afford a new dog. She walks a lot because it's cheap and it's such a beautiful autumn. She tells us she always removes all the red toadstools in case any of the dogs mistake one for a ball. Find little heartsease, still surviving, wrapped around with frost-starched red-gold chestnut leaves, like a fox fur tippet.

Wednesday, November 5th

Bitter wind. Plane leaves cling all the way up the Pineapple Walk wire fence, turning it into a golden hedge. Pine needles lie all over the path down the right of Barnes Graveyard, like the result of a savage shearing on the hairdresser's floor.

Saturday, November 8th

Bitterly cold. So many plane leaves are blown into the porch that the milkman fails to see the empty milk bottles. The rattle, as I walk through the dead red chestnut leaves, is like waves on the shingle.

Sunday, November 9th

Heavy rain; walking through dampened leaves, it sounds like someone frantically pulling Bronco in the office loo. Notice human ageing process is reversed in the white willow. The silvery grey leaves turn blonde and then fall off. It is the same with the white poplars.

Barbara eats a toadstool. Terrified by a description of warty caps in a book I've been reading about gypsies, which says they have little poisonous hooks which attach themselves to the inside of the throat of the victim, who dies a slow and lingering death. Barbara, however, seems to be in the pink, and eats the toe off one of my best pairs of black shoes for pudding.

Tuesday, November 18th

Meet old man with snarling bull terrier called Oboe, who, he says, is a terror for dogs.

'If he hears barking outside, he goes straight through the winder. Every time he meets another dog, 'e sets abart him.'

Oboe always sleeps on the verandah at home, and in cold weather the old man steals out and puts his cardigan round him. Often he finds other members of the family have stolen out and put their cardigans round him too.

Monday, November 24th

Two Alsatians, who bay like the hound of the Baskervilles, appear to be living on top of the Spencer Arms Function Room. They pace up and down and, from boredom and probably despair, bay at every dog that passes. A bicycle hangs from the plane trees above the bus shelter. How did it get there? Not much fun having it land on one's head.

Tuesday, November 25th

Exquisite day – but fraught with danger, all the cats, wild and tame alike, crawl out to enjoy the pale mild sunshine.

See two goldfinches. They are so neat and merry with their black and yellow wings, red and black muzzles, and breasts the soft brown of sycamore leaves. They are delicately picking seeds out of the thistles.

The path up to Oedipus Corner is laced with yellow willow spears. A tennis player in a blue track suit stoops to pick up a ball near the fence. He tells me Barbara is a lovely little dog and very friendly. Barbara belies this by flouncing off in a swirl of plane leaves.

The buds, already sticky on the bole of the horse chestnuts, give a promise of spring. In the morning sun the little oaks shine like orange Hallowe'en lamps. Meanwhile the bees are going berserk in the yellow ivy flowers hanging over Putney Cemetery wall. They smell rather like elder flowers but less potent. I always think of Shelley:

> He will watch from dawn to gloom
> The lake-reflected sun illume
> The yellow bees in the ivy bloom,
> Nor heed, nor see what things they be:
> But from these create he can,
> Forms more real than living man,
> Nurslings of Immortality.

Oh, I want to be a great writer, but I don't believe I ever will be. Anyway how can I watch anything from dawn to gloom, unseeing and unheeding? – Fortnum would have chewed up a thousand Yorkshire terriers.

Wednesday, November 26th

Poor Tommy thinks he will have to put his dogs into kennels, as the bank where he works has changed and lengthened its shifts. He daren't risk changing jobs, as he might blow the mortgage on his new house. To rise is indeed to feel less secure. Clarissa's daughter has got engaged; she is about to meet her fellow in-laws and is very apprehensive about the whole thing. She has also slipped a disc. Rosie, with the whole of Cambridge at her disposal, has fallen madly in love with a London architect; she says she hates Cambridge and misses Michelin, her Peke, who's had to stay in Putney.

Barbara has had dog 'flu and didn't eat from Saturday to Thursday. I had to take Fortnum and Mabel out on their own. Mabel adored it, and tugged playfully at Fortnum's lead for the first time since Barbara came, making me feel a louse.

Thursday, November 27th

Away doing television. Came home to snow. The conservatory is temporarily blotted out, the bamboo tree is weighed down like an English sheepdog, the stiff leaves of the magnolia hold up flat slats of snow, the yellow leaves of the mulberry are lovely against the white garden. In our warm brown newly-painted kitchen the crimson azaleas and pink cyclamens crowd along the window ledge.

I am reminded of Louis MacNeice's poem, *Snow and Roses*.

Friday, November 28th

The dogs love the snow. Mabel finds a green ball, and Fortnum circles her, snorting and biting at the snow. Sadly it is not settling: the flakes are too big and it gathers in huge wet points on the end of my gumboots. But it is so beautiful. In close-up the grass bristles blackly through the whiteness. At a distance, tawny or green patches of the grass show through, giving the snow an emerald or gold tinge. The church roof, All Saints' School and the church-warden's house all have their icing of snow; so do all the big houses along the Common. The richest people's roofs seem to melt first because of central heating. Leo says this is rubbish, the poorest melt first because they haven't had their roofs insulated properly. He pooh-poohs it when I say they may not have any heat on either.

Snow is nestling in the groin of the lime trees, and along the privet hedge, thickening and whitening the grass.

Fortnum pinches and punctures Mabel's ball, hooking it onto one of his teeth, like a gooseberry; then he buries it in the snow so Mabel can't have it – he is the original dog in the manger. Mabel looks for it everywhere, but as the churchyard is full of broken glass I take her home.

Saturday, November 29th

Barbara still ill. I pass the vicar on the way out with Fortnum and Mabel, and ask him to pray for Barbara. He asks what's the matter with her.

'She hasn't eaten since Saturday,' I say. The vicar throws his hands in the air crying: 'Are even dogs anorexic these days?' But, like jesting Pilate, doesn't stay for an answer. Grumble about vicar to Mrs Bond who says since his daughter got engaged to a Bishop's son he's got very uppity. Vicar's lack of prayer works dramatically

– in the evening Barbara has a bowl of milk and two mouthfuls of chicken.

Sunday, November 30th

Walk with Tommy and Clarissa. Clarissa's meeting with her fellow in-laws went off very well. Tommy is very red-eyed, poor angel, because he is about to put Treacle, his great Dane, and Zelda, his saluki, into kennels. He is terribly worried Treacle will pine because she had such an unhappy early life.

Crispin joins us, just back from New York, which he says is full of pin-stripe-suited men on roller skates and grand pianos being played in banks. Girls kept asking him to smuggle in Yves St Laurent lipsticks which are banned in America because they're supposed to give one cancer. There is also a terrible witch hunt going on about deodorised Tampon poisoning people and being a male capitalist plot to kill off women. Evidently one woman in a million has died. As we discuss this, Fortnum is just stopped from murdering a Yorkshire terrier. Crispin says Fortnum ought to appear in a butch commercial for me and my Yorkie.

Sunday, December 21st

Molly and Rachel have been attacking Barbara and saying how naughty she is. Barbara has chummed up with Clarissa's cocker spaniel, Hugo, and keeps swooping down on Rachel's dog, Bridie, in a pincer movement. She also bullies Molly's Dalmatian, Ophelia, endlessly.

Monday, December 22nd

Walk with Rosie, who's back after her first term at Cambridge. She says the Common is very parental, which means people treating people like children. We then discuss rape. Rosie says she knows a husband who says his wife is quite safe alone in winter as she always wears eight layers of clothing because their house is so cold, and any rapist would get bored trying to undress her.

Thursday, December 25th

Very mild and summery in between showers. Birds all singing

carols as they sunbathe on the bare trees. Willows all gilded by the sunshine. Heavenly rainbow rises out of red houses along Rocks Lane – first just straight up, then arching into a bow. Rush off to find someone to show it to. Meet Clarissa and her husband, who say, in a somewhat blasé way, that they have already seen it.

Friday, December 26th

Very hard frost. Leaves white and crackling, nine-sixteenth moon on its side looking over the tennis courts from a clear, pale blue sky. Green woodpecker laughing its head off at Christmas festivities. The oak copse is still dazzling orange in the sun. Clawing bracken gradually collapsing down the trees.

Monday, December 29th

Get up early; walk with Rosie who's been to a dinner party where everyone was very unpleasant.

'You know the sort of thing – piranha fish in the finger bowls.'

Molly joins us and says how snobbish people are in Barnes and Putney: 'I may be poor,' she goes on, 'but I'm all right.'

While she stops to chat to a friend, Rosie and I discuss Fortnum's increased aggression.

'One has to accept the fact that he's a delinquent,' I say.

'A de who?' asks Molly catching up and excited at the prospect of French genealogy.

Go to butcher to buy hearts for the dogs for a treat. I get the last one. A fat woman behind me in the queue asks for five hearts, like a bridge game. I feel very guilty and offer her my heart, but she flounces off to the butcher down the road.

Tuesday, December 30th

They are cutting the undergrowth along Beverley Brook; it looks tidier but less romantic. Pass couple gathering winter fuel and two men in tweed coats playing tennis. Struck in the Graveyard, by contrasting beauty of silver-green softness of lavender and sharper spinach green of the box. Running past, Barbara looks quite patrician with her flowing tail and her ears flat. Then she sees a skewbald Italian greyhound in a coat, which is total anathema! Her tail curls over, her back ridges, one ear pricks up, the other drops and her eyes narrow: plebeian as ever.

1981

Saturday, January 3rd

South-west wind continues for three days – very mild and gentle.
The lack of rain has made the leaves very dry; they circle and eddy
on the pavements then rattle across the road.

Find huge political meeting of seagulls on Barn Elms playing
fields. As I reach the grassy Hillocks in front of Beverley Brook,
they are suddenly overhead, being blown like a snow-white
blizzard against an angry dark blue sky with the trees lit up behind.
They seem to enjoy their joy-ride, then suddenly they all get bored
and go back to the playing fields. Why do birds go around in flocks
at this time of year? Is it safety in numbers, ganging up against the
elements, keeping warm together; or are they looking for future
mates, and feel they are most likely to find them at a party? At a
time of year when food is short, it would seem more sensible to
forage on one's own.

Elizabeth and Philip, a local couple, have broken up. Leo says
it's a clash of the lack of two cultures.

Sunday, January 4th

Bump into Rosie, who says Frances the feminist has just sent her manuscript on sisterhood to a publisher. She told Rosie she was convinced she has produced a small masterpiece. Rosie and I agree that we cannot bear the thought of the book being accepted, because Frances will be *so* smug. On the other hand, says Rosie, it might mean that Germaine, the poor vegetarian dog, gets a better diet. After Rosie slipped Germaine a pork pie last year Frances didn't speak to her for a month.

Thursday, January 8th

Wake up to pale orange light and sky, and snow, and blizzards outside whirling and turning in the bitter east wind. It is so bad that the school run is cancelled. All down the street people are revving up and grumbling and scraping ice off the windscreens.

The man down the road, who always seems so *much* more interested in his ancient Ford Escort than his wife that we call him the Car-Respondent, is now pulling back the tarpaulins to reassure himself his car's still there.

Set out as late as possible with the dogs, find snow thick on the pavements but not settling on the roofs because the wind keeps sweeping it off. There is no colour on the Common: just the odd blade of grass sticking through the snow, like badly-shaved legs. The dogs adore it. Fortnum plunges his face in a drift, then bounces out with snow all over his forehead and round his collar, so he looks like a seedy vicar with scurf.

Meet Scottish Molly, her cheeks bright red, coming from the west into the vicious acupuncturing wind. I turn round and walk with her. The snow is murderous, like little bits of glass stabbing away at our faces. Soon you'll be able to drive to Cornwall on my red veins. When we get back to the Lower Richmond Road, my hands are so cold that I can hardly put on the dog's leads. A robin flashes by the Barnes–Putney junction – like a drop of blood on the white snow.

Tuesday, January 20th

I bump into Frances the feminist, who says she has had the manuscript of her book on sisterhood acknowledged by the publishers.

'The only reason your books sell,' she goes on, 'is because you always have your picture on the jacket.'

She then says one shouldn't descend to such sexist ploys, and serious writers never have their faces on the jacket. But as she is a one-parent family, and, unlike me, has to support her numerous children single-handed, her friends in the Women's Movement have persuaded her to allow her photograph to be put on the front of her book when it is published.

I send up a fervent prayer that the book will be turned down, then catch the lacklustre eye of the sad vegetarian dog, and add, by at least one publisher.

Wednesday, January 21st

Rosie and I walk with Clarissa. Rosie and I make some dismissive comments about Frances endlessly blowing her own trumpet. Clarissa says very kindly:

'It's only insecurity. I've studied psychiatry,' she goes on. 'I think such people deserve every sympathy.'

'Clarissa, you're *so* much nicer than I am,' says Rosie.

'And I am,' I say. 'You've got a lovely nature like Mabel!'

Clarissa looks pleased, and starts to beef about her ancient aunt, then remembers her lovely nature, and says: 'Of course the old girl did give me a beautiful scarf for Christmas.'

How one can manipulate people.

Tuesday, January 27th

Go out late at night. Fog coming down like a blanket. The trees look cloudy, like X-rays of lungs full of tubercular patches. Surrounded by beams of light from the orange street lamps, they appear as though they're wearing long pleated dresses. The mist is orange from the neon lights, which are in turn softened by the mist, which is coming down so fast that trees keep vanishing before my eyes. I turn back to the warm, comforting gold of the lights of Lower Common South. Suddenly a ghostlike figure in a hood comes creeping past, and as suddenly vanishes – like Christ on the road to Emmaus.

I call the dogs nervously, not even giving Mabel time to have a pee, and run home.

Thursday, January 29th

Just about to go out on the Common at lunchtime, when Maxine shouts, 'Fortnum's being sick.' I rush downstairs; he tries to come to meet me, leaping on the spot like a dolphin, but his little back legs keep collapsing. He is frothing at the mouth and having some kind of fit. We wrap him in a towel and rush him round to the vet. When he fails to attack a handsome male collie on the doorstep, we know he must be ill.

In the surgery he recovers, following me round, and then leaping fatly onto Maxine's lap. Mrs Fraser, the new vet, who has just taken over from Dr Findlay, says he must have had a terrible fright, because his pupils are vast. She thinks he's probably eaten something poisonous, but being such a strong dog, and so well muscled, he's thrown it off and managed to sick it up.

We keep him very quiet for the rest of the day. Maxine agrees it's like a.. Agatha Christie novel, and there are probably lots of people who would be only too happy to bump off Fortnum.

In the evening Leo comes home and says Fortnum hasn't been poisoned at all, he's just suffering from too much sex.

Friday, January 30th

Emily develops a raging temperature and retires to bed. Leo comes home and claims she's caught it from Fortnum. God – men are irrational!

Sunday, February 1st

First snowdrop buds sighted on the edge of the Eternal Triangle – sticking skyward like space rockets.

Saturday, February 7th

Snowdrop buds turn over and droop their heads.

Saturday, February 14th

Bitterly cold; sun smouldering through the mist turns the frozen grass into a cornfield. Fortnum, having recovered from his fit, celebrates St Valentine's Day by getting stuck once more inside Mandy the ginger bitch – this time outside Cedric's house.

Mandy's mistress says I ought to take Mabel and Barbara home, as it's such a bad example for them to see their father in such a compromising situation. Mabel, Barbara and I go home and have a cup of tea. Then I go back alone, and Fortnum decides to detach himself. He returns home very uppity, and eats all the other dogs' dinners.

Thursday, February 19th

Bitterly cold still. Two furry silver shoots have forced their way out of the brown buds on the osiers by the corner of the football field. Pass rather shabby man by the tennis courts gathering vast quantities of leaf mould in Harrods plastic bags. Perhaps he's a distressed gentlefolk. On the way home, Barbara, who has no sense of proportion, picks a fight with a large grey police horse.

Friday, February 20th

Frances the feminist's book on sisterhood has been turned down – by a woman editor, which makes matters worse. The Common rallies. Clarissa rings her up and says there are plenty more publishers in the sea, and Molly rings up and says all your friends are worrying about you, Frances. Frances, now the blow has fallen, is rather chipper and embattled, and enjoying the luxury of everyone feeling sorry for her.

'The person I feel sorry for,' says Rosie, 'is that vegetarian dog who now, no doubt, will get its lentil ration cut.'

Saturday, February 21st

Walk with Molly who is having a dinner party that evening, and flapping about what to cook. Say the only thing I can't eat is veal. Molly who isn't listening says, 'I'm going to give them Osso Bucco.'

'That's easy,' says Clarissa, who's just joined us.

'Thank you, Clarissa,' says Molly waspishly.

We then have the recipe twice over from Clarissa.

Sunday, February 22nd

The Common is getting quite ridiculous. Evidently Molly ticked off Clarissa the other day for walking with Crispin, the budding artist.

'Crispin is Jilly's friend,' Molly went on firmly, 'and Vic the printer is my friend, and Syd the carpenter is your friend, Clarissa.'

'Like some ridiculous barn dance,' snorted Clarissa to me afterwards.

The whole thing's like adultery. Crispin evidently went to have a drink with Clarissa to see her paintings, but was not allowed to tell Molly.

Leo says we're all menopausal. Mugwort is supposed to cure it, but is unfortunately not in flower at the moment. Roll on summer.

Wednesday, February 25th

See first celandine, very cold and tucked up, near the three poplars. Snowdrops still unopened, but don't blame them in this cold.

Bump into Mrs Bond. Her nephew has piles, she says, her doctor told him it was because he'd got a sedimentary job.

Saturday, March 7th
Snowdrops finally open.

Monday, March 9th
It is the crimson stems and tiny red buds on the wild rose bushes on the Flower Garden which give them a lovely dark red haze. Discover Clarissa lurking by a very pale and anaemic clump of daffodils in Barnes Graveyard.

'Lack of nitrogen,' she mutters darkly. 'I wonder what was the matter with that corpse.'

Friday, March 13th
I bump into Old Dick's darling wife. She says he is very poorly, and she doesn't think he's going to last long.

Saturday, March 14th
Week of incessant rain and very mild weather has brought the spring on in seven-league boots. The osiers are now a haze of softest silver angora, ghostly and bridal against the gaunt dark planes behind. Look for the first coltsfoot. Find a dazzling gold bed open on the second Hillock, with their strange mare's-tail stems and crimson buds. Find more out on the Flower Garden.

Meet sweet man with beautiful black and white collie. He bought it, he says, as a puppy from a farmer in Wales, during a rain storm. The farmer was smoking his pipe upside down so the rain didn't soak the tobacco.

When asked how much he wanted for the puppy, the farmer replied, 'About fifty.' When the prospective owner said that seemed a bit steep, the farmer said he would have given the puppy away, but felt he ought to charge something. Eventually the prospective owner twigged that the farmer only wanted 50p, and refused to accept a penny more. He evidently now boasts to all his Welsh farmer friends about his dog living in London. Collie *de grandeur*.

Lunchtime: Terrific thunderstorm. Walk when it's over. The privet round the church is absolutely loaded with raindrops, turning it into a marvellous silver bank.

The alder catkins are crimson by the Brook. The snowdrops, having waited a month to come out, are all blown in a week. The floor of the blackthorn thicket on the west of the Flower Garden is carpeted by ivy. Soaked with rain, it gleams in the shafts of sunlight like silver treasure at the bottom of a dark cave.

Sunday, March 15th

After three months in kennels, because Tommy was moving house and is on longer shifts at the bank, his two dogs are back on the Common again. Treacle, the great Dane, who was the one Tommy was most worried about because she'd had such an awful start in life, seems unaffected by her stint in kennels. She looks terribly well, and bounds round the Common today like a prep school boy who suddenly realises, after separation, that his parents are rather nice after all.

Zelda, Tommy's saluki, who's always been very undemonstrative, has grown a huge red woolly coat like a yak from living in a kennel outside. At the sight of all her dog friends – Ophelia, Michelin, Hugo, Mabel, Barbara and Fortnum – who all gather round to welcome her, she suddenly stops in her tracks, and lets out a series of long earth-shattering howls, and then cries real tears, which course down her silky ginger cheeks. Fortnum licks them away for her. It is so touching. We all have lumps in our throats. Zelda, like Mabel, is so much less demanding than other dogs, that one is inclined to forget how deeply things affect her.

Monday, March 16th

Cold weather sets in: all the little birds caught on the hop. Spring came much too fast this year. I prefer it like Christabel: 'Spring comes slowly up this way.'

Meet Clarissa and Rachel striding across the Flower Garden, like bathers wading in shallow water. They have been examining the white blossom on a copse near the two blasted oak trees.

'We think it's wild pear,' announces Clarissa.

I think it's damson, but keep my trap shut.

I am reminded of a frightful prissy girl at my primary school, who said her mother would never allow her to ask for damson jam, because it had the word 'damn' in it.

Friday, March 20th

Out in a sweater. All the blossom has come out in a whoosh, and there are misty palest green haloes round every tree. Find little bluey-purple flower on the banks of the Brook. Clarissa says it is water speedwell. The Common is being mown for the first time. Breathe in glorious smell of wet earth, blossom and grass mowings.

Saturday, March 21st

Took the dogs out on the Common at about seven in the evening – it was already dark. Barbara started playing up, refusing to be caught, and dancing up the middle of Egliston Road like Gene Kelly. Thought: 'Oh to hell with her, she'll follow me' and set off for home. Next minute a car came round the corner, there was a hideous bump, and a terrible screaming. Barbara charged past me into the house, covered in blood like a foetus, her little back leg a pulp of red flesh with all the bones laid bare.

The driver of the car knocked on the door and came furiously into the house, saying, 'My wife's pregnant, and is very upset by the accident.'

Got on to our vets, who were off duty, and then on to a relief vet somewhere in Upper Richmond Road West. Couldn't hear the exact directions because I was shaking so much, and the washing machine was spinning.

Maxine, Emily, Barbara and I set off to find him. It was a nightmare. Barbara was so brave, she sat shuddering and pouring blood with me in the back. We couldn't work out where Sheen Lane ended and Upper Richmond Road West began, because all the numbers were hidden by trees or shop fronts, and we couldn't stop because it was a main road. After several abortive consultations with Italian restaurants along the way – who seemed to have neither customers nor telephone books (do they never ring anyone up?) – we finally found the relief vet's house: a gaunt Victorian building with no lights on. We rang and rang the door bell. Finally a pale girl answered, and said they'd been operating on a cairn who'd swallowed a bear claw. At the smell of antiseptic Barbara started shaking even more violently; she bit the assistant once, and the vet twice before he could inject her, and she pulled back terrified against me when he took her away.

The cairn was still lying, out like a light, in the operating theatre and a bald cat was mewing in a cage. Maxine and I got home and sobbed our hearts out. Poor, darling Barbara, and it was all my fault. There was blood everywhere – all over the carpets, the kitchen floor and the skirting-board. Maxine washed most of it out, but it had soaked deep in the carpets. Neither of us felt up to consulting Mrs Beeton on how to remove it.

The relief vet rang at ten, to say he'd operated on Barbara, she had two severed tendons, and had lots of stitches, and would have very sore toes for a bit, but would recover. For this relief, much thanks.

Sunday, March 22nd

The vet rang at 10 am to say we could pick up Barbara. Took the other two dogs out first; then Maxine and I went to pick her up. She is a game little duck. When she saw us, she flattened her ears, wagged her tail and gave the ghost of a wiggle. The one most upset is Mabel. When Barbara came back she couldn't stop whimpering, and kept going up to Barbara's basket and trying to get her to play. Fortnum doesn't give a stuff.

Monday, March 23rd

Barbara eating well – chicken, scrambled eggs and lamb chops – and hopping around on three legs. Mabel, poor disaffected angel, won't touch a thing.

Maxine went out and bought Barbara a vast circular basket, so she can lie with her legs stretched out comfortably. She lies on my old black fur coat, like Juliet performing theatre in the round, flanked by 'Get Well Soon' cards. She got one from Battersea Dogs' Home, saying: 'All 550 of us at Battersea are thinking of you.'

Sunday, March 29th

Mothering Sunday. The children are wonderful. They tidy the whole house. Felix types a breakfast menu, complete with VAT. Barbara has chewed off her bandage, and is now so neurotic about

going to the vet's that she has to be given an anaesthetic to put her out every time.

Monday, April 13th

From you, dear Diary, have I been absent in the spring, finishing a book on mongrels.

Today Clarissa shows me spotted medick on the second Hillock above the Brook. It has little yellow clover heads and clover-like leaves with black crescents in the centre. According to folk lore, these were caused by Christ's blood dropping onto clover growing at the foot of the cross. It is often called Calvary clover.

The dogs crop ecstatically at the spring grass.

Tuesday, April 14th

The turkey oak is out on the Fair Triangle. It has tiny catkins and red oak apples like Worcester pearmains. The sweet chestnut near it has strange creamy flowers shaped like starfish. Even the moss by Mill Hill is putting out tiny red shoots with bobbles on the end. The blackthorn is browning and over, but bluebells are coming out. Poplar smell, suddenly evoking the autumn, is very strong by Barnes Station. Once again the steeplejack snails hang in triplicate on the stalks of last year's nettles, above the stings of the new growth. The north-west corner of Barnes Graveyard is at its most enchanting with purple periwinkle, blue-grey rosemary, pinky-purple dead-nettle, stinging sapphire bluebells, and dark purple and yellow heartsease.

Wednesday, April 22nd

My waistband is very tight as a result of Easter Choc-in. Try and walk a bit faster. Now I am forty-four, I find it is not as easy as it was of yore to jump from the path along tennis courts up onto the little two-foot wall edging the Graveyard.

Notice the chestnut candles on the south side of the tree always come out first. Lime leaves are all hanging downwards out of their pink coral buds – like tiny green handkerchiefs on a black clothes line. Daily the handkerchiefs get larger and paler. Some ash leaves are out – some still in the sooty hoof bud stage. Garlic mustard is out by the Brook.

Walk with Frances the feminist. Dare not ask about her book on sisterhood, as it may have been turned down by another publisher – or, even worse, accepted. She uses the words 'caring' and 'supportive' a great deal. She says gays are very lucky because they have 'caring' relationships, and both partners in a couple bring in plenty of money. Says there ought to be a national wage of £6000, and one should be paid less if one loves one's job.

Reply that I should find it difficult to support a husband, two children and three mongrels on that.

'Why d'you trivialise everything?' snaps Frances.

Thursday, April 23rd

Glorious day. Little pink holly buds coming out. Notice it is the catkins on the oak tree that make it so saffron in the spring: they are much yellower than the leaves.

Saturday, April 25th

Near catastrophe. Dogs corner wild cat up rowan tree by the Ranelagh Estate. Thank God it jumps clear and escapes. All the fishwives come out and scream at me. Fortunately, dear Clarissa strides up and silences them:

'Those dogs have never killed a cat in their lives.'

Hope she isn't done for purrjury.

On the way home, I hear sad news from Ken, the Common ranger, that Old Dick is dead.

Such a slow rotten end – and such a dear man. I will miss him very much. He was certainly the only person who'll ever refer to me as the Goddess of the Common.

I remember the way he used to come out, like celandines at the first warmth of spring sun, and sit outside the ranger's hut in his black beret. I remember his kindnesses: the bunches of wallflowers and daffodils he gave me in the spring, the roses in the summer, and the endless generosity to Emily, a packet of Polos, or even an apple, every time she passed.

'Anything I can do for you?' he used to call.

His wife Lily is a saint, and has had such a bad time nursing him at the end when he was so ill, but she never lost her sense of humour.

'I've had the better of my marriage,' she would say. 'Now I'm having the worse.'

Thursday, April 30th

Go to Dick's funeral. All Saints' Church is packed. The Lady Deaconess takes the service quite beautifully; we are all moved. Old Dick's poor wife Lily looks frozen. It's awful the way one's eyes are drawn helplessly to the bereaved at a funeral.

Tuesday, May 5th

Meet Henerietta, who announces that her mother is going into hospital for a minor gynaecological operation. Say (very nobly, I feel) that I will go and see her. Then wish I hadn't as Henrietta replies that as her mother is so loved by everyone, and will have so many visitors, I will have to make an appointment first.

Wednesday, May 6th

Rosie gives a birthday party on Lurker's Paradise for her Peke Michelin's tenth birthday.

'Seventy today,' says Tommy, counting in dog years, 'and he's kept his teeth, and his figure.'

We all drink Yugoslav Riesling at ten in the morning out of paper cups. The dogs each have a slice of a chocolate birthday cake. Michelin, being a Peke, jolly nearly snuffles out the ten candles, but has to be helped a little by Rosie. Rachel's West Highland, Bridie, who's been put on a diet, although she's not at all fat, is only allowed a small piece of cake, and no second helpings. All the other dog walkers surreptitiously feed bits of cake to Bridie when Rachel isn't looking.

I am rather surprised that Scottish Molly isn't here; wonder if she's fallen out with Rosie again. Adrian the Munsterlander, belonging to Syd the carpenter, waits until everyone is looking the other way, then wolfs the remaining half of the cake, and the paper plate on which it is sitting.

'Don't you ever feed him?' says Rachel putting on her Archers voice.

Mrs Bond says she expects they'll all be under the vet tomorrow.

It is a nice and very jolly party.

On the way home, I notice that someone has carved the words: 'Ronald thinks Tits are Ace', on the second bridge.

As Clarissa's husband is called Ronald, I wonder if Scottish Molly is responsible.

Wednesday, May 20th

Common is gloriously thundery; there are boiling cauldrons of midgy shade under each chestnut. Every puff of wind is a snowstorm of blossom. Egliston Road is strewn with lilac flowers.

Thundery weather is not improving mood of dog walkers. Walk with Scottish Molly, who says she feels absolutely awful that because of some domestic crisis she completely forgot to go to Michelin's birthday party. Afterwards, Rachel had rung her up and been terribly mean, saying what a wonderful party it was, and how everyone thought she hadn't been asked.

Thursday, May 21st

Beautiful warm day. Walk in a cotton dress. Fortnum has his first dip in the Brook, bending his legs like Dixon of Dock Green.

Walk with Scottish Molly. We meet an architect with two King Charles spaniels called Edward and Percy, who chat up Barbara and Mabel in an eager but ineffectual way. I say they love girls just like chinless wonders.

'Love sleeping with them, you mean,' says Molly. 'Mind you the cavalry were always queer. One could never understand why they never reacted to one.'

The sea of green along the Brook is broken suddenly by a heavenly bright pink clump of campion against donkey-brown nettle stalks; then by the pale lilac comfrey bells swinging gently in the breeze; then by a yellow, newly-glossed clump of buttercups, all facing south, holding their innocent faces up to the first sun in weeks.

Monday, May 25th

Tommy and his boyfriend have been to a fancy dress ball. The boyfriend went as the Bride of Dracula. Tommy went as a Roman in a sheet. Tommy was doorstepped by an elderly queen dressed up as Margaret Thatcher, and said rather sharply, 'Don't tread on my sheet, it's the only one I've got.'

'Well you're not going to have much fun then,' said the elderly queen, and flounced off.

'I know one Conservative life wouldn't be better under,' Tommy yelled after him.

Rosie, who joins us, said that when Macmillan met Mrs Thatcher for the first time, she lectured him for two hours on the Common Market. At the end of which Macmillan said, 'You really ought to be teaching O-level geography.'

Tuesday, May 26th

Find purple goat's-beard called salsify on north side of the Brook, opposite a clump of alders on other side of the bank.

No one has seen a flasher this year – like the swallows, they're very late.

Wednesday, May 27th

I have a new menace figure. A man with three lurchers. He usually stands on the Big Common at the foot of Dogger Bank and lets them run round and exercise themselves. They are all male, very fast and appear pretty out of control.

Go out at lunchtime, and see Lurcher Man *in situ*, with the lurchers prowling round like tigers. Avoid him by walking over to Barnes Station. Rewarded to find tiny pale purple violets out by the path that runs along the railway lines. They don't smell so they can't be sweet violets, yet look too small for dog violets. Also find buttercups, with an unfamiliar jagged leaf, and forget-me-nots. On the Yarrow Meadow, the broom is out – white, yellow and red – and giving off the most wonderful combined smell of sweet tobacco and aftershave, like the poplar smell but sweeter.

Saturday, May 30th

Heavenly wet wet day. Very few dogs on the Common for a Saturday. The cow parsley is on the way out, and every day looks like gooseberry fool with less and less cream in it. The boles of the planes are ravishing. There are still holes in the canopy of leaves;

thus the patterns on the trunks have so much variety – part-dry, part-wet, part-sunned, part-shaded; ochres, greens, browns and greys all drying streaked like a snake skin. You could never capture it in a painting, or enhance the beauty of the young shiny green ivy clambering up the trunks.

Friday, June 5th

Life is rather stressful – as Frances the feminist would say.

The dogs put up what I think is a fat grey squirrel one hundred yards in front of the Mill Hill complex of houses. It turns out to be a grey cat, definitely not a stray, crouching precariously at the top of a seven-foot oak tree. By some miracle I catch Barbara and Mabel, and with twisted collars drag them 400 yards away where I sit for twenty minutes listening to Fortnum's hysterical yapping.

Just wondering whether to knock on the door of one of the Mill Hill houses, and ask if I can use telephone to summon Maxine's help, when Fortnum scampers up looking as though squirrels wouldn't melt in his mouth, and then does a Dixon of Dock Green knees-bend in a nearby puddle to cool his stomach.

Saturday, June 6th

Rachel and I find horrible mutation of the plantain on the north side of Beverley Brook. Instead of the usual single brown head like a woolly cigar, the head is forked into three and covered by disgusting black seeds like a swarm of ants. It is like the start of a horror film: two women on a country walk finding the first sinister clue – particularly as on the other side of the path we find an elder, prematurely aged, covered in red leaves and choked with ivy.

To add to the horror, the zombies in orange space suits have been killing off the wild flowers on the west side of Barnes Graveyard, with their haphazard spraying of weedkiller. Weeds go untouched, while heartsease, periwinkle, stonecrop and berberis are drenched and burned to death. Several lady dog-walkers (myself included), avarice masquerading as altruism, uproot heartsease and take it home to plant in the garden to save it from cruel orange zombies.

The far end of the Graveyard, on the other hand, is alight with dog daisies, bright pink rambler roses, and foxgloves – lovely against the purple of the periwinkle.

The cotoneaster has shed its white flowers, but is garlanded with goose grass turning a lovely rose madder.

Sunday, June 7th

Find melilot like a small yellow lupin on the Pineapple Walk. The sycamore keys hang in coral pagodas. Evidently the pollen count is very high – which always sounds like some glamorous French emigré getting plastered. The long grass is also as high as a springer spaniel's eye, which means one cannot see dachshunds or Yorkshire terriers coming. This is sometimes an advantage when Fortnum misses them – although sometimes he doesn't.

Meet sweet man who owns Blossom, Fortnum's inamorata, a white woolly dog who leaps off the ground four feet at a time with joy when she sees him. Today she is daunted by the long grass.

'Come on Blossom,' says her master, 'put your stilts on.'

Wednesday, June 10th

In the afternoon, walk to Barnes Station. On the Yarrow Meadow find the little white burnet roses and blackberries in pale purple flower. Also find a patch of stitchwort. Apparently a concoction of stitchwort and acorns infused in wine cures stitches – which would be helpful for all the joggers. The broom has green pods like tiny mange-touts.

Walk dogs at midnight. Bump into David the sculptor. On the way home we pass twelve-year-old local child prodigy, still up doing his homework.

'He ought to be in bed,' I say in tones of outrage.

'Perhaps he got pissed at lunchtime,' says David.

Saturday, June 20th

All the tents have been going up for the Putney Show. The dogs went berserk – every guy-rope and paling had to be inspected.

The Show itself is a great success. I judge the Fancy Dress once again with Anthony Andrews. His wife, Georgina, has grown her hair and looks very pretty. He is much jollier and more self-confident and has become a big star as a result of *Danger UXB*, and because he is playing Sebastian Flyte in the new television production of *Brideshead Revisited*.

We knock back several large gins in the steward's tent, and then insist on every single child who enters the Fancy Dress competition getting a rosette – like the Caucus Race. Even so, all the other competitors' mothers who've probably toiled all night are annoyed when we give first prize to some *Star Wars* child covered in Space antennae.

Fortnum has his first bath ever, as a result of rolling in horse-manure with Rosie's Peke, Michelin. They both turn bright olive green. The bath water afterwards looked like curry soup.

Monday, June 22nd

Find ten-foot-high cow parsley in flower on the Barnes Graveyard side of the Lower Richmond Road. It seems a complete anachronism. Cannot find it in any flower books. Grass is high and all seeding. I love the pinks of June: the rose mist of the wavy hair grass, the soft grey-pink of Yorkshire fog, the closed-up crimson lake of the hogweed buds, and the bright cerise of the clover. On the Common near the station the oaks are half-red, half-green with new growth.

The black poplars in the middle of the Squirrel Wood and the south edge of the Lower Richmond Road are shedding white very fluffy catkins, cocooning nearby hawthorns and silver birches like a heavy hoar frost. This process is far heavier than in previous years.

On the Flower Garden find melilot, toadflax, bird's-foot trefoil, tormentil and knapweed. The long green skinny arms of the brambles shoot out like the Ancient Mariner, resting on nearby thistles. Through the long grass creeps the hairy tare, a tiny vetch with a pale purple flower. This seemingly innocent plant is the enemy tare sown overnight which caused such strangulating havoc among the wheat in the parable of the good seed. After dolphining through the long grass, the dogs are very tired after each walk.

Monday, July 6th

At night the peppery smell of the privet flowers round the churchyard overpowers the heavenly waft of the lime flowers.

Sunday, July 12th

Our street party. I was very uptight about work and only stayed half an hour. Leo, Maxine and children evidently had a terrific time at the party. 'Daddy danced and danced with two punks,' said Emily next morning.

Frances the feminist had baked lots of rock-hard wholemeal loaves.

At midnight, Leo, Felix and Cedric had a shot-putting competition with one of them.

Monday, July 13th

Come down first thing and find bowl of potato salad from the street party among the lobelia in the tub outside the house.

Walk with Clarissa, who gives me another four-leaf clover. She tells me about an old lady in Barnes who has always had a breed of dog called griffins. Now at the end of her life, she wishes she'd owned dogs of other breeds as well, as when she tries to remember her individual griffins they all merge into one.

Barnes Graveyard is strewn with brown pine needles, rust-brown pine tassels and yellow yew needles. Notice the conkers of the pink horse chestnut are smooth like lychees.

In this hot muggy weather, I am constantly on the look-out for flashers and irritable dogs. Only men approaching with briefcases or women with handbags are safe.

Monday, July 27th

Do very bad interview for *Start the Week*. Janet Street Porter has a go at me about being a raging snob and writing the *Class* book.

Tuesday, July 28th

Meet Clarissa, who says: 'We all stripped while you were on the wireless,' which sounded like a mass orgy. Evidently, she took her wireless and her stripping comb out on the Common, and was joined by Rachel and a woman called Joy. They all sat on the bench backing onto Putney Cemetery, and stripped the fur off their dogs as they waited for me to speak. All the dogs look very spruce now. Wish I had been more articulate.

Clarissa says she's just bumped into Mrs Bond who has some cock and bull story about a flasher in the bushes.

'More cock than bull,' I say.

Wednesday, July 29th

Lady Diana's wedding day. Heavenly weather, French grey sky on the horizon, clear forget-me-not blue overhead. The grass is corn-coloured but dewy, with inky black depths to the trees. The forecast rain never materialises.

Walk early with Emily. We meet Blossom and her owner, to whom I introduce Emily. He says Emily is going to be a smasher.

Emily goes very quiet, and five minutes after we have left him says indignantly: 'What did he mean? I don't smash things.'

The wedding is lovely, very moving, and cheers everyone up. We have a party at home. Rosie announces she is writing a book. What with me, Old Dick, Frances the feminist and now Rosie, it seems to be catching.

Saturday, August 1st

Find strange cow parsley plant with leaves like hen's feet on the bank of Beverley Brook beyond the second bridge. Pick some and put it in my dog biscuit bag, hoping to identify it when I get home.

Saturday, August 8th

Discover that cow parsley-like plant I found by the Brook, which has now vanished mysteriously from my dog biscuit bag, is the deadly poisonous hemlock water dropwort – do pray I haven't handed it out to the dogs in a moment of vagueness. They look quite well.

Horrified also that oak trees all over the Common are producing, instead of acorns, very beautiful bright green shiny mutation discs, not unlike amateurishly applied sealing wax. Do hope it's just a temporary aberration. With the mutations on the plantain as well, it is all rather frightening.

Sunday, August 9th

Fortnum has fearful public flight with Mac the cairn. Crispin, Clarissa, Rachel, Molly and I all try to get him off. Finally, Crispin and I drag him away. A man with two King Charles spaniels rushes up, and tells me I am a very wicked woman and ought to put Fortnum down. Go home feeling suicidal.

Sunday, August 16th

Boiling day. Leo comes out on the Common with me. To ward off fights, he brings an umbrella. Fortnum and the other two dogs walk in Indian file behind Leo all the way round, as though they expect to be awarded the Nobel peace prize.

Sunday afternoon: walk across the Yarrow Meadow. The haws are turning crimson. Barbara and I eat wild raspberries. The oak trees are lovely, dark ivy green in the centre, with palest lettuce-green new shoots on the outside. In the wood, north of Barnes Station, the chestnuts are already turning, and the willowherb is whiskering. White and fleecy, it is massed above the dark gorse, like an army of baby ostriches. Suddenly there is a sound of a rusty door swinging. Barbara is searching everywhere, then a flock of grey geese fly over.

Coming home I listen to the rattle of the red 22 buses, as, turning round, they bash against our hanging plane trees, ready to start on their journey back into London again. Meet nice old-age pensioner, who's been rehoused from Paddington to Putney. Says he's knocked out by 'the country smell' of the privet.

Monday, August 17th

Radiant morning. At 10.30 am Maxine sees Rosie walking arm in arm with one of London's leading publishers across zebra crossing in Upper Richmond Road. In the other arm, she is holding a two-litre bottle of white wine. They look excited and conspiratorial. Perhaps he will publish her book. Venus, according to the papers, sets an hour after the sun and can be seen only through binoculars.

Wednesday, August 19th

Lovely morning, heavy with dew, landscape softened by the thistledown which drifts everywhere despite the lack of wind, as though a pillow had suddenly burst. All along Beverley Brook, massive inroads have been made into the thistles and the nettles, as the police look for a little Indian boy, who tragically disappeared – believed kidnapped – in the Upper Richmond Road, on his way back from Lady Diana's wedding. He said he wanted to walk home from the bus, and was never seen again.

The green copse of trees west of the Flower Garden is scorched with the flame-orange leaves of sycamore dying of sooty bark. As you walk past Oedipus Corner, you are aware of broken sycamore branches lying horizontal like roof-racks up in the trees. It is very sad. I hope they don't go the same way as the elms.

Thursday, August 20th

New stair carpet being laid. Dogs sit in martyred row on tin-tacked underfelt. Barbara, oh God, is on heat. Mabel has become very sapphic and upset, and keeps whimpering pitifully and jumping on Barbara. Fortnum, surprisingly, is showing no interest at all, but has become very short-tempered on the Common, and screams with rage if any dog approaches Barbara. Barbara is behaving like a complete tart, whisking about, waggling her bum, and adoring her new-found sexual power. All those breed dogs – Hugo, Michelin, and Adrian, are running after her – driving Fortnum demented.

Friday, August 21st

Barbara goes to Bellmead Kennels in Egham. After being run over earlier this year, she is terrified of lorries. On the way down, she ducks every time we overtake or are overtaken by one. Despite two tranquillising car sick pills, she trembles and trembles. I realise her terrible insecurity when she is no longer backed up by an adoring elder sister, and a tough protective father. I do hope she doesn't bite anyone, like she does at the vet's. Looking back, I see her dancing off with a kennel maid. I try not to cry.

Tuesday, August 25th

Great excitement. Fortnum and Mabel are going to appear in a television commercial to promote mongrel book serialisation in *Daily Mail*. How sad that Barbara is stuck in kennels.

Take the two dog stars out for a walk. They promptly disgrace themselves by routing out a plump tabby between the two bridges, and chasing it up a tree, in the heart of the densest clump of nettles. I wade into the breach, catch Fortnum just in time, and, five minutes later, Mabel. I am stung to death all over the ankles and hands. Even worse, Mabel is frantically rubbing her eyes, which start watering and streaming. Terrified it's a cat scratch and her beauty will be ruined for tomorrow's commercial, I take her to the vet, who diagnoses nettle stings and gives her the same tube of ointment that Barbara has for pink-eye. We now have six tubes.

Cheered up by other Barbara, the receptionist at the vet, who tells me that her daughter went out to a party leaving her Airedale at home. When she got back the dog had eaten twenty-six yards of tinsel and four boxes of Christmas coloured glass balls to no ill effect. This brilliant dog also opens dog food tins with her teeth when she's hungry.

Go home and ring kennels for the third time that week. Barbara has settled in, and is very happy. She's doing a lot of barking and all the kennel maids think a lot of her. Absurdly pleased by this information.

In the evening, the director of the commercial, who is called Jonah, came over, and we went out on the Common to look for a 'location'. What a pompous director's word it is. Fortnum was out on some jaunt, so we set out with Mabel. Amazed to find Fortnum

218

sitting under a chestnut tree, and having amiable conversation with two of his very worst canine enemies. Leo said they were all smoking their pipes.

Immediately Fortnum saw us, he curled his tail up tightly, and trotted over to us on poker legs. Rather like a small boy at prep school saying 'my people have arrived', but definitely no public displays of affection.

Out on the Big Common it was all grey blue and misty, the ravages of the summer heatwave softened in the half light. Snow-white flowers of the bindweed hung luminous – evidently they stay open all night if there's a moon. In bed by midnight. Make-up girl due at eight the next morning. Realise I am hypochondriacal about lack of sleep when I want to look good the next day.

Thursday, August 27th

Rise at six, and wash my hair. Dogs droop, thinking I'm going out, then become ecstatic when I walk them on the Common. A heat haze dances above the dewless grass, it's going to be a scorcher. Comforted when very attractive make-up girl turns up, because she's my age, wears a commendable lack of make-up and has bags under her eyes. Are they referred to as 'make-up girls' even when they're over seventy?

Made-up, I take up my position on a bench on the edge of the Flower Garden. The crew who are all sweet, say I look nice on film. Dogs, heavily sedated by car-sick pills, droop in the shade. Usual rat race follows about remembering my lines, looking into the camera, and keeping that nice little laugh in your voice, Jill, and not forgetting to turn the *Daily Mail* face upwards. Memorising all these things is not helped by planes coming over every two minutes, frenzied dog barking and sounds of squirrelling issuing from nearby wood; or by the make-up girl continually stepping forward with huge powder puff to de-shine my sweating face; or by dog walkers rearing out of the bracken avid with curiosity to see what's going on.

Fortnum's enemies also troop past – including the lurchers, Buster and several snarling sneering Labradors doing V-signs. Fortunately, for once Fortnum ignores them and behaves with quiet dognity. At 11.30 we have a brief break. I take the dogs down to the Brook for a drink; Mabel goes straight in and emerges black and glistening, and has to be filmed behind Fortnum for the next hour until she dries off.

We then don't break for another two hours, by which time my concentration has snapped. I fluff line after line as script and business are continually changed. The children, who are watching, keep raising their eyes to heaven and saying, 'Can't you get it right, Mummy?'

Feel miserable and unprofessional. Jonah, the director, then sends poor Felix across the Common to the local off-licence to stagger back with a whole crate of Perrier in the boiling heat. To Felix's disgust, Jonah gives him only 10p. Nice assistant director gets Mabel and Fortnum a drink in a film can. We break for lunch, I go home and have three gin and tonics, and nothing to eat, and feel better. Mabel eats three slices of mortadella, Fortnum has six; they both have a lot of pâté and cheese and all the bacon left over from everyone's 11.30 rolls, which makes them very thirsty.

In the afternoon, in order to fake a shot of the dogs appearing to pull me across the Common on the bench as they chase after another dog, I have to sit on a bench on top of a platform on wheels, pulled by three men with ropes, and held back to stop it running away too fast by three more men with ropes. Long to shout, like Tamburlaine, 'Holla ye pampered Jades of Asia, what, can ye draw but twenty miles a day?'

Instead I have to say, 'It's all in my new book *Intelligent and Loyal*,' as I am tugged away. It's the same rat race. First they want me to drop a rolled up *Daily Mail* forward, then backwards behind the bench, then keep my eyes on the camera, then keep my foot off the ground, so I appear to be falling sideways.

Concentration not at its best, because I am so worried that the minicab won't arrive to pick up Mr Knight, a friend who owns a beautiful black mongrel, who is coming over from Hounslow to appear in the commercial. The PA keeps saying everything is fine. I send Maxine home to check. Sure enough she gets home to find Mr Knight on the telephone: the minicab hasn't turned up, and, when it does, how does he find us? Arrange for the cab to bring him to the Eternal Triangle, and say PA will meet him.

'Can't one of your children wait there for him?' says Jonah.

'And get raped,' I snap, becoming irrational.

Finally Mr Knight arrives with beautiful shaggy dog, Sam, and nice wife. They all eat lots of mortadella, and don't seem at all rattled by the cab arriving an hour late. Mabel barks furiously when they turn up, and has her bark recorded on the boom.

Sam is filmed very quickly. 'You must pay him,' I hiss to Maxine.

Then it's my turn again. Jonah wants to film Mabel and Fortnum rushing after an imaginary dog, and pulling the bench with them, but they won't rush anywhere if I am sitting on the bench behind them – only if I walk away. So Maxine has to change into my jeans, sit on the bench and pretend to be my legs, while I walk off and the dogs strain at their leads to follow me.

Maxine and I then retreat behind a hawthorn bush and swap trousers, she is wearing white knickerbockers – at least I can get into them – but I am acutely conscious of my purple unshaven legs and fat ankles from the heat. Fortunately this bit is filmed very quickly and I can get back into my jeans.

Then we have reaction shots from Fortnum and Mabel. By now Fortnum is almost ODing on tranquillisers and keeps full frontalling and looking neither intelligent nor loyal.

Finally we are allowed to go home.

Arrive home to find Mr Knight has left in a state of ecstasy, having been paid twice, first by Maxine, and then by the film company who were ignorant of the first payment.

We then record Mabel and Fortnum barking. I keep them in the garden, at the back, while Leo bangs dustbins, and Maxine gouges out the non-existent doorbell. The next-door-neighbours' hose starts, their little boy starts to cry, and Jonah says:

'For Christ sake, turn that child and that hose off.'

Fortunately Next-Door doesn't hear, or she'd have no doubt leapt over the fence and socked him. At last about eight o'clock they depart. I eat three eggs scrambled and share twelve degrees of Brie with the dogs and fall into bed.

Thursday, August 27th

Walk on Common with Emily. Fortnum and Mabel look everywhere for mortadella and pâté. Notice pink columbine entwined round and bending double a stinging nettle, two dangerous enemies, locked in mortal combat, like China and Russia.

Friday, August 28th

Heatwave continues: blazing sun beating down on smouldering sand-coloured grass – just like the south of France. Go out at lunchtime and south of France image is intensified by stumbling on incredibly bronzed youth in bathing trunks. Seeing me, he executes a brilliant backward somersault. Fortnum stops admiringly in his tracks. I burst out clapping, so the bronzed youth grins and executes two more somersaults. On the way home Fortnum and Mabel get plugged into vole hole. I am just bawling them out with a stream of vile language, when a ravishingly good-looking boy in a striped shirt and grey flannel trousers, with black rings under his eyes passes by. I smile apologetically, he smiles back and walks on, then comes back and with a lot of stammering asks if I mind if he talks to me.

He is in anguish, he says, because he has found out that his girl is being screwed by his best friend.

'What's the best friend like?' I ask.

'He's called Harold,' he says, 'and works on an oil rig.'

'Well,' I say dismissively.

'He also writes very good poetry,' says the boy.

His girlfriend, he goes on, keeps saying she loves him, and not Harold, but he's not sure if he can trust her. I try to explain that her jumping into bed with Harold probably meant nothing to her, certainly compared with the immeasurable agony he's going through at the moment. The only solution, although it's difficult, is to get tough and insist she packs Harold in. Why doesn't he punch Harold on the nose, I go on, warming to my subject?

He half smiles and says Harold is bigger than he is. He is certainly the most heartbreakingly attractive boy I've seen in years; his girlfriend needs her head, or rather her heart, examined or someone else will snap him up – wish it were me.

Fortnum, however, is bristling after a passing Doberman, who is about to be let off his lead, and I am feeling hot, shabby, dirty-haired and unglamorous, so I say I must go. He looks desolate. I ask his name. He tells me, I give him my telephone number, and tell him to drop in if he gets desperate. But he'll never remember it in the numbed state he's in.

I do hope he'll be all right; I wish I'd been kinder. Dmitri, who's taking the photographs for this book, rings up when I get back. I tell him about the boy: Dmitri thinks he's a cousin of Edward Montagu's and says a solicitor was very kind to him in Wandsworth Park once when he was absolutely distraught with grief after his wife left him and let him talk and talk. Later Leo catches me feeding chocolates, given to me at a signing session, to the dogs. He says I love the dogs more than him. Say I don't but dogs are sometimes nicer to me than he is. That shows how stupid they are, snaps Leo. Go out and sulk in the twilight. I can see Arcturus, and the beautiful constellation known as the Swan. The Great Bear is playing hard to get behind a wisp of cloud.

Saturday, August 29th

Heavy storm in the night. Outside, jet-black trees and the catalpa flowers are brilliantly creamy white against an emerald-green sky. Next morning the Common is wonderful. Most of the torrential rain has been drained off because the ground is so parched, but the trees are marvellously glossy and dark. The storm has had an amazing effect on the pine needles in Barnes Graveyard: they have been driven together like tiny logs racing down a winding narrow stream. Fortnum very clinging and edgy. Thunderstorms have exactly the same effect on him as Leo does.

Walk by Barnes Station at lunchtime. Lots of bees sucking at the purple flowers of the burdock; surprised they don't get trapped by the burrs. Dogs have started voling again: all you can see and hear is frenziedly wagging tails, and the equally frenzied crackling of last year's knotweed stalks. Far too many of the oaks over here have those emerald-green sealing wax formations instead of acorns. They squidge like pickled walnuts underfoot. Terribly miss the crunch of acorns. The police helicopter is buzzing overhead still searching and searching for the poor little Indian boy who was kidnapped on the Upper Richmond Road after Lady Diana's wedding.

For some days I didn't write my diary. During this time we went to

France. The dog commercial appeared on television and was lovely. The mongrel book was serialised in the 'Daily Mail', who printed a full page picture of Mabel, Fortnum and Barbara (who had returned from kennels with pink-eye, a rash and the inevitable hacking cough, but soon recovered). As the 'Daily Mail' included an extract from the book about Fortnum's addiction to fighting, people started gathering up their dogs and bolting as we approached on the Common, which made things very peaceful.

Thursday, September 17th

Shower of rain makes everything smell lovely. Find two arm-chairs and a sofa set out like deckchairs on the Eternal Triangle. Fortnum sits on all three, then lifts his leg on the sofa. Brilliant red berries are catching the sun on the holly at corner of Putney Cemetery, but berries are still green on hollies facing north by the tennis courts. Passers by already rustling through fallen lime leaves in Egliston Road.

Friday, September 18th

Lovely soft afternoon but not muggy. A picker's rather than a flasher's afternoon. Women with plastic boxes are gathering haws, hips and blackberries. A nice man, wearing a very smart red and orange striped blazer, has balanced a ladder rather precariously against the blackthorn and is picking sloes – to make sloe gin. Sloes are very unpredictable he says. There were none at all last year. In the oak wood, the squirrels are busy gathering nuts. There is also a conker glut. They thud into the puddles and litter the paths – sad when Felix is away at school and can't take advantage of them.

Saturday, September 19th

Emily returns home and says the 'jun-yers' have been throwing up sticks to bring down conkers. A passing old lady complained that they were going to fall on the Infants' heads, and Mrs Roberts says they will be severely punished if it happens again. She says she hates her form mistress today for calling her a chatterbox, and can she go onto packed lunch at once, as soon she will be the only one in her class eating school dinners? Quailing at the thought of staggering down every morning and finding no bread on which to put Sandwich Spread, I say, 'We'll see.'

Wednesday, September 23rd

Walk very early in the morning. The slanting rays of the sun through the big pine tree are so beautiful – white and unearthly – that you can understand why in the old days people believed in heavenly visitations. A greenfinch is singing sweetly on one note. At our approach he bolts into a holly tree.

Thursday, October 1st

Mild, gentle, flickeringly sunny day. Pick two gigantic mushrooms on the first Common.

Tommy has rescued yet another great Dane, and called her Rowena. She, like Treacle, had a ghastly life before he took her on. She is brindle with a sweet, sooty black face, not unlike Mabel's. Understandably, thinking she's being abandoned again, she howls when he goes out and she's left behind in the house.

Walk over to Barnes Station at lunchtime. The maple on Putney–Barnes boundary corner is already turning dark red, enhanced by white keys like translucent fairies' wings. Dogs frantically squirrelling: they charge every tree like Don Quixote.

On the way home I meet old Mrs Woodward, who is nearly eighty-seven but still full of gusto. She admires the dogs, and says she'd once had a bobtailed sheepdog when she was young, and a ewe called Elsie, which they'd reared as a pet lamb. Elsie wouldn't touch grass, but liked ice cream and pudding and cake and everything humans ate. They all loved her, and she was great friends with the sheepdog, but she bleated when they all went out – she hated being alone, and so the neighbours complained.

'So we took Elsie to the butcher. We said, "After you've killed her, can we have the skin?" and we kept her as a rug.'

Monday, October 5th

Lovely soft evening. Trees still incredibly green. Except for a slight rusting on the first Common, and the maples turning on the Fair Triangle, it might be midsummer.

Meet poor Tommy who's having more trouble with his new great Dane, Rowena. Like Mrs Woodward's Elsie, she still loathes being left behind and howls when he goes to work. Last night, his bloody neighbour knocked on the door, and said he was on night shifts, and he couldn't sleep in the day because of Rowena's howling, and his Nan had cancer, and it upset her, and he was going to bring a court order against Tommy, and did Tommy know he was a police officer?

Tuesday, October 6th

Beautiful day. Eiderdown of thick mist lying just above the grass, echoed by a thick band of dark hyacinth-blue cloud against a sky of very pale Cambridge blue. Cobwebs hanging in dew-drenched hammocks from the thistles. Michaelmas daisies a mauve haze on the Flower Garden. Their centres start yellow then slowly turn dark crimson like a crumb-filled jam-tart.

Wednesday, October 7th

Clarissa finds spearmint – the flower not the chewing-gum – fifty yards out opposite the nurses' home. Blue chicory is still flowering in the centre of the Big Common. Triffid burr marigold is out by the bog. I also find a tall beautiful pale yellow plant like a hollyhock in Barnes Graveyard which I think is Aaron's rod.

The willow tree opposite the hospital has lost another huge

branch, like an old lady who somehow struggles on, although every part of her is riddled with cancer.

Thursday, October 8th

Hard frost, grass flattened and whitened like tagliatelle. Three-quarters moon hangs muffled and aggrieved above Putney Cemetery. Cobwebs on the thistles look very messy, as though the spiders were doing a last dance of death, or stumbling about like explorers crazy with cold. On the tallest grasses, the spiders have woven over-webs, like a dowager's rows of pearls. One particularly beautiful chestnut, two down from the slide, and the first to go every year, is turning golden orange.

Friday, October 9th

All the dogs very lippy. Fortnum even takes a bite out of Rosie's Peke Michelin, who is his only entirely male friend. Rosie says the book she is writing is going well, and divine Henry took her out on Saturday, and is taking her out again on Tuesday. Ashamed how jealous I suddenly feel. Wish my book was going well. Then Vic the printer joins us with his two Dobermans. He says the senior Doberman hasn't eaten for three days, and won't even touch chicken or hearts. I say Rosie has obviously touched Henry's heart. We giggle and I cheer up. Tommy turns up with his two great Danes and the saluki; he says Rowena's howling is much better, and the sadistic policeman neighbour hasn't complained any more.

Monday, October 19th

Take dogs out late at night. I am admiring Pegasus and Andromeda, when suddenly the dogs charge across towards the church barking hysterically at three men who are having a pee against the privet hedge. The men zip up frenziedly and do a bunk. Feel this is dreadfully hypocritical of Fortnum, as he is always doing the same thing.

Tuesday, October 20th

Walk with Molly and Rachel. Torrents of rain, and lovely glaucous green light. In the Squirrel Wood it is like walking in an aquarium. All the turning leaves swirling down like goldfish. We pass sweet old man with a poodle, who always raises his hat and says 'Good morning ladies,' when we pass. 'Good morning fish-wives' would be a more appropriate greeting. At variance with his old-fashioned courtesy, is the very obscene turquoise plastic coat worn by his fat white poodle, which zips up under the waist, but has holes for the usual offices, like some rubber fetishist's kit from Soho.

Walk at lunchtime – feeling very jumpy. Yesterday a woman walking an Alsatian was raped by a black man on the Common near Barnes Station. Another girl escaped from a rapist in All Saints' churchyard, and Rosie has been followed home from the bus stop by a horrid lurker. Almost worse, a flasher flashed at the lurcher man's wife, who ran home shrieking leaving the lurchers at large on the Common to create mayhem. Added to this the glue-sniffers are out in force along Beverley Brook. Any idea that they are quite harmless has been shattered by three of them stabbing a policeman on the north side of Beverley Brook a couple of weeks ago. Finally my three guard dogs are so heavily into squirrelling and voling, they couldn't give a damn what happens to me.

Go out on Common and sight potential glue-sniffer/flasher/rapist swinging from the second bridge in a Prussian-blue jersey. I tear round Barnes Graveyard to avoid him, but as I cross the Flower Garden, he emerges from Flasher's Point and leaps laughing inanely and waving, from oak sapling to oak sapling. I run for home stumbling in vole holes, then turn from the safety of the middle of the Big Common, where I am in full view of the Lower Richmond Road, the hospital and a middle-aged couple walking arm in arm. The glue-sniffer proceeds to wave and wave at me. Perhaps we've met at a party.

The summer has been so bad that all the nutters are packing their nuttery into the last days of a warm autumn. We need a hard frost to kill them off like greenfly. Appropriately wild oats are springing up in front of the hospital where the King's Troop had their stables during the Putney Show.

Thursday, October 22nd

Common swarming with dogs, fortunately all friends: Treacle, Rowena and Zelda, Michelin, Hugo and my three. All their different browns, reds, golds and ambers are reflected in the turning trees: sycamores, oaks and planes, which are all blued and softened by a dozen bonfires. The birds are all singing – tits are appropriately swinging from a sycamore near Flasher's Point.

No flashers, glue-sniffers, rapists, or lurchers, or cats about at lunchtime. Have magic walk, full of double gins after BBCFA broadcast. Notice maple on the edge of Queen's Ride, is red and orange on one side, and green on the other, like me going grey on the right side of my head. Meet handsome jogger from Festing Road, who says, 'Don't tell anyone you've seen me walking.'

Go out at night. Little maple in front of Cedric's house is dropping leaves in the orange lamplight like yellow butterflies.

Monday, October 26th

Vile afternoon. The lurcher man stands in the middle of the Big Common while his lurchers frolic around him. Go round by the keeper's cottage to avoid him. Coming back by the football pitch, I go slap into him. Notice he has black hair, black eyes, and wicked gypsy face. He snarls at the lurchers, who decide not to eat Fortnum. I flee to the right across the Flower Garden.

Out at dusk with Emily. Barbara finds a turkey carcass and cavorts around crackling bones and refusing to be caught for at least twenty minutes. I could murder her. Emily gets furious, too, and lets out a stream of dreadful language to the horror of various passers-by. Then she rushes off to get Maxine, and the three of us manage to corner Barbara. I beat her when we get home, Leo beats her, but she is not at all contrite and indulges in a lot of fluted whining.

At 11.15 I go out into the garden. Not prepared to risk Barbara on the Common again. Gemini and Taurus are brilliant overhead, but I can hadly see Pisces. No wonder I'm born under this ineffectual sign. Cygnus, the lovely constellation of the swan, is flying away over Chester Close, and Orion is just climbing out of Erpingham Road and pulling on his sword. What glamour is attached to each new star as it comes over the horizon! In a month or so, we'll be able to see the Dog Star. Poor Leo is deeply bored with my new preoccupation with star-gazing and is asleep when I get to bed.

Lurchers monopolising the Big Common again. Feel that sense of frustrated outrage other dog walkers must feel when they see me walking towards them. Very envious that lurcher man manages to stand still, and his dogs gambol and exercise themselves around him. If I stand still, my dogs come and sit at my feet and gaze up at me.

In his lively book, *An Englishman's Flora*, Geoffrey Grigson says that if you take a boat up a river or wide stream in October, you will be subjected to the continual rifle fire of seeds shooting out of the balsam. Alas there is a fat chance of sailing up Beverley Brook with all its mud and detritus.

Almost knocked flying by the mother of Crispin, the budding artist, by the first bridge. She has bright pink hair today, but is as white as a sheet. She says she was just taking Emma, her poodle, along the towpath, when a glue-sniffer jumped out of an elder bush, and leered at her. She threatened to call the police, but he just waved his arms at her, so she and Emma ran away. She had a funny turn when she got home. It seems no time at all, she goes on, since she saw a flasher last summer who dropped his trousers in the Flower Garden.

'Crispin,' she goes on, 'says "Those sorts of men never hurt you, Mum," but you can never tell. The Common's not what it was.'

I sigh and agree with her that the Common is indeed not what it was, what with muggers, flashers, rapists, lurchers, not to mention lurking wild cats.

In full flood, we pass a man with a West Highland terrier, who hates Fortnum. He is swinging a golf club.

'He doesn't like me much either,' I say.

'Oh don't bother about him,' says Crispin's Mum. 'He takes that club out for protection, not golf. I asked Crispin to look out for a club like that for me, next time he goes to a jumble sale.'

We are joined by Tommy and his great Danes. The new one, Rowena, now she's settled in, is really happy and cavorts like a drunken dinosaur, to Barbara's intense irritation.

Crispin's Mum says Crispin is always surrounded by pretty girls, but she expects he'll settle for a homely body.

'I wonder who he'll be,' mutters Tommy hopefully.

Saturday, October 31st

Great dramas on the Common – apparently Molly had a go at Rachel and Clarissa. They were evidently so frightened by what she said that they clung to each other for mutual support. According to Clarissa and Rachel, she also said fearful things about me. Dying to find out what they are. Clarissa and Rachel refuse to tell me, but say they will never speak to Molly again.

Sadly, amidst all this acrimony, the Common is looking breathtaking; the limes went in a week – just a few gold leaves are left like rings on fingers. You can see Orion's belt every night now, rising resplendent out of the bare trees.

Monday, November 9th

Pollarding certainly arrests decay. The little poplars flanking the bowling green which were cut right back last summer, still have their leaves. The privet hedge round All Saints' Church has also been cut down from seven feet to three feet, virtually stripping it of all its greenery. As a result, all the lovely proportions of the church are revealed.

Saturday, November 14th

Bewitching morning. Sun comes out of the clouds above All Saints' and lights up the last curled leaves of the planes against a dark grey sky. On the Fair Triangle, one brilliant chestnut holds on to all its leaves like a red tea cosy. Strange how trees protect one another: the one in front quite bare, the one behind still full of leaves – a symbol, perhaps, of marriage.

Tuesday, November 17th

Walk late, having just finished a *Sunday Times* piece.

Meet John B, a television producer with whom I occasionally walk, on the Big Common. He says he feels he's at last getting over his wife's death a year ago, and beginning to exist again.

'How awful,' I ask, 'Did she die of cancer?'

'No, no,' he says impatiently, 'she committed suicide.'

I express shocked surprise.

'But you knew that,' he goes on.

I say I probably did, but I'd forgotten, which won't do at all.

The awful thing is that I've been walking with John B on and off for months not realising his wife had died and just babbling on about this and that, when he must have been in such anguish. I ask him if he thinks he'll get married again. He says it's like Superman II, a question of Follow That.

Wander home pondering on death and mortality. Notice new coral buds on the churchyard limes already pushing off the last yellow leaves, and dead plane leaves mingling by the church door with the confetti from last Saturday's wedding.

Wednesday, November 18th

Meet Rosie, who says Graham, the male hairdresser up the road, who owns an immaculately kept Yorkshire terrier, has fallen in love with an architect: 'Well spoken, well dressed, fancied him rotten,' according to Graham. When they got into bed, the architect evidently made Graham blow up a pile of balloons, and pop them all at the moment of climax. Talk about having a bang, says Rosie, in order to have an orgasm. This ribald conversation is brought to a sharp halt by Fortnum nearly murdering a cairn, and Barbara cannoning off a Peke.

Thursday, November 19th

Heavenly day. Go out at 7.45. As the sun rises orange over Common View, its rays, coming through the bare plane trees, throw thick snake shadows onto white bands of mist across the first Common. All the trees are gold above it.

Putney Hospital is open once more – thanks to courageous and persistent local lobbying. Just shows what you can do if you persist. Feel very guilty I had no part in it, as I never got around to writing to the Minister of Health, but thrilled to see it in action once more, with smoke coming out of the chimneys, and the snowman no longer peering wistfully out of the ground floor office. The only problem is cats. I pray the hospital don't start feeding and attracting them to the area again. Please don't bring back the cat.

L'affaire Molly has become most unpleasant. I am really devoted to her, in the same way that I am devoted to Clarissa, and even, underneath it all, fond of Rachel, when she's being nice.

This morning Clarissa lets slip that Molly in her great attack said

that Leo employed slave labour and never paid bills, and he'd never paid Biffo for some German translation. I hit the roof, deny stoutly that Leo hasn't paid Biffo, and rush home in a whirl of self-righteousness to ring Leo, who says he actually hasn't paid Biffo yet.

Oh God; Leo then fires off incensed letter to Biffo plus cheque for translation saying he hopes this will go some way towards paying his wife's slander bills. Oh dear, oh dear, what have I started? Cry havoc, and let slip the dog walkers of war.

Friday, November 20th

Terrified of bumping into Molly, in case Biffo gets Leo's letter first post. But can't be frightened for long, because it's so beautiful on the Common. I do love November. The trees are all stripped now except for the oaks, and a rusting of plane trees along the paths. It is all bare bones, new angles and views, and everything laid open to the sky. The nights are beautiful too, you can see so many more stars, and the atmosphere is so much clearer. Last night the Dog Star rose brilliant and flickering above All Saints' Church.

Saturday, November 21st

Get anonymous card from Molly, with picture of a kill out hunting; inside she has written a quotation from *Violets and*

Vinegar, the anthology of women's quotes I collected with Tom Hartman. It says:

> Who can begin conventional amiability the first
> thing in the morning? It is the hour of savage
> instincts and natural tendencies, it is the
> triumph of the disagreeable and the cross.

Feel very sad, as I really love Molly so much.

Friday, November 27th

Still nervous that Molly will suddenly leap out of Lurker's Paradise and shout at me. It is a lovely mild, grey, damp, leaf-moulding day. Blackbirds and thrushes singing in gratitude, note sooty black buds on the ash, and inverted arrow heads on balsam poplars by the bowling green.

Saturday, November 28th

Walk with Rosie. She tells me the sad story of Tommy's great Dane, Treacle. Her tail, which kept knocking against the furniture, has gone gangrenous, and two inches have had to be amputated. Now she keeps chewing the bandage off. Rosie dreamed up the brilliant idea of covering the bandage with a French letter, and went into a chemist's to buy one.

The chemist, who fortunately had a sense of humour, said he hadn't a French letter to fit, as he couldn't imagine a male member as long or as thin as a great Dane's tail.

Last night, Rosie goes on, she went to see *Richard II*, played by Alan Howard, which was evidently magic. During the interval, however, an Aston Villa supporter in a woolly hat and scarf came up and said:

'This is the most boring play I've ever been to, I wish I'd stayed at home and watched *Coronation Street*.'

Notice one little south-west corner of the privet hedge round the bowling green is yellow like an elbow patch.

Thursday, December 3rd

To everyone's horror and shock, a poor schoolmistress in her thirties has been raped by three glue-sniffers on the Common near

Barnes Station, at four o'clock in the afternoon. As a result we are all very nervy and frightened; women walk in twos, jumping at the slightest sound. Trees have become flashers. Behind every hawthorn thicket is an imaginary Gaberdine swine.

Sunday, December 6th

Walk with Rachel. Meet Clarissa and her husband, Ronald, who says: 'You're both looking very solemn.'

'We're talking about rape,' I say.

'Surely not before lunch,' says Ronald with a shudder.

Returning from the Common, Rachel and I pass two men in woolly hats who are painting the newly visible iron railings round All Saints' Church in orange, crimson and red. They assure us, wearily and obviously for the hundredth time today, that this is only the undercoat.

Rachel then stiffens at the sight of a carrier bag, a battered Thermos, and two paper bags, nestling in the roots of a nearby lime tree.

'That's what I call disgusting,' she says. 'Leaving litter like that on the Common,'

I agree with her rather more forcibly.

We are both embarrassed when one of the workers points out that this is their lunch.

Monday, December 7th

Woken by shrieks from Emily. There is deep snow and it is still falling thickly. The magnolia and the bamboo are weighed down to the floor.

Outside, the traffic is grumbling and crawling along the Lower Richmond Road, and snow is hurtling down, stabbing and unpleasantly horizontal. Meet Tommy being towed along by a troika of dogs.

The silver birches by Barnes Graveyard are particularly beautiful, each slender twig etched like marvellous black hair heavily streaked with silver. Tommy and I both decide we would like to go grey like that. In the Flower Garden the brambles crouch like an army of white praying mantises. Gradually on the walk the outlines of the trees are blurring and thickening. The orange street lamps glow out of the gathering whiteness.

Still looking nervously for Molly. Imagine she may have put on a white fur hat to blend into the scenery like an arctic fox.

Clarissa joins us on the way home. Like the Bertram sisters in *Mansfield Park*, we all wonder rather scornfully who's 'out' – and are very contemptuous of those who won't brave the snow.

Clarissa, in fact, is very nervous of walking on her own, and keeps saying: 'Where's Rachel? She's usually tough on these occasions.'

Get home to find children snowballing in the churchyard, and Emily and her cronies very over-excited because the snow has slowed down the minicab (none of the mothers felt like taking the school run) and they'll miss lessons. Maxine and I feel totally blanketed against disaster and reality as one always does with snow.

Tuesday, December 8th

The Common is deserted except for a lady in a green Husky, with a springer spaniel; but don't feel this is a day rapists will venture forth. The sun comes out, but, despite the faint drip of melting ice, the snow is holding. Notice it has only covered half the trees: on the north side they're thickly coated, on the south side they're bare. Suspect this is because the blizzard has been blowing from the north all day. The alders are incredible. The little black fruits like tiny fir cones are all coated with ice, which has been turned yellow by the emerging pollen; the result is a glittering lemon sherbet or butterdrop tree, straight out of Edward Lear. The tall grasses are bent double like gnomes' fishing rods. The kestrel, which Clarissa claims is a sparrow-hawk, sits morosely on the football wire, watching a mouse. He has a black forked tail, and a striped dappled chestnut back.

Barnes Graveyard has suddenly dropped a storey with all the tall trees weighed down with snow. Each angel has a white mob cab, every grave a feather quilt.

In the centre, the hawthorn glitters metallically silver as though fashioned by a craftsman. The evergreens are painted more slap-dashly with several coats on each leaf. Crossing the path on the edge of the graveyard, which is now made impassable by holly trees bent double, I go into the Squirrel Wood, which is quite breathtaking. The snow has entirely doused the red flame of the oak trees and whitely clings to each tiny twig to form a ceiling of light overhead. It is like some icy palace, subtly spot-lit by a pale gold sun.

In all this ecstasy, I lose yet another lead.

Wednesday, December 9th

Snow continues beautiful, but it is a two-edged sword. The pavements leading down to the Common are incredibly treacherous. Each new layer of snow, ice and sleet melts and freezes hard at night. Progress at a snail's pace, clinging to fences, lamp-posts, cars, privet hedges and walls, until I reach the safety of the grass on the first Common. Know I am being wet, but if the dogs see a cat or an enemy or even a friend, coming, they will bolt and down I'll go, slap on my coccyx.

Today the sun is shining, but the snow is blue creped by the wind. It is a beautiful colour: very light powder blue, with a touch of lavender, with no suggestion of green. Perhaps Winsor and Newton should market a new colour – snow-shadow blue. After yesterday's hard frost there is a layer of ice on top of the snow. In the early morning it's like treading on *crème brûlée*, but in the afternoon like meringue. The dogs are wildly excited by all the delicious crackling. Barbara barks a lot at the snowmen. Why doesn't one build snow women? I expect they do in Hampstead.

Thursday, December 10th

Walk very early with Rosie who presents me with a huge gold punk safety-pin onto which to clip my leads, so I won't lose any more. She says she overheard two youths on the 22 bus yesterday. Waiting for it to start, they were watching me shambling dog-bound, duffle-coated, with my hair flying, across the Common.

'You see that bird over there with the three dogs?' said the first youth.

'Wot abart 'er?' asked the second youth.

'To look at her,' said the first youth, 'You'd never think she was loaded.'

Later in the day, I go to Leicester to award a cup to the most

237

lovable mongrel. He is called Gunner (pronounced Gooner) and unbelievably jolly. Realise afterwards, rather shamefacedly, that I have chosen a smooth-haired brindle mongrel: a combination of Fortnum, Barbara, Mabel and Sexy Rexy. Are all judges as partisan? The editor of the *Leicester Mercury* tells me a lovely story about the Christmas performance of *Toad of Toad Hall* at a local school which is fifty per cent Asian. All the children who haven't got speaking parts play spare badgers. The English children have a black stripe down the centre of their faces, the Asian children a white stripe.

Leo meets me off the train; we go to a drinks party, and take a taxi home as far as Putney Hospital. Walking back, the stars are dazzling; Orion bestrides the snowy churchyard. The orange street lamps warm the white trees; the gold windows of Lower Common South gild the white drives; the church with its little white turret and mother-of-pearl roof glitters in the moonlight. It is just like a Christmas card. It's freezing so hard, I ought to be much more frightened of falling over, but, in vino, I cross the snow without a slide or a stumble.

Friday, December 11th

The mist lies like a blanket over the snow. From the hospital one cannot see Putney Cemetery 200 yards away. The sky is putty coloured, the privet on the corner of Barnes Graveyard weighed down like a weeping willow.

Saturday, December 12th

It snows all day – heavy flakes like goosefeathers suffocating everything in pillow cases of white, filling up the hood of my duffle coat, clogging up my eyelashes, and settling in the metal clips of the leads. Going towards the Brook was murder, like Scott struggling polewards, then once one reached Oedipus Corner it was sheltered. The flakes were coming down dark against a pug-coloured sky, white against the dark trees, then getting lost from view as they reached the snow level, there was no colour, just sepia, white and black.

Barbara rushed about catching snowflakes and spitting them

out, and eating all the crumbs Rachel put down for the birds before the snow laid a shroud over them for good. Tuesday's snow was exact: each red blackberry cable defined like a mound of spaghetti. Today it splodges down, making igloos over each clump of brambles.

For me it was bliss because it emptied the Common, except for me and Rachel, who was in one of her nicest moods. Her son is having a party on Saturday night – twenty-five people in his bedroom, says Rachel. She hopes the snow will last so none of them come.

Monday, December 14th

Dazzling blue sky; icicles two feet long glisten from our faulty gutters. Avalanches fall off the roofs in a great crash. An epidemic of snowmen has sprung up on the Common, so Barbara did a lot of

239

barking and Fortnum a lot of leg lifting. Everyone was snowballing and tobogganing, aided by bouncing excited dogs.

Sadly, many trees have been wounded by the weight of the snow. The pine in the churchyard has lost three huge branches; the green fir cones, ripped off in their prime, give off a heady smell of Badedas, laced with mint. Under the trees, the dripped-on snow is the texture of boiled rice. The tunnel through the blackthorn up into the Flower Garden is quite impenetrable because the trees are so weighed down. The brilliant sunshine gives the snow a marvellous rhinestone sparkle.

Tusday, December 15th

Freezing hard. Go out on first Common. Heavenly flush of the sun setting above Chester Close matches a red 'sold' sign on Lower Common South. What a symbol of prosperity, as the house has been up for sale for only about five minutes!

Meet Rosie, who says she was pulled over by Michelin, outside her house, whereupon he rushed back indoors and refused to come out for forty-eight hours. Most people are just letting their dogs run down the road off their leads.

With traffic moving at a snail's pace, and everyone walking up the centre of the road to avoid the polished pavement, there is a feeling of being back in the old days, and one realises what a tyrant the motor car is.

Wednesday, December 16th

Thaw followed by a frost. The Common is patched with snow, like children's cut-out doilies stretched over tufts of bleached grass. On the paths between the Squirrel Wood and Barnes Graveyard, the leaves are bleached and moulded into a khaki pattern, like one of the nastier carpets in Putney High Street. The puddles are frozen three layers deep, white, grey and black and too hard for the dogs to break.

Thursday, December 17th

Snow continues. People mince down Egliston Road, terrified of being knocked over, like little old Japanese ladies. Great chuntering because no one has sanded the pavements, although the milkman and the postman soldier on. The dustmen, frightened of slipping, haven't been for days; the stench is positively mediaeval. Rachel is in a state of apoplexy.

Saturday, December 19th

Bitterly cold. Beverley Brook is frozen over. The landscape is lovely: snow the colour of dirty seagulls, grey and white sky, and the soft warmth of the bare trees in between. Blending in with the scenery, totally disregarding his master's despairing cries of 'Chester, Chester,' a large English setter lopes into view by the football osiers, stares at us with his mouth open, then, seeing Fortnum, like the moving finger, moves on.

The sun is nowhere, the sky is heavy eyed with snow.

My safety-pin is a boon. I haven't lost a single lead since Rosie gave it to me, and I can also put my frozen hands in my pockets.

Monday, December 21st

Poor Mabel has fractured her foot and has to have it in plaster, and is not allowed on walks. She is terribly low, poor darling; feels she is being punished when she gets left behind, and whines piteously. The vet says if her bandage gets wet she might get gangrene.

Walk with Felix, who is home from school. His new punk hair style is so short his ears go bright red under his cap. Coming home with both Barbara and Fortnum on leads, we are pursued by a West Highland terrier, who first bites Barbara, and then attacks Fortnum. The Westie has an ancient ineffectual owner, who does nothing but say 'Oh dear', and wring her hands when I ask her to take him away. Fortnum promptly weighs in for the kill. I try to separate them, to no avail, and send Felix off to Cedric's house for a bucket of water. The door is answered by Cedric's beautiful wife, who spends ages asking whose dogs are involved – 'Anyone we know?' – by which time, a wonderful man, whom I didn't have time to thank, had leapt out of a passing van, and thrown his coat over Fortnum who promptly drops the Westie. I am bitten to pieces and dripping blood in the snow.

Go out at dusk with Barbara and Fortnum. I am in vile temper because *The Sunday Times* want to come and photograph me at

9.30 tomorrow morning, which means getting up at crack of dawn to wash my hair. So deep in thought I don't notice that Barbara is suddenly being chatted up by one of the three lurchers.

'Come away!' I shriek.

Next minute Fortnum pitches in, poker-legged, pug-tailed and sinks his teeth into what he hopes is the lurcher's throat, but turns out to be his shaggy shoulder. After a ten-second spat, they break up, and Fortnum is just weighing in for the second round when suddenly like smoke up come the lurcher's two grey, even larger, stablemates. Fortnum suddenly looks like a bubble car hemmed in by three double-decker buses; his tail curls up even tighter. I look in despair for the lurchers' master. He is nowhere, but I can see his wife running away as fast as her legs can carry her, towards Beverley Brook.

Thank God Fortnum realises when he's beaten, and trots off trying to look nonchalant: 'Nice to see you, lads.'

The lurchers confer, shrug their shaggy shoulders, and lope off to retrieve their mistress from the Brook. At least it's frozen over so she can't drown herself.

Tuesday, December 22nd

Very hard frost. Mabel still ill.

Shopping in the afternoon I pass rather drunk punk and his girlfriend in Lower Richmond Road.

'Shall I compare thee to a summer's morn?' he cries out to the girlfriend.

'No, no,' I tell them pedantically, 'it's "day" not "morn".'

They both look at me as if I'm crackers, and move away. Later Emily comes for a walk with me, and tells me her cousin Clemmie's best things in life are dressing up, putting on make-up and eating crisps.

Feel Clemmie has a fine sense of priorities. Return home to find Felix having maths coaching. He is lounging at the kitchen table, swinging a can of beer, and saying, 'Algebra, I've never heard of it.' Feel that this attitude will not get him through Common Entrance.

Friday, December 25th

Being driven crackers by a middle-aged New Zealand Nanny,

who is looking after us while Maxine's away. She is very efficient but cannot stop telling us all about her problems. The children and Leo run out of the room when she enters. To cheer her up, today I take her out on what must be the most beautiful Christmas Day ever. The snow is flushed pink from a setting sun flecked with black branches. The sight of Putney Hospital, however, launches her into a thirty-minute description of her migraines and her torn shoulder. As we return past Putney Cemetery, she tells me she hasn't had sex since 1964.

Quite unable to think of anything to say but: 'Oh dear.'

Then she tells me she has a vet lover in Wolverhampton, but they only went to bed once, and she didn't go the whole hog, because they didn't want people to know.

Say: 'Oh dear,' again, twice.

She'd come up to London, because she and her vet lover (who's called John Lewis), didn't want to get talked about in Wolverhampton. Feel poor John Lewis is certainly getting talked about in London.

Saturday, December 26th

Spitting with rage, because yesterday New Zealand Nanny got us through Christmas dinner in thirty-five minutes flat, whipping away our plates before we'd finished eating, and crashing them into the washing-up machine. Poor Felix didn't even get a second helping.

Today Fortnum spends his time whining to go out, and returning half an hour later, cheeks bulging with turkey leftovers.

The Common is full of male joggers, working off their Christmas pudding, and grumbling about departing mothers-in-law.

Tuesday, December 29th

Yesterday we had our Christmas party. It was great fun, except for a cock-up over the food. Leo ordered curry for twenty from the Indian restaurant. In a panic that I'd asked too many people, I rang up the restaurant, and, unknown to Leo, upped the order by fifty per cent. The bill came to £291. The only thing Leo and I could do was scream with hysterical laughter. It looked as though we were feeding the entire Indian Army.

At midnight during the party, the New Zealand Nanny cornered me in the kitchen, and with a trembling lip told me she'd just rung up her vet lover – rather late for a social call, but I suppose vets are used to being rung up at all hours – and he'd told her he was in love with a married woman. But at least the married woman won't have him, she goes on, 'which makes me feel happier'. She now says vet lover is called Peter Robinson, and is always falling for women, but is a super beautiful human being. No doubt he'll be called Harrods tomorrow.

Out on the Common to escape curry fumes. The snow has disintegrated into small hard, dirty grey patches, like symbols of Polish resistance to the Russians. I feel so sorry for the Poles.

Bump into Molly on the Flower Garden, who sent me a Christmas card with a dove on it. So pleased to see her again, I greet her with huge hug. We have a lovely chat, and frantically keep off the subject of Clarissa and Rachel, both of whom I'm terrified will suddenly appear over the horizon and who are still not speaking to her.

Further on we meet Horsey Miriam. Miriam is wearing a mink.

Molly says: 'Haven't you got a mackintosh, Miriam?' three times.

To which, Miriam replies: 'What?' three times.

So Molly says: 'Oh well, a raincoat, if you must call it that.'

Miriam, says: 'No.'

Rosie joins us – pray that she won't thank me for last night's party. I meant to ask Miriam, but never got round to it, and would have asked Molly, if we'd made it up yesterday. Everyone says their Christmas was quiet.

Crispin, the budding artist, rolls up looking just like Charles Ryder in *Brideshead Revisited*. He is wearing short gumboots, a long fawn coat, and a trilby. He says his ceiling has just fallen in.

'Is that why you're wearing a hat?' asks Rosie.

Wednesday, December 30th

Rachel and I see shadowy heron flying over the Brook. Everywhere grass and leaves are wonderfully bleached by the snow.

244

Another lovely mild day, with midges, and a fat bullfinch singing from the sycamore at the edge of the Flower Garden.

Thursday, December 31st

Go out at dawn, bump into Rosie, looking radiant, and walking on air. She says she's in love. She finally got talking to David the sculptor at a party the other day. They left all the other guests, and went upstairs to the children's nursery and watched *Gone with the Wind* together. He was delighted because she said Rhett Butler was a berk. Feel a stab of envy for her Ritzy single life.

Then go home to full dress row. Felix has been sent to his room by Leo for refusing to chop logs when the temporary asked him. He refused quite politely, Emily tells me in an excited stage whisper, and said he didn't know if Mummy and Daddy wanted a fire.

At that moment we both jump out of our skins, as the temporary walks in.

'I don't want the boy punished,' she says pursing her lips. 'But I won't put up with children cheeking me,' then she turns to Emily and asks: 'I bet you're longing to have Maxine back, aren't you?'

'Yes,' says Emily, who has no tact.

'I bet she's not as strict as I am,' says the temporary.

'No, she isn't,' says Emily.

Find Leo pouring large whisky in the drawing room, it is only 10.30 am. He says New Zealand temporary's menopause is like *The Mousetrap*, it will run for ever.

Overwhelmed with love for him and the children, could never change a minute of them for all Rosie's Ritzy existence.

1982

Friday, January 1st

Change over to new diary. Riddled with guilt at all the telephone numbers I wrote down on the back pages of the old diary and never did anything about. Who could I possibly have been going to ring up at the Kensington Hilton? I thought only airline pilots stayed there.

The nutty temporary has gone; Maxine is back. Never so pleased to see anyone.

Monday, January 4th

Felix goes back to school today. We have a last walk together. I am always reminded on these occasions of Meredith's *Modern Love*:

> Love that had robbed us of immortal things,
> This little moment mercifully gave.

Alas, today we didn't even have 'this little moment', because Clarissa bears down on us. I love her but I wish that like all dog walkers she realised that I get precious little time with my children, and when I walk on the Common with them we want to be left alone.

Today Clarissa is very worried that in a flippant moment, she quoted:

> Adultery do not commit,
> Advantage rarely comes of it,

to Frances the feminist, then remembered one of Frances' frightful children was the result of a bunk-up with a married man. Did I think Frances would be terribly hurt? Before I have time to answer, she tries to engage Felix in conversation. He was so enraged at having our tête-à-tête interrupted, he answered only in monosyllables. In a pathetic attempt to keep the conversation going, I find myself answering for him – which I know Clarissa, as an ex-headmistress, regards as a heinous crime.

Walk the dogs late at night after taking Felix back to school. Orion is brilliant above Cedric's house. It is difficult to pick out the fainter constellations because they are overshadowed by a dazzling, diamond-hard, five-eighths moon. Think of the same moon shining on Felix at school; oh, I hope they take care of him.

Tuesday, January 5th

The dustmen still haven't been. We'll be asked to bring out our dead soon.

Out at lunchtime – very mild, midges everywhere, and a marvellous bilberry-blue blur on the wet trees. Blackbirds, thrushes, sparrows, chaffinches and robins all carolling, like a lunchtime concert at All Souls', Langham Place.

Wednesday, January 6th

Walk with Rosie, who is looking ravishing – thin and 'sheeny' as Leo calls it from desire and being desired. She is still besotted with David the sculptor. He drops in every day. Her mother approves and thinks David has a very sexy voice. Rosie also had breakfast yesterday with an old lover, lunch with a glamorous man in advertising and dinner with an actor.

The man in advertising evidently said they must lunch once a fortnight for the rest of their lives. He's just paid off all his debts, his business is going brilliantly, his marriage is wonderful, in fact he was all poised for the big dive – falling in love with Rosie.

She returned from lunch to find the telephone ringing, it was David the sculptor, 'How can you possibly lunch with anyone in advertising, they're so superficial!' Then to get his own back he raved about some ex-girlfriend in the BBC.

'So we had our first quarrel,' sighed Rosie. 'But we made it up half an hour later. He calls me his sylph.'

'Ha, ha,' I say. 'Then when he doesn't see you, he can say I'm not feeling my sylph today.'

As we walk home, the safety-pin holding my trousers together slips and plunges into my stomach. Make mental note to lose weight and look less repulsive. Coming across the first Common on a bicycle, cloak and long skirt flying, rather like a very pretty version of the witch in *The Wizard of Oz*, comes Pandora, our local biographer, who, unlike Frances the feminist, gets her books published. I introduce her to Rosie, who says she's also writing a book.

Pandora says she has been asked to write for some travel magazine, and the editor keeps pouncing on her, but she's not going to give even a fraction of her all, until he's written her a letter officially commissioning the piece.

'Piece now,' I say, 'or forever withhold your pounce.'

Pandora then informs us she hasn't had sex for four years which makes all the men she meets absolutely insane with desire, and they rush round with champagne and intentions. This must all be part of the New Celibacy that is being so bandied about in London.

I get home to be greeted by an ecstatic Maxine. Her boyfriend has rung, he's taking her out tonight, and she's aleady got butterflies in her stomach.

'You are lucky,' I say, unable once again to suppress a stab of jealousy for all these wildly desirable ladies. 'I haven't had butter-flies over a man for years.'

Maxine looks amazed: 'I always think how lucky you are,' she says, 'having Leo coming home every night to you, knowing he'll always be there.'

This pulls me up with a start. I shouldn't presume he will always be there, but it makes me realise how immeasurably fortunate I am.

Thursday, January 7th

Very cold suddenly, with a bitter north-east wind, which makes the unsheltered walk down to the first bridge extremely unpleasant. The birds appalled by the change in the weather have suspended their matings and are totally silent. Hope the same thing doesn't happen to Rosie, Pandora and Maxine. The crimson mugwort stalks are brown now, the knotweed has lost its orange fire, all the undergrowth along the Brook is drained to a pale donkey brown.

Meet Mrs Willis with her darling plump, piebald mongrel, Spot, who says she had a nice Christmas but quiet, and Spot enjoyed his turkey dinner. She then wishes me ''appy new year' twice, in case I hadn't heard the first time. Otherwise the Common is deserted, which is lucky because the low winter sun at twenty-five degrees shines blindingly into the eyes, so I can't see any enemy dog coming.

The dustmen come at last: they are so anxious to ingratiate themselves with the public after their strike, that they don't even kick up when they have to carry a thousand and one empty bottles out of our house – the result of Christmas excess. Several bottles are dropped in the road, covering it with green glass. Horsey Miriam comes out with her BMW, sees the glass, and rushes inside for a broom. She is joined by the Car-Respondent also with a broom. They click their tongues and sweep the street talking loudly to draw attention to their act of philanthropy. Deliberately don't let them see me looking out of the window.

Friday, January 8th

Mornings are so dark – I find it impossible to get up early. Walk with Emily – it is her first day back at school but she doesn't have to clock in until eleven o'clock. It is bitterly cold. Emily wants to discuss rape, which seems to be dominating all the papers, particularly since a Judge ticked off a Devon girl who got raped, for hitching a lift at night after a party.

Emily wants to know *all* about it. I tell her about rapists being let off, which is wrong, but also add how stupid any girl is who hitch-hikes at any time of the day. We are joined by John B the television director who says I am quite wrong. How can I be *so* sexist as to think of men as creatures who cannot control their appetites? I stammer that I don't really, but I still think girls who hitch-hike after parties are daft.

John B says he *always* gives lifts to hitch-hikers. He hitch-hiked so much in his youth and feels he is paying people back. His car can carry four people and it is a sin for it to be empty, when people sometimes have to wait for hours for buses in the most terrible weather.

Warming to his subject, he goes on that the transport is so awful in Yeovil, that there's often only one bus a day, and if you miss that you've had it.

He makes me feel middle-aged, and horribly unphilanthropic, particularly when Emily keeps pausing to bounce on puddles, and break up the ice so that the 'poor birds' can get a drink, and I, getting frozen with waiting, tartly tell her to buck up. John B then shoots me a shocked look, and goes back and jumps on puddles with Emily, telling her what a 'good, caring little girl' she is to think about the birds. Emily, scenting conquest, goes and swings on a dead bough of the nearby acacia.

'Don't do that, it's dangerous,' I snap.

Whereupon John B goes back and very carefully explains to Emily the branch is dead, and she might fall and hurt herself. Emily beams up at him, and he gives me a reproachful 'they'll do anything, if you treat them properly' look.

Get my own back by saying that by an extraordinary coincidence Maxine lives in Yeovil, and as John B is so keen on giving people lifts, why doesn't he give her a free ride every time he goes home. Immediately he looks at his watch, says he must rush and vanishes like smoke.

Midday: even colder than this morning. All the runnels and ridges in the quagmire forged by dog walkers, dogs and bicycles over the last week are now frozen razor sharp, and cut through the soles of my gumboots. Push leaves aside by the Bryant's grave on the edge of the Eternal Triangle, and find first snowdrop shoots.

Monday, January 11th

Go out early. A huge aggrieved full moon looks down the white gardens of Lower Common South, like a gardener complaining that the frost has got his roses. The birds are all shouting and congratulating each other on surviving the rigours of the night.

Tuesday, January 12th

Prettiest morning yet: even colder and icier with a brilliant gentian-blue sky above soft grey-blue clouds and a saffron sun, warming all the trees and putting a gold rinse on the grey and yellow boles of the plane trees. The traffic is so bad that a coloured necklace of cars, still shining with melting ice, is strung motionless along Lower Richmond Road and Queen's Ride. No one smiles or waves you through – bad temper is rampant. A new layer of ice has formed like windows over the patches of grass showing through the snow.

Meet Clarissa and Rachel, who point out that some strange mediaeval monster appears to have come up the Brook, and bashed up all the ice to let the water through. Is it the friends of Barnes Common on a trip of altruism? It looks more like a sinister lava path, or a bomb site with broken window panes. It is such a lovely day, and we are all progressing happily, when a jaunty grizzled red setter bounces round the corner and starts chatting up Barbara. Fortnum rushes up, and despite Clarissa's bellows and my shouts goes straight for the setter's throat, but, thank God, catches hold of only his collar and red fur.

Remembering how effective the driver of the van had been when he threw his coat over Fortnum, Clarissa, Rachel and I all whip off our coats and throw them over Fortnum. Despite looking like the hostess's bed at a party, Fortnum takes no notice. Only when the owner comes up and kicks his ribs in does he finally drop the setter. The setter owner, who is very handsome, with red hair slightly grizzled like the setter, is understandably very cross. He says Fortnum ought to be put down, and what will happen if he attacks a child?

Later we pass him again in the Squirrel Wood, and I go up and apologise profusely. Would I have bothered if he hadn't been so good-looking? He is very nice, and says the setter had started a few scraps himself in his youth. Rachel and Clarissa mutter about muzzling.

Go out in the afternoon. See man who owns two beautiful grey deer hounds having a shouting match with a man with a stroppy Alsatian. Evidently the two deer hounds chased the Alsatian across two main roads, and he nearly got run over.

A kind old man, who caught the stroppy Alsatian and took it back to its owner, tells me he thinks those 'two German dachshunds', are very dangerous and should be kept on a lead.

Try to identify pine tree in Barnes Graveyard: it has long needles in bunches of five, and long curved cones. Could be Mexican white pine, Japanese pine, Bhutan, pine, or a Weymouth pine. Give up – it's just a pine.

On the Eternal Triangle, I appropriately pass two women discussing kitchens: 'I don't know how to describe it really,' says the first, 'but it's one up from pine.'

Wednesday, January 13th

Heavy, heavy frost makes snow more magical than ever. Underfoot it is absolute murder; the Common paths are as treacherous as the pavements. Fortnum is very hepful, and pulls me up hills whenever I have him on a lead.

Out in the afternoon, the frost has gone leaving the trees the softest taupe above the white sparkling snow, with a grey-blue haze above gradually blending into an almost hyacinth-blue sky overhead. Winging overhead comes a seagull, its snowy undercarriage almost incandescent. Feel my heart expanding with love for its beauty. As a result almost fall over a sweet man with a mobile, lined, character actor face and two Alsatians. He agrees that the snow is beautiful, but adds that it puts some people like him out of work. He explains he is a roofer, but at least 'wevver' like this makes people realise their roofs need mending. Remember two-foot icicles hanging from our gutters and say he'd better come and have a look at ours.

Thursday, January 14th

Beverley Brook is completely frozen over.

Bump into Rachel and Clarissa, who are getting terribly thick, and make me edgy because they have lots of private jokes. We discuss Mrs Thatcher's son who has disappeared on some safari rally.

Rachel says very beadily: 'There are other people lost on the rally – why all this fuss about Mark Thatcher?'

I say I hold no particular brief for him, but I just feel very sorry for Mrs T.

We progress towards the Flower Garden, where Clarissa claims that she has seen some poor model being photographed in tennis clothes in the snow. We round the corner, and sure enough rearing out of the bracken is a huge amazon with oiled brown legs and arms, wearing nothing but a skimpy tennis dress. A male photographer and his assistant, both in fur coats, are leaping about taking pictures.

We all mutter loudly about sexist photographers exploiting women *and* on the coldest day of the year.

'Oughtn't we to remonstrate with them?' says Clarissa.

But on getting closer, we discover our sympathy is wasted: the model turns out to be a dummy. We tramp off towards the Flower Garden feeling foolish.

Clarissa goes on to say that she once worked on a magazine and had to organise models. If they were tiresome, she made them wear awful clothes. She then broaches the subject of Fortnum's muzzle yet again, and what a good idea it would be. She's been discussing the problem with several dog trainers, she says. Her sister also had a fighter, and muzzling worked on him, so why don't I try one on Fortnum?

She leaves us. I walk miserably home with Rachel and make a crack about the Dog in the Iron Mask.

Rachel puts on her Mrs Thatcher voice (if she dislikes our Prime Minister so much, she shouldn't try to sound like her) and says this is a serious matter. Clarissa is only trying to help, and sooner or later someone will make an official complaint.

Find it impossible to explain that if they didn't lecture me so much, I wouldn't be so uptight and Fortnum would fight less. Think about Fortnum in a muzzle, never being able to bark or vole or fascinate, and feel horribly depressed.

Back home, Emily is reading about rape. She explains that her form mistress has told her to read the papers, as in the forthcoming exams for their secondary schools they may well get asked general knowledge questions. 'What,' she goes on, 'does "semi-naked" mean?' Do not feel this will really help her get into St Paul's.

Saturday, January 16th

Hooray it's thawing. Like an army defeated, the snow has retreated. Everything is dripping. Rape has been superseded as the chief subject of conversation by grumbling about dustbins not being emptied. On the one hand the local *Borough News* congratulates the council workers for putting in a twenty-four-hour day to grit the road and pavements (which is rubbish – they've never come anywhere near our road), but on the other hand there has been no dustbin collection for ten days, because the pavements are supposed to be too dangerous for anyone carrying heavy loads. Discuss this with Crispin the artist and Rosie.

'What,' says Crispin, 'about old-age pensioners coming home weighed down by two carrier bags?'

'Old age pensioners,' points out Rosie, 'rarely have enough spare cash to fill two carrier bags.'

We pass Mrs Bond. We are all horrified when she tells us that the temperature in her front bedroom the other night was thirty-two degrees.

After she walks on, we all ponder gloomily on the fate of the aged and hypothermia, until Crispin tells us about an old lady who fainted by the cheese counter in Sainsbury's last week. A doctor was called, who examined her and went into a long rant about hypothermia and how badly the English treated their old people. Finally, however, he removed her hat and found she was harbouring a frozen chicken underneath.

Sunday, January 17th

Woken by terrible wails and groans. Think it's one of the children being murdered, rush upstairs and find Felix, who's home for the week-end, singing to Adam Ant with headphones on. As a result get out early on the Common, overtaken by Clarissa, Rachel and Crispin. We are all watching the sparrow hawk, which I think is a kestrel, being mobbed up by a troop of magpies, when we suddenly realise Scottish Molly has crept up on us. Rachel and

Clarissa, who are still not speaking to her, turn away in disgust. To their intense irritation, Crispin and I say 'hullo'. Molly winks and passes on. Barbara takes advantage of my inattention to roll in goose's crap, and later has to have a bath.

Monday, January 18th

It is lovely to see green grass again. The snow has thawed in patches, leaving fantastic shapes – a sea horse there, a camel here. Across on the Barn Elms playing fields, the snow stretches in sheets like flooding.

Go out in the afternoon. By Beverley Brook, we see one of Fortnum's rivals, a little black mongrel mounting a terrier bitch. They are having a lovely time. Fortunately Fortnum is on a lead, but Barbara, enraged by evidence of sexual enjoyment in which she is not participating, charges the happy couple so fiercely, that they both fall into the icy Brook. It obviously has the effect of a cold shower. They emerge two minutes later, chastened and trot off home in separate directions.

Friday, January 22nd

The latest hideous development is joggers who have earphones plugged into transistors attached to their wasists. How can they enjoy the rustle of poplars, or the song thrush on the sycamore or the merry barking of dogs, if they're listening to pop music all the time?

> It's not their fault they do not know
> The bird song from the radio,

claims John Betjeman.

It bloody well is.

Green lichen on the trees is beautiful – particularly on the sycamores where it is a violent Dayglo green. There seems to be more lichen on parts of the tree that are facing north.

Meet sweet old man who admires the dogs. He says he once had a bull terrier like Fortnum who was terribly aggressive and fought on until he was seventeen. One night he started a fight with another dog, just as the crowds were coming out of the cinema. The old man was so frightened his dog was going to bite someone that he hoisted both dogs on top of a car, where they carried on fighting on the roof rack.

I ask him if his bull terrier ever attacked cats.

'Attack them!' he says. ''E once swallered an old lady's cat whole.'

I don't know why but these stories made me feel better. Tell Rachel who's not amused, and says fighting is a serious business.

Saturday, January 23rd

Cheered up walking with dear Rosie. Things are going wonderfully well with David the sculptor. Gradually she seems to be shedding her other admirers. The other day, she said, she and David were walking down the street and bumped into Graham (the hairdresser, who was having a walk-out with the architect who liked having balloons popped at the moment of orgasm).

Afterwards, Rosie asked Graham the hairdresser, what he thought of David.

'Well dear,' said Graham, 'he's all right if you like that sort of thing. But for my money, the sexiest man in Putney is that butch Leo Cooper.'

When I get home I ring up Leo to tell him.

'Ask him round for a drink,' says Leo. I can detect his smirk down the telephone wires.

Barbara has been spayed. She's so brave, bless her. She came out of the vet's very tucked up, with flattened ears and tail, and rushed upstairs the moment she got home, and jumped up over the brass rail onto our bed. Mabel as usual seems much more upset than Barbara, and stood over her whimpering, and nudging her with her nose. I'm so relieved it's done – I couldn't have borne sending her to kennels again.

Sunday, January 24th

Happy because Barbara is much more cheerful; she's eating well, if pickily (rump steak and chocolate biscuits), but not going out yet. I love the way she preserves her energy, and won't romp because it hurts so much. Mabel is blissful, going out without Barbara.

Meet Clarissa and Rachel. Clarissa looks pointedly at Fortnum and then says she's been looking at long leads in the pet shop. At that moment, dear Hugo lets her down by attacking a passing shaggy dog. Resist the temptation to say Hugo should be muzzled and put on a long lead. Clarissa, by way of exoneration, says Hugo always mistrusts dogs with shaggy faces whose eyes he can't see. What is so unfair is that Hugo often attacks other dogs, but because he's castrated they feel it is below the belt (or the collar) to fight back.

Monday, January 25th

Walk with dear Tommy. We discuss Rosie. He says people are like their dogs. Michelin is very secure and serene like Rosie. Wonder where that puts me? Am I a belligerent sex maniac like Fortnum, or a shy, lovely-natured darling like Mabel, or a lippy clown like Barbara?

Tuesday, January 26th

Walk over to the Yarrow Meadow at lunchtime, it is a lovely mild afternoon. On the apple tree with its grey sooty buds, a robin is singing, its little orange throat vibrating, its black eyes so shiny. I throw it some biscuit crumbs, which Fortnum immediately snaps up.

Go to seek out the aspen on the corner of Rocks Lane. According to Kenneth Allsop in his book, *In the Country*, it should have pink and purple shoots in the spring, but when I get there these are too high for me to see.

Talk to darling elderly lady who used to have a black spaniel. She says she still misses him particularly on spring-like days like this, but she still goes on the same walk, even without him, and wasn't the snow lovely? It came over her gumboots one day, but she didn't mind because everything looked so beautiful, and she saw the television reporter, Jon Snow, ski-ing on Barnes Common.

'In the bleak mid-winter,' I say.

She looks blank.

'Snow on snow,' I say.

'He's just as nice in the flesh as he is on television,' she goes on. 'Very natural.'

Meet woman coming out of Putney Hospital, who admires Fortnum and Mabel, saying they're beautiful dogs. She had a setter, she says, who lived until he was thirteen; she misses having a dog, but it's difficult at her age. At this juncture, Fortnum starts straining after a passing hospital cat, so I say, 'It's difficult at any age.'

Wednesday, February 3rd

Notice alder catkins by Beverley Brook; they are made up of tiny yellow checks edged with red like Harrods golf stockings. Meet Clarissa by the second bridge.

'Enjoy your dogs while you may,' she cries, advancing towards me over the bridge.

'Oh God,' I say, 'Is there a writ out for them? Is a dog catcher going the rounds?'

'Crackers,' she says. 'Went to the vet yesterday, who diagnosed cancer – evidently his lungs are quite eaten away. He's on steroids and will have to be put down at the end of the week.'

Oh poor Crackers. He was the most beautiful, gentle, liver and white pointer, and only seven.

'How dreadful,' I say. 'How did he get it?' (Resist temptation to ask if he smoked heavily.)

'It's the level dogs are,' says Clarissa, 'They just breathe in all the exhaust and fumes from cars.'

'Does his owner go to our vet Mrs Fraser?' I ask.

'No, one in White Hart Lane,' says Clarissa. 'He's a very caring vet, and is always sending dogs to dog training classes.'

At this utterance, Fortnum gives Clarissa a very old-fashioned look, and even Mabel starts walking to heel.

The next weeks were gruelling. Emily took exams to get into four different schools. This also involved interviews with all the head-mistresses, so Emily and I were racketing around London like the proverbial foxes with burning tails in the Bible. Towards the end of the exam stint, Fortnum, Mabel and Barbara were invited to go to Cruft's to appear on the Russell Harty Show, and take part in an obedience test.

Thursday, February 11th

Evidently Rachel and Clarissa are apoplectic at the news that Fortnum is doing an obedience test at Cruft's, and think that I'm going to make a complete fool of myself. Happily I don't. We have a lovely day. All the dogs went to a photo-call outside Cruft's in the morning and posed with Judy Geeson, Bill Pertwee, Bob Wilson, and Faith Brown and their dogs. Fortnum's photograph appeared in the *Daily Mail* under a Smirnoff Vodka poster saying: 'It bites.' He looked absolutely sweet, except that the *Mail* caption called him Barbara, which is a slight affront to his doghood.

In the evening, all three dogs went on the Russell Harty Show; and, because Leo was there (whom Fortnum regards as his pack leader), Fortnum, relieved of his responsibilities, behaved impeccably. Throughout the proceedings, despite growling from Vince Hill's English sheepdog, barking from Faith Brown's Labrador, and snarling through chair legs from John Noakes' sheepdog, he maintained a quiet dognity. Just before the transmission, when I wasn't looking, Leo gave all three dogs massive doses of tranquillisers. As a result, although the programme was live, Mabel and Barbara jolly nearly weren't. Both kept collapsing cross-eyed onto the floor, and falling asleep – although Barbara did manage to struggle to her feet, when Russell Harty came up to speak to us.

He asked me why I like dogs so much. I stammered because I was basically shy, and found dogs easier to communicate with than people. At that exact moment, Barbara stepped forward and goosed Russell Harty vigorously.

I said: 'You see I'd love to be brave enough to do things like that.'

The audience were in stitches. Fortnum appeared totally unaffected by the tranquillisers, and did a brilliant obedience test; the judge said if it had been an official test, he would have won. So boo sucks to all the ladies on the Common.

The loveliest moment was after the programme, when I let the three dogs loose and they ran round the huge Cruft's exercise ring, which tomorrow will be full of breed dogs and champions.

Friday, February 12th

Bump into Rosie ad Tommy who say Fortnum and the others were smashing on telly. Rachel and Clarissa join us – they make no comment.

Tommy says: 'I've given up smoking, so I'm going to jump all over that bunch of snowdrops.'

Monday, February 15th

Emily goes off to school to take her last exam for a boarding school in Berkshire. She is very tired and depressed – so am I. I go for very cold walk feeling miserable. As I am shambling towards second bridge with Rachel, a bird comes whirring towards us.

'The kingfisher!' I cry. 'Look, look!' And there it was, flashing past: the most ravishing streak of turquoise and pinky coral, like the colours of some Derby winner, dazzling against the beiges and greys of winter – then it is gone.

Tuesday, February 16th

Out about nine in the evening. Meet the Brigadier returning from the pub in merry mood. We admire the Pleiades. The Brigadier quotes a line from Tennyson, about a shoal of silver fishes in a net. Then he says that three of his old aunts have recently died, so now he and his wife don't have to worry so much about money, and can even take taxis.

I say the nice thing about money is that it gives you the freedom to do everything you want.

'Not everything,' says the Brigadier, giving me a foxy squeeze round the waist.

Friday, February 26th

Find beautiful dead fox with blood seeping out of its mouth, lying in the middle of the Fair Triangle. It is about three feet long; it must have been hit by a car. The foxes are barking a lot along the back gardens at night – I suppose it's the mating season.

Saturday, February 27th

In the first minutes during the past few weeks when I haven't been worrying myself sick about Emily getting into a school, we receive a letter telling us she's got into the boarding school in Berkshire. I burst into tears of joy and hug her until I nearly crack her ribs.

Go floating on air out on the Common. Find the first coltsfoot, or coltsfeet I suppose, below the osiers on the second Hillock.

Monday, March 1st

Very proud of darling Emily. She ploughed St Paul's, but got into three other schools. The Common is swarming with bitches and amorous male dogs. But perhaps because I'm so relaxed and happy about Emily, Fortnum picks up the vibes and hasn't had a fight for ages. Rachel and Clarissa, however, are still stepping up their campaign to get him muzzled and put on a long lead.

Thursday, March 4th

Clarissa and Rachel are getting thicker and thicker. Meet Clarissa who is pacing up and down saying, 'Rachel's late today,' then she remembers: 'Oh it's Thursday, she'll be doing her double wash.'

Find speedwell and celandine out along the Brook. Once again the green woodpecker is laughing his head off. The green flames of the hawthorn are out, and there is a lovely red haze of lime twigs round the churchyard.

Wednesday, March 10th

Meet Clarissa and Rachel in a state of chunter. They were

walking quietly along with Crispin, they tell me, when Molly suddenly emerged like a jack-in-the-box from the bushes in Lurker's Paradise, and called out: 'I don't want to drag you away from your harem, Crispin.'

'We ignored her,' says Clarissa.

'Disgusting,' says Rachel.

Poor Crispin evidently rang Molly afterwards and said despairingly, 'But I like you all!'

Fortnum loses a fight with huge blond dog, who pursues us across the Common. The dog is so tall, Fortnum can't reach his throat. Instead the huge dog gets Fortnum's head in his teeth. The owner sensibly keeps his distance, and eventually the big dog drops Fortnum who trots back to me very bloody but unbowed.

Tuesday, March 16th

Find heartsease and red dead-nettle in Barnes Graveyard; the ground is littered with red poplar catkins, and last year's black alder hops. So busy supervising Fortnum, I miss a glorious row on

the Common. Tommy and Rosie rush up gleefully and tell me about it.

Evidently Tommy was walking along the Pineapple Walk with Clarissa and Rachel, when suddenly Molly reared out of the knotweed on the opposite bank crying out: 'Haven't you two ladies had your pound of flesh?'

'What?' shouted back Clarissa.

'Haven't you two ladies had enough revenge?' yelled Molly.

'Don't be childish, Molly,' bellows Clarissa.

'What?' echoed Molly.

'Clarissa said "don't be childish",' snaps Rachel.

'What?' said Molly, and passed on. And all ringing across the sluggish mud of Beverley Brook.

Tommy evidently got the giggles and lurked behind to walk with Molly.

Next day, Rachel, all of a chunter, sidled up to Tommy saying, 'I'm so sorry we left you in the lurch with Molly, yesterday.' Whereupon darling Tommy snubbed her very politely saying he was devoted to Molly and hadn't seen her for ages.

Thursday, March 25th

Meet nice deputy headmistress with red-gold dachshund. She says when she had some friends over to tea at the weekend, the dachshund sneaked in and devoured all the cake, doughnuts and buttered buns beforehand. When she scolded him, he waved his brown plumed tail and looked quite unrepentant.

Friday, March 26th

Hear tragic news that Mrs James, a local schoolmistress, has finally died of cancer – she was so young, and so brave, and hung onto life so tenaciously. It must be terrible to leave a dear husband and three such beautiful children, and never to see them grow up. The youngest child, Sybilla, is only seven. I feel eaten up with sadness for the whole family.

Sunday, March 28th

I think this is the worst day of my life and it started so beautifully. I had a lovely walk with Emily. We looked at the closed-up celandines rising like crowns of lamb by the Brook. Fortnum had a long flirt with his girlfriend Blossom, who gets so excited when she sees him that she bounces around lifting all four legs off the ground. Then Maxine, who'd gone out the night before looking smashing in white tie and tails, slightly startled the Sunday morning car washers by returning in broad daylight in the same kit at 11.30 am. She'd had a riotous night with two young bloods which involved playing bears round the furniture in some flat in Sloane Square and getting whacked on the bum with a copy of *The Sunday Times*.

Then Mr James came for a drink. He was *so* brave about his wife's death. He looked shattered, but still thank God retained his sense of humour.

His seven-year-old daughter, Sybilla, had evidently said:

'Now Mummy's dead, Daddy, why don't you make some money selling your double bed, and buy a single one?'

Then we went to have a drink with Rosie and drank a lot of Bloody Marys, and came back home and had roast pork for lunch. In the afternoon Felix took Mabel for a walk, and later Emily and I followed him with Fortnum and Barbara. Floating along in an alcoholic haze, I insanely let Fortnum off his lead. The next moment he'd shot round the corner and was swinging what I thought was a squirrel – shaking it like a rat. I rushed forward yelling to stop him, together with the conductor and the driver from a parked 22 bus, then realised, to our horror, that it was not a squirrel but a tiny Yorkshire terrier. By the time we reached it, it was dead. The men from the 22 bus found me a cardboard box, and I carried it home. It had no collar or identity disc. Poor little Emily fled crying to one of her friends down the road.

Back home, I telephoned the police, and told them Fortnum had killed the Yorkshire terrier. A sweet policeman came straight round. He was a 'dog 'andler' himself, he said, stroking Fortnum, and Fortnum was obviously a nice calm dog, who didn't bite people. I then said numbly that I'd have to have Fortnum put down. The policeman didn't agree.

'It's 'uman nature,' he kept saying somewhat illogically, and I would be being very hard on Fortnum to put him down. Then he rang the RSPCA who arrived with a van and took the little dog away, they were terribly kind too.

Then Emily returned very tearstained from down the road. She'd told poor little Sybilla James about Fortnum. And Sybilla said: 'Poor Emily, poor Jilly, but a much worse thing's happened to me this week.'

Then the children and I mindlessly watched a James Bond film on television, and the nice policeman turned up in the middle. He said he'd found the owner of the Yorkshire terrier; it was a policeman, but actually the dog belonged to his thirteen-year-old daughter. And I wasn't to ring now, as the child was so upset, but could I telephone tomorrow afternoon? Oh poor, poor little girl – I know what she must be going through.

Oh God, what am I to do? Everyone says don't put him down. But if he lives, chaos will come again. The witch hunt will start. Dog wardens will come to Putney, and pick Fortnum up every day, when he's off on his outings around the streets. And if we ever move to the country, sheep certainly won't graze safely. And what about all the dog owners who are terrified by Fortnum, and terrified for the safety of their dogs? Once blooded, he may kill others. And, worst of all, what about the poor little policeman's daughter and wretched little Yorkshire terrier?

But I love him so so much – with his fat paws, and his lovely solid body and grey scarred face, and his merry canter and his blazing neurotic loyalty. Can I possibly bear to take him round to the vet's tomorrow?

Monday, March 29th

Midnight: Fortnum is dead. Christ, I wish I hadn't done it. I took all three dogs out very early. It was very cold and grey. Fortnum never left my heels the entire walk. He knew something was up. Then I saw two magpies for joy rising out of Barnes Common boundary; their credibility is gone for ever.

Coming home, I met Rachel on the edge of the Lower Richmond Road, and started to cry, as I explained I was taking Fortnum to the vet to have him put down.

'Don't do it,' she said. 'Have him "carstrated", put him on a long lead for the rest of his life, and never let him out in the street.'

But I couldn't do this to him. Life would be unendurable. No outings, no kingdom, Fortnum's occupation gone.

Then Fortnum and I walked up to the vet's. All the blossom was out and shivering in the icy wind. We didn't have to sit in the waiting room, thank God, but went straight in. Mrs Fraser was angelic. She was the one person who agreed with me. She said Fortnum would reduce me to a complete nervous collapse soon, and there was no guarantee that castration would work; and it would not take effect anyway for six months or so, by which time he could easily have killed another dog.

She told me not to stay, but I wanted to. I felt I'd let Fortnum down in life, without leaving him at the end. I warned her he'd need a massive shot because he was such a powerful dog, so she had two injections ready.

I held him in my arms, and as the first shot went in, he turned round and gave my face a last lick and then collapsed, but it wasn't enough, because he went into the most frightful convulsions, and she had to give him the second injection to finish him off. She said it wouldn't have hurt him, that the convulsions were just anginal spasms, but I think she was being kind. I don't remember going home. But I took a minicab back later in the day to collect him, while the gardener came over and dug a grave.

I wrapped him in the blue and orange knitted blanket he'd arrived with seven years ago, and buried him at the bottom of the garden beside the gooseberry bushes that he'd spent his life proving puppies weren't found under. He looked so sweet and at peace. I made a wonky cross out of bamboos and stuck it on the grave.

About 1.30 there was a terrific thunderstorm. I felt crucified, because I wondered if Fortnum was aware of it, and would be panic-stricken if there was no one up there to comfort him.

Maxine, who was in floods all day, said the thunderstorms must have been Fortnum arriving in heaven and showing everyone who was boss. I hope he is with Maidstone. What a disastrous dog owner I've been. What a squandering, through my soppy indulgence and inability to discipline a flea, of two marvellous dogs.

Emily was at school, but Felix was absolutely angelic, he kept saying: 'Put your head on my shoulder, Mummy, and have a good cry.' The next hurdle was ringing up the policeman whose daughter owned the little Yorkshire terrier. He was incredibly kind and understanding, and refused my offer to buy the little girl a puppy. Then later I had to tell Leo who is heartbroken, too, but won't talk about it.

Saturday, April 3rd

Life goes on. Thank God, I am desperately busy finishing a piece on men and how wet – or wimpish – they've become for *The Sunday Times*. I took the dogs out today and poor Mabel who's been searching for Fortnum everywhere, suddenly barked in delight and took off after a brown dog. Then slunk back to me despondently when she realised it wasn't Fortnum.

Shambling through Barnes Graveyard, I find an urn lying among the pine needles with 'Dead Dad' engraved on it, and am tempted to pinch it for Fortnum's grave. Adding her usual note of bathos, Barbara bounces out from behind a tombstone with a rotting fairy cake in a plastic bag attached rakishly to a pointed bottom tooth.

Wednesday, April 7th

Walk with Molly, who wrote me a lovely letter about Fortnum. Young goosegrass is rampaging everywhere, cow parsley and speedwell are out on the Hillocks. Molly immediately gets onto the subject of Rachel and Clarissa. Do I think they'll ever bury the hatchet? I sigh, and say I don't know. (Feel privately that I will never forgive either of them for being right about Fortnum.) Molly says Rachel refuses to look her in the face – 'like a sacked housemaid,' she adds. But the other day she could have sworn that Clarissa's husband, Ronald, gave her a ghost of a wink as he passed.

Today Barbara riots so joyously with Molly's Dalmatian Ophelia, that she hurts the leg that was run over, and can only just hobble home.

Thursday, April 8th

It's like the ten little nigger boys. Fortnum gone, Barbara confined to barracks with a bad leg – just Mabel and me, desolate on a cold grey morning.

The leaves that come before the acid-yellow flowers are out

fizzing like sherbert on the two Norway maples on the Fair Triangle and on the south of the first Common.

Deeply saddened that the Spencer Arms by the 22 bus shelter has been gentrified. It has been painted bottle green with gold lettering, festooned with carriage lamps, and surrounded by tables with blue and white striped umbrellas. Saddest of all, the words 'Function Room', which used to make Leo and me giggle so much, have been painted out. I suppose this tarting up is all to compete with the old French Revolution pub, across the road, which has been mock-tudored and gentrified up to the eyeballs and renamed the Beefeater.

Saturday, April 10th

O God – I miss Fortnum. But I feel relieved: I have finally dispatched the piece on wimpish men to *The Sunday Times*. I pray that they like it – it's awfully contentious.

Sunday, April 11th

Work and Fortnum dying have distracted me from the Falklands Crisis – it's all very alarming. The euphemism 'task force' is being bandied about. It sounds like a posse of debs from an agency converging on one's filthy house to blitz it at £2.50 an hour.

Today I talk to the man who instead of walking always sits under the trees in a deck chair reading *The Sunday Telegraph*, while his dog barks after the squirrels. He works at Peter Jones, he says, and is on his feet all day, so he comes out on the Common for a rest and to read the paper. What a refreshing change from all those joggers! We discuss the Falklands Crisis, and admit a sneaking admiration for Mrs Thatcher, and agree What Else Could She Have Done?

I have been reading about gorse in a flower book. Evidently when gorse is in flower, England will never be beaten. But alas on the Common no gorse is out.

Return home to find Felix, who is home for the weekend, and who should be mugging up the Old Testament for his Common Entrance exam next month, reading a comic and watching television. I tick him off for not working. He replies airily that he has given up scripture for Lent.

Monday, April 12th

Barbara better and back on the Common. Liberated from Fortnum's belligerent chaperonage, she is busy acquiring admirers. Chief among them is Rufus, a very handsome golden retriever. Today Barbara meets Rufus in the Squirrel Wood. She behaves exactly like a socialite at a drinks party, chatting animatedly to him, but glancing over his shoulder all the time, searching the trees for squirrels.

I was worried that, with Fortnum dead, Barbara and Mabel wouldn't defend me; but comfortingly if I go out with them at night, they bark their heads off if anyone comes within twenty yards of us. Last night walking home up Egliston Road, I nearly died when what appeared to be two huge figures, leapt over a flowering currant bush, and landed at my feet. Both dogs went berserk and opened curtains all the way up the street with their barking. I screamed my head off, but felt a bit silly. The 'huge figures' turned out to be two local twelve-year-olds returning from Scouts.

Saturday, April 17th

Not a word from *The Sunday Times*; I do hope the Wimp piece is all right. Paranoia is not helped by Emily who comes for a walk with me, and gets wild with rage when anyone else tries to join us. Seeing Rachel and Clarissa bearing down on us, Emily looks bootfaced: I'm going to be like Daddy from now on,' she announces loudly, 'and be rude to people.'

Tuesday, April 20th

Out on the Common. Beautiful radiant blue day. Just crossing Flower Garden boundary when I see my roofer friend, with the two Alsatians and the character-actor face, running towards me shaking with rage and horror.

Some bastards, he says, attempting a vile black magic ritual, have killed a puppy and hung it on the stone cross in Barnes Graveyard. It is about Barbara's size – a little brown and black very thin bitch, still with its woolly puppy coat. Blood is dripping from its mouth, and oozing all over the white steps of the grave. One can imagine the terror the little creature must have felt. The murderers had trailed bramble strands in parallel lines from the steps of the grave and put a large broken branch of cypress across the bottom to form a ritualistic square.

My roofer friend says he can't get the puppy down, because his dogs will grab it. I go and find Ken the Common ranger. Crying all the while, I find I have no paper handkerchief, and have to resort to my sleeve. Ken, mercifully, probably, is very matter of fact about the whole thing. When we get back to the Graveyard, the roofer man has lifted the puppy down. Lying dead on the gravel, she reminds me so poignantly of Fortnum. Go home utterly sickened and miserable. I can't stand living in Putney much longer.

Wednesday, April 21st

Walk early in the morning – no one about. It is very spooky; death seems to lurk everywhere. Still haunted by the little brown and black bitch.

On the way home Mabel meets a ginger mongrel and, as Barbara is on the lead, immediately goes into her sweet flirting act, flattening, ears back, followed by a lightning pirouette, then flattening again. Perhaps she is going to have a Roman Spring.

Next minute, however, we bump into Buster, the collie, one of Fortnum's great enemies. Barbara, who has no filial loyalty, immediately charges up to Buster, and starts chatting him up. Mabel, however, the dear principled creature, snarls, wrinkles her nose and refuses to be friendly. Buster's mistress, who can now afford to be magnanimous, says that Fortnum was a fine-looking dog, and that Buster still barks at Fortnum's ghost in the churchyard.

Thursday, April 22nd

I do miss Rosie. Most of her time is taken up with David the sculptor, and as Michelin, her Peke, had a heart attack last week, she no longer takes him out on the Common.

Friday, April 23rd

Leo and I have a long, long discussion and decide we're definitely going to move to the country soon. As it may be our last Boat Race in Putney we decide to go and watch it for the first time in ten years. On the way, Barbara rolls liberally in goose droppings, and then plunges into the muddiest part of Beverley Brook, emerging with thick shiny black leg warmers. I suppose it's one way of dispersing the crowds along the towpath. Actually the race is boring. Just two crews flashing by, followed by a lot of red-faced men in launches yelling into speaking trumpets. Until we get home we don't even know that Oxford have won.

Saturday, April 24th

Still no word from *The Sunday Times*, but bolstered by nice talks yesterday to the *Mail on Sunday*, who would like me to go and work for them. Their first issue is due on May 2nd, but after thirteen and a half years it would be a terrible wrench to leave *The Sunday Times*. Also cheered up by exquisite day and warm weather bringing out the lilacs, the double cherries and the wisteria in all the gardens.

Bump into Mrs Bond, who is exploding with indignation. One of her daughters (deserted by her hubby, and left with five kiddies) is living with a lorry driver, and evidently drawing social security. A German woman who lives in the council flat next door has, says Mrs Bond, tipped off Social Security that her daughter was living with the lorry driver.

Her daughter, she added, 'When she 'eard about it, followed the German woman down the street with language and other fings. And what are Germans doing in our council houses anyway, after what they did to us in the war?'

Having regaled me with this tale for at least fifteen minutes, Mrs Bond says she can't waste time chatting all day, and scuttles off to char for Henrietta.

On the way home I pass the lurcher man and his three lurchers, who gambol most charmingly with Mabel and Barbara. Also very ashamed to notice that the lurcher man himself is not black-eyed, black-haired and gypsy-faced, as I've always claimed him to be, but blond, brilliantly blue-eyed and very good-looking with his arms full of bluebells. I've heard of *names* being blackened by prejudice, but never eyes and hair. I hope I never have to be a witness in a murder case. And talking of murder, I really think we're right to think of leaving Putney. On the way home I bump into Rachel, who tells me an old tramp has been battered to death near Barnes Graveyard. Everyone is very jumpy.

Wednesday, April 28th

Still no word from *The Sunday Times*. The woman's page editor rings me up about my next piece and I ask her if she knows anything about the Wimp piece: 'Ah,' she says, 'none of the top floor like it,

they're all going round saying: "Jilly's got men wrong, my wife says I'm not like that."'

Whether this is true or not, it makes me feel deeply irritated. Ring up *The Mail on Sunday*, and say would they like me and the Wimp piece? They answer yes to both questions. Go out to lunch with the editor of the *Sunday Express* colour magazine, who left *The Sunday Times* about three months ago. He very kindly offers me a job, too. We proceed to drink far too much champagne.

Walk from Barnes Station through Mugger's Tunnel and along the path by the railway line. Find clumps of palest purple violets in the copse opposite the last platform. Above them on a lime tree, two fat squirrels are guzzling nuts – little hands working, black eyes sparkling, cheeks bulging like Timmy Tiptoes. Their coats are half-rust, half-grey. They are totally unafraid.

Get home at 5.30, to find the woman's page editor of *The Mail on Sunday* has sent me armfuls and armfuls of white freesias and bluebells, like the lurcher man, plus a note saying the Wimp piece is marvellous. Feel gratified and quite sick all at the same time. After thirteen and a half years on *The Sunday Times*, it is rather like walking out on a husband.

Maxine tells me that Barbara, in anticipation of new riches, has chewed up a five pound note.

Friday, April 30th

Walk with Syd the carpenter, who tells me that on the morning the old tramp was murdered, he (Syd) was out very early about 7.30, when a strange figure lurched towards him then lurched away. Syd then rounded the corner, bumping into a pretty girl with a Munsterlander bitch, who was in a frightful state because she'd just found the tramp's bashed-up body by the tennis courts. The poor girl, understandably, hasn't been seen on the Common since. Syd is convinced the first man was the murderer. He's been interviewed by the police. Having exhausted that subject, we then talk about El Alamein. Syd says he was a sergeant fitter. He thought Monty was a twerp and a butcher.

Saturday, May 1st

Very cold and blustery. Walk with Rachel who has had her

blonde perm cut very short. She is fuming because she is going to a wedding today, and the cotton suit that she's spent a fortune on is going to be too cold. Still utterly shell-shocked from leaving *The Sunday Times*, I suddenly feel faint crossing the Lower Richmond Road, and nearly black out.

'Perhaps it's the Change,' says the ever-tactful Rachel.

Change of newspapers more likely, I mutter under my breath.

Sunday, May 2nd

Leo and I take the dogs for a walk at dusk. The Fair is here. There is a new roundabout composed of coloured umbrellas flying round, lovely against the soft lit-up massed spring greens and bronzes, topped by pink and white chestnut candles.

Go home and watch a programme showing clips from the last Russell Harty series. And suddenly there is Fortnum, taking his Obedience Test at Cruft's, looking so alert, well behaved and sweet. He was such a beautiful dog. It is nice to remember him during his finest hour.

Wednesday, May 5th

Rosie rings very early to say Michelin was put down late last night. He had throat cancer. She is incredibly brave; she says she is going to have him cremated rather than buried at the bottom of our garden beside Fortnum, because, if we're thinking of moving, the new owners might dig him up. Feel desperately sorry for her.

Go out on Common – it is bitterly cold. As a result of making a commercial for *The Mail on Sunday* yesterday, I have bright scarlet nails, which clash horribly with my butcher-red and purple hands. As there was no time to cook last night, we had take-away curry. The dogs who wolfed all the leftovers are now desperately eating grass.

Meet Tommy who admires my nails then says he's very worried about Rosie, and is going to ring up Peke Rescue and see if he can get her another dog.

We are then joined by Crispin, the artist, who also admires my nails. He said that in America women come up to the counter after a manicure, hands with still-wet nails turned out, and say to the girl behind the till: 'My credit card's in my blue jeans pocket.'

Walking along by the tennis courts, I am horrified to find that the council have been at work again with the weedkiller, destroying all the wild flowers growing on the west end of the Graveyard, burning the blossom and leaves off the nearby chestnuts, as well as the needles off two pine trees. They have also left a disgusting smell of chemicals.

Rachel joins us also in a high state of chunter. I say I will write to the *Richmond and Twickenham Times* and complain – I bet I never get round to it.

On way home we meet Mrs Willis and her lovely mongrel Spot. She says her neighbours on the Ranelagh Estate have complained because 'sometimes Spot has a bark of a night,' and aren't dogs 'better than 'oomans?'

After she's gone, Rachel puts on her Mrs Thatcher voice and says, 'Isn't it tragic?'

'What?' ask Tommy and I.

'That dog,' says Rachel, 'is younger than Bridie, and look how fat it is.'

Thursday, May 6th

Photographed for *The Mail on Sunday* by Norman Parkinson. He is divine. Like a kindly Great Agrippa in *Struwwelpeter*. He says he was born in Putney, and used to go to Westminster School every day in a top hat, and all the louts of Putney threw all sorts of *dee*-tritus at him. His mother had an allotment on the Common with lots of roses. As usual Barbara insisted on getting in every photo.

Saturday, May 8th

Just walking down to the Common, when a silver-grey BMW screams to a halt; it is Horsey Miriam who says ecstatically, 'She had a little girl, all by herself in the night.'

Totally bemused by this piece of information – surely Miriam can't be referring to her daughter, who is unmarried and only eighteen. Then suddenly twig she's talking about her mare who's just had a foal. She is utterly enchanting, says Miriam, and striped like a humbug. Such is her euphoria she doesn't even mind Barbara standing on her hind legs scrabbling at the silver flanks of the BMW.

Out on the Common, meet Bea, a very pretty girl with a splendid rotund sleek black mongrel called Otis, who dotes on me because I always give him dog biscuits. The Fair, says Bea, has been all too much for Otis. He discovered two chips dropped by the 22 bus stop, and was dragged past them on his long green fishing rod lead (the kind Clarissa wanted me to have for Fortnum) like a great black whale. Let loose by the Brook, he ran the quarter of a mile back to the bus stop, across the two main roads, to collect the two chips.

Rosie comes round for a drink in the evening. She is so brave about Michelin, and not a bit self-pitying. She was immensely cheered because the vet wrote her a lovely letter afterwards, saying, 'We see a lot of dogs, but even we could see Michelin was special.' (I suppress ignoble thought that vet probably fancied Rosie rotten.) As the vet said, Michelin *was* special. Rosie says she misses him terribly. She got him just after she split up from her husband eleven years ago. It's been the longest relationship she's ever had with anyone.

David the sculptor, says Rosie, has been quite marvellous about the whole thing.

'What about his wife?' I ask cautiously.

Rosie shrugs and says the marriage is in injury time anyway. Hope to God it is.

Sunday, May 9th

Leo and I return at midday from a dance in Oxfordshire to find Felix with a huge black eye. He got beaten up by a gang of thugs at the Fair, after winning the jackpot on the fruit machine. Fortunately, he fended the thugs off, until the man who owned the fruit machines came to his aid. Leo bawls Felix out for going late to the Fair, but adds privately to me that this is one more reason for leaving Putney. Details of country houses are flooding in from house agents all over the place. The ones in Berkshire and Oxfordshire are ridiculously expensive. I am having slight cold feet about country life, but Leo is hell-bent on moving.

Felix and I walk on the Common. He has his French oral Common Entrance exam next week. So I attempt to question him in French round the Common. When I ask him his favourite food, he answers, '*Amburger et Cheeps*'. Suggest it would be better if he replied '*Harry Co Vert, et Pommes Freets*'. Felix says he can't cope with that. Then I ask:

'*Combien de chiens avez-vous dans vôtre maison?*'

'*Un chien, Monsieur,*' replies Felix.

'But we've got *two*,' I protest.

'I know,' said Felix, 'but I can't remember the French for two, and anyway the examiner doesn't know we haven't got only one dog.'

Gloomily feel that his chances of passing are rather *mince*.

Friday, May 14th

To my incredulous delight, Felix rings up from school and says the examiner has told him that he has just scraped through his French oral. Wonder all the same if French is actually still taught in schools.

Sunday, May 16th

Leo and I leave for a week's holiday in France. God I hate going away; I know I'll love it when I get there but the garden is looking so exquisite, full of lilies of the valley, wallflowers, bluebells, lilac and Solomon's seal, which was given me last year by Rachel. On the Common the hawthorn is just coming out, and the chestnuts are in their full glory.

As we leave, the dogs look at me with huge reproachful eyes. The children get up at six in the morning to say goodbye, both fighting back resentment. How can I ever move to the country, if I can't bear to leave Putney for a week?

We take the car on the ferry from Portsmouth and watch all the ships sailing out of the harbour waved off by cheering crowds as they set off for the Falklands. It gives me a sick feeling inside to see all those spruce young sailors lined up on deck. Will they ever return?

Tuesday, May 25th

Back from France, having spent a week renting a house in the heart of Normandy. It was so beautiful and so quiet. I manage to read fifteen books on how animals have been used in war, for my next book. Decide I will be happy in the country after all, but are holidays different from real life? Will I get bored without Putney bustle and gossip?

Friday, May 28th

Very late walking the dogs because we watch the Pope arriving at Gatwick on television. Cedric does the commentary quite admirably.

Leo, who violently disapproves of the Pope's visit, puts on a black shirt and tie this morning. His disapproval turns to horror when he sees the papal helicopter landing on a cricket pitch. Will the wicket ever recover? Having just come back fat as *beurre* from France I can only admire the nimble way the Pope bends down to kiss the earth and think how fit he must be.

Sunday, May 30th

Leo and I spend the weekend at Longleat, where Mabel and Barbara take part in a sponsored dog walk called the Great Paw Trek. Leo and I sleep in the Kama Sutra room in a huge four poster with a mirror in the ceiling. After a heavy evening, we fall into bed too exhausted to realise that Barbara is slumped between us. Waking at dawn, Barbara sees her reflection stretched out in the mirror above, thinks it's another dog, barks her head off, and rouses the entire household.

At lunch the next day, Leo gets tipped off about a ravishing house in Gloucestershire which is just coming on the market.

Tuesday, June 1st

Gorgeous weather. Lovely row over official opening of Putney Hospital. Two hundred people from NUPE (and very un-COHSE) chant rude slogans throughout the ceremony, in an attempt to drown all the speeches. According to the *Wandsworth Borough News*, the canteen staff were on strike, 'and the Friends of the hospital had to provide refreshments in the form of tea and biscuits for the visiting dignitaries'. After that din, all they probably longed for was a stiff drink.

Wednesday, June 2nd

Meet my director friend Peter Duffle, who says he is soon to start work on a film of *The Far Pavilions* in India. I haven't seen him for ages because he's been living in the country for several years. He says he is terribly glad to be living in London again. One of the things that put him off the country was his beautiful bearded collie getting kidnapped, and then being found a few days later run over on the motorway.

He now has an adorable new bearded collie puppy called Pompeii, who gallivants wildly with Barbara.

'Beardies,' the breeder told him, 'are very anxious to please.'

This beardie has eyes covered in hair, cannot see his master, hares enthusiastically up to everyone else in an attempt to find him, and sends Clarissa and Rachel flying.

Thursday, June 3rd

Emily and I stop to talk to Rachel, who has been gathering stones on the Common for her rock garden. She is resting on the much graffitied bench backing onto Putney Cemetery. Emily insists on reading out the latest graffiti in her piercing voice:

'Virginity is like a balloon: one prick and it's gone.'

She then asks: 'What does virginity actually mean Mummy?'

Hastily point out new post-Pope graffiti.

'JPR has made more conversions than JPII.'

Friday, June 4th

Heavy thunderstorms just before dawn. So strange not to have Fortnum's terrified trembling body in my arms. Pray for the thousandth time for him to be all right in heaven.

Common is rough mown for the first time – grass lies white like shorn locks on the hairdresser's floor.

Meet Clarissa who gives me a four-leaf clover, and says: 'Last night I'd just put on my housecoat, and taken a sleeping pill, when one of my battered wives rang in hysterics from the police station. She had two black eyes, and the police insisted on sending her home.'

Clarissa then nobly got dressed and drove down to the police station to take the battered wife back home at 1.30 in the morning.

'What does your husband look like?' asked Clarissa.

''E's short,' said the battered wife.

So Clarissa and the battered wife crept back dodging short men.

I think Clarissa must have read somewhere of the importance of getting bereaved people off the subject of those they have lost. Every time I mention Fortnum's name, she cuts through the sentence and starts talking about her mother-in-law or some book she's been reading. I wish I could explain. It helps if I can talk about him occasionally.

Saturday, June 5th

Still very hot and thundery; smell of elder and white valerian particularly strong. Meet Molly with heavenly friend Mrs Tomkin who has a big black mongrel called Max.

Max is a great barker, explains Mrs Tomkin, and the police called to complain, so she now keeps him in a play pen in the garden during the day.

'At night,' she says, 'Max likes to use Father's artificial leg as a pillow.'

'Isn't it rather small?' I said, mishearing, and thinking she said 'egg'.

'No,' she says, 'it's the same size as his other one.'

She then says Mabel and Barbara (who are charging about romping with Ophelia) ought to join the IRA, they're so good at bashing kneecaps.

While I am pondering why I don't in the least resent Mrs Tomkin making cracks about my dogs, when I mind them so passionately from Rachel and Clarissa, the latter two come over the brow of Dogger Bank, and catch me giggling with Molly. Why do I find myself going scarlet with guilt, as though they've caught me stealing sweets? Vow to try and mind less what people think.

Go home and write a stern letter to the *Richmond and Twickenham Times* complaining about the wantonly haphazard use of weedkiller which has destroyed the wild flowers, shrivelled the chestnut candles, and finished off two perfectly good pine trees in Barnes Graveyard.

Sunday, June 6th

Everyone revving up for Putney Arts Festival. Drop into the church and find people hard at work arranging pews front to front, and pinning orange felt over them, so objets d'art can be displayed.

The butcher's daughter has produced the most ghastly mirrors decorated with coloured tiles. Would it be worth buying one for the sake of perfect steak for years to come?

Frances the feminist, in a caftan, is handing round cucumber sandwiches made with wholemeal bread. Perhaps she should put her spurned book on sisterhood on display. She hopes I'm going to be 'supportive' and buy a lot of pottery. A girl with bright crimson hair tied up in a ponytail going blonde at the roots is going mad trying to catalogue brooches.

The south-east corner (where dreadful paintings of celebrities are being hung) is known as the Top of the Flops. Michael Foot, Ted Heath, and George Melly are only too glaringly recognisable.

'I'll give you £100 if you take one away,' says a jolly lady in a folk weave skirt.

Monday, June 7th

The poplar fluff is drifting, but not covering all the adjacent trees in a total grey snowstorm as it did last year.

Attend the opening of the Putney Arts Festival. Talk to Cedric's wife.

Cedric is standing beside her trapped by a ring of admiring bores. Notice him pressing her collar bone with his thumb, harder and harder, like a duchess imperiously ringing for a butler. Suddenly she winces, starts, and says:

'Oh gosh, we must go or we'll be late for dinner.'

Ten minutes later I see them deep in conversation with Our Member. Perhaps it was *me* she wanted to escape from.

Tuesday, June 8th

Very hot but less muggy. Meet great friend called Bruce who used to be a stockbroker, but whose firm went to the wall in the great crash of 1974. He now works as a chauffeur, and has just acquired an adorable Jack Russell puppy.

Barbara, Mabel and the Jack Russell suddenly see a tramp with a bicycle standing deep in the nettles on the north side of Beverley Brook, and all go into a frenzy of barking.

My suspicions expressed to Bruce that the tramp may be a flasher or a glue-sniffer are quite unfounded. He turns out to be a middle-class man with a beard and a paint-stained smock, who is clipping elder flowers to make wine. He gives Bruce and me the recipe. When he reaches the words 'Yeast Extract', I start glazing.

He says if he puts a carafe of elder flower wine on the table it always goes before the red or the white. Bruce asks him to make him some whisky.

We overtake Clarissa and Rachel who are in high indignation because a two-feet-wide edge of grass has been mown along Beverley Brook, cutting down the salsify in its prime.

'Sappho,' I say wistfully, thinking of the poem about the plough share slicing through the poppy.

'No, no,' says Clarissa impatiently, 'salsify.'

I give up. The charming clump of yellow irises, that always get nicked within twenty-four hours, has come out on the edge of the football pitch.

Out in the afternoon. Alas, the wild roses are nearly over in the Flower Garden, but delighted to find a new bush has seeded itself. The flowers are whiter and more anaemic than the pink roses on the other bushes, but the smell is heavenly.

Wander through Barnes Graveyard and put a bunch of dog daisies on the grave of Francis Turner Palgrave, sometime professor of poetry at Oxford, born September 28th, 1824. He also produced *Palgrave's Golden Treasury*, an excellent poetry anthology, much used in schools in my day. I suppose he'd need to be born in Libra to be diplomatic enough to cope with all the poets who were livid with him for leaving them out, or not putting in the poems they liked best.

Finally identify the pine in the graveyard as a Weymouth pine; it is already putting out pale green cones beside the old brown ones.

Friday, June 11th

Meet nice man with tiny moustache and tight-skinned mongrel called Edgy. Edgy's master, he says, is in the Falklands in the Welsh Guards. All the family sat down and cried when the Welsh

Guards copped it, but he thinks Edgy's master is OK. He says it won't be easy to capture Port Stanley, because of all the Falklanders living there. Feel depressed by this piece of news. Wish I wasn't always influenced by the last person I've talked to. Wish the war was over.

Meet Emily and Maxine back from the shops. Emily has had an appallingly short haircut. I know it's fashionable, but it's dreadful. Try to pretend I like it.

Leo comes back from seeing the house in Gloucestershire about which he was tipped off at Longleat. He is very pale. He says it's the loveliest house he's ever seen but he doesn't want to pressure me; will I go and see it very soon?

Sunday, June 13th

The Putney Common show has grown so large it is spread over two weekends. The first weekend includes a horse show – and, for the first time terrier races. They are terribly funny. The competitors are all Jack Russells who bark and bark at each other, and break off to have tremendous fights in the middle of each race. They rush down the straight after a fluffy rabbit on a piece of string. The finish is piled bales of hay, with a hole big enough for one winning terrier to race through after the rabbit. The rest nearly concuss themselves on the bales, or surge over the top, and are grabbed by the scruff of the neck by their owners, before they lay into one another again. The din can be heard from Egliston Road.

In the middle a kind local policeman comes up and says I'd better tell my son to pick up his bicycle from the grass, as this lot are likely to nick it.

Emily, deeply affronted at being thought a boy, decides maybe her hair is too short.

At the show I judge the Fancy Dress. It is the usual rat race of trying to distinguish between the professionals who clean up at all the shows, and the amateurs whose mothers have toiled all night over their costumes. Nor do I have the support of Anthony Andrews, who is too busy to judge this year. According to his wife, he's 'up to his neck in the Pimpernel'.

I've just reached Beauty and the Beast in the line up, when a horsey female steward cries out, 'Look out, she's staling,' whereupon Beauty's horse lets out a stream of pee, and a succession of very loud farts. I, after several gins in Miriam's caravan, get dreadful schoolgirl giggles, and have to bury my face in the shoulder of a nearby Arab Chieftain's horse.

In the end I give the prize to three adorable children carrying candles and their pony, who was covered in white net. They are supposed to portray a nightmare. Everyone afterwards tells me who else should have won. Judge not that ye be not judged.

Monday, June 14th

After watching terrier races very carefully yesterday while she was on the lead, Mabel rushes back to the track this morning to find the fluffy rabbit. Both she and Barbara examine the hole where it went through, and not finding it, wee on the bales in disgust.

Felix starts Common Entrance today. Pray so much that he passes.

Tuesday, June 15th

Everything revving up for the second big Show on Saturday. Attractions include steam-rollers, mowing machine races, the Marines (wildly popular since the Falklands Crisis), and the King's Troop. The Common is now overrun with roaring Rotweillers, caravans, washing and jolly whistling soldiers, saying, 'Nicest thing I've seen today,' to every girl who passes.

Council workers, racking their brains as to where all the tents should go, mark their territory with lengths of string, which trip up unsuspecting old ladies. Yet another Fair has also arrived with a roundabout, reducing Rachel to apoplexy. She is very cross there is not an arts and crafts tent at the show.

Meet old lady with adorable little dog. She says it is an Australian breed called a healer, and what absolutely delightful habits healers have. Fortunately she cannot at this moment see little healer and Barbara who are busily guzzling manure behind a hay bale.

Wednesday, June 16th

Walk with Clarissa and Rachel round the football pitch, from which we're really forbidden. Excited by fresh territory, the dogs snort a lot. We find cranesbill, speedwell, and a beautiful white and purple vetch like a lupin that none of us can identify.

I am about tell Clarissa that I haven't slept for a week worrying about the results of Felix's Common Entrance exam, but decide not to because I know any reference to public schools will enrage Rachel.

In the afternoon after a jolly bibulous lunch with two senior boys from Radley, who'd come up to interview me for the school magazine, I am photographed in Barnes Graveyard by the *Richmond and Twickenham Times* who are actually going to publish my letter. In vino I find it very hard to look suitably outraged and upset by the devastation caused by the weedkiller. Hope Rachel and Clarissa are pleased with me.

Thursday, June 17th

There is nothing as beautiful as the whitening grass on a warm June day, the weather is perfect. The Falklands War is now over. Lefties and Liberals are finding it very difficult to curb both elation and emergent jingoism. Nor do the media make any attempt at impartiality. I heard a man on Capital Radio today saying: 'I'm sure we're all absolutely – I mean I'm sure *Mrs Thatcher's* absolutely delighted that we've taken Port Stanley.' I think it's wonderful. Hurray for Maggie, she should call an election now. How disgustingly right wing I've become.

Yesterday, I fell in love with the house in Gloucestershire. I drove down with Leo who is right: it is utterly magical. We make an offer, even though we haven't looked at any other houses. All the same I wish Putney wasn't looking quite so enchanting. Warmed by endless lovely days, then fierce rain refreshing everything at night.

Friday, June 18th

Muggy, still day – grey sky lovely against the deep summer greens. The King's Troop are rehearsing on the Big Common for Saturday's display. Goodness, some of the officers are glamorous. I know I'm a sexual snob, but they do look so much more attractive than the men, principally I think because they're allowed to have longer hair, growing at least an inch under their caps, which is far more becoming than the troopers' crew cuts. Also their chargers have long manes, while the troopers' horses have hogged manes. To emphasise further that there is one law for the rich, the six officers' chargers are stabled in separate loose boxes – three in a row, and back to back – while the troopers' horses are tethered in the horse lines, tied by their off fore and near hind legs.

I talk to Paddy, the King's Troop vet, who owns an enchanting lame Labrador who spends his time slavering outside the cook-house. Paddy tells me about some of the individual horses: Wincanton, known as Cyril, who bites and kicks but is a brilliant ride, and Rebel who is forever kissing you if you've got nuts and sugar, and Yum Yum ridden by trumpeter Mason – who one year at the Royal Tournament was enjoying the applause so much that he refused to leave the ring and Trumpeter Mason was reduced to setting about the horse with his trumpet.

Paddy, the vet, also said the men were devoted to their horses: 'They'd kill a comrade, screw a girl, beat up their wives, rifle their mother's handbag, rather than let a hair of their horses' heads be hurt.'

Out in the ring, the Troop were practising pulling their gun carriages in figures of eight with a tremendous jangling. Some of the turns looked terribly hazardous. Paddy said the ground was very bumpy, and a gun carriage might easily overturn.

The Troop, he tells me, are due to do a display in Aldershot early next week, but may have to rush back to London to fire the salute in Hyde Park if Princess Diana's baby is born.

Any further chat was drowned by the deafening crash of the thirteen pounders, now firing blanks, but all used for real in the First World War. If Fortnum had been alive, he would have bolted halfway to Hyde Park by now.

Saturday, June 19th

Putney Show. Out early. Barbara and Mabel suddenly see a Peke beside the first bridge, and charge over, thinking it's Michelin. When they get there and realise it isn't, they start snarling in rage and disappointment. Find that more of the lovely lupin vetch that we discovered on the football pitch is growing in white and blue on the north side of the Flower Garden. Finally identify it as goat's rue. It is strange that when you discover a new flower (like learning a new word) it suddenly seems to crop up everywhere, and you can't imagine how you've missed it all these years.

Barbara, who's thoroughly over-excited by the Show (so much to roll in), follows a man in braces into a wooden privy. He swears at her, she shoots out again, like a jack-in-a-box, straight into the jaws of a huge Rotweiller.

The King's Troop display in the afternoon was truly splendid; all dressed up in their scarlet and blue, they are a magnificent sight. I notice the officers' quarters are strategically placed under the nurses' home, with a large sign saying Orderly Officer. I wonder if they'll scale the wall in the middle of the night and catch some matron unawares.

Monday, June 21st
Out on the Common, find the King's Troop packing up and in considerable disarray. Princess Diana, says Paddy the vet, has gone into labour. Half the troop are on their way in horse boxes down to Aldershot, and will have to do U-turns on the motorway and come back to London again.

I bid them a fond farewell and walk on, passing an earnest woman in rubber gloves with a bawling child busily trowelling manure into a black dustbin bag.

'I am getting it for the garden,' she says with a defensive laugh.

Borne down on by Rachel and Clarissa.

On the north side of Beverley Brook, Rachel suddenly asks if Rosie is having a walk-out with David the sculptor. Cornered I hum and haw, and say yes she is, but it's all right because they're terribly in love. And David the sculptor's been miserable for ages because his wife's had lovers dripping out of her ears (not sure she has at all) and Rosie has picked up the pieces wonderfully.

Hope I haven't landed Rosie in it. But all worry about Rosie or Clarissa or Rachel is driven out of my head by Leo ringing up and saying we've got the house in Gloucestershire.

Tuesday, June 22nd
On the Common meet Otis, the greedy black mongrel on his

green fishing rod. Bea, his pretty mistress, says he is still disgracing himself by charging across main roads after rubbish, and eating one of the Show Rotweiller's dinner while it was barking impotently inside a caravan. Worst of all, yesterday, he rushed into the tent, where all the soldiers were having their breakfast.

So she called in a high voice: 'Come here at once, Otis.'

And all the soldiers shouted back: 'No, no, you come *here*, sweetheart.'

On the way home, I bump into a nice minicab driver in his sixties walking five dogs: two Bedlingtons and three mongrels. He says he has just got married to a rich wife also in her sixties. Both were widowed before. Now they have five tellies, three video machines, three mowing machines, five children and five dogs between them.

Tonight Leo is going to an Old Boys' dinner and committee meeting. He says he may get an intimation whether Felix has passed Common Entrance and got into the school or not, but he won't be back from the dinner much before midnight, so I'll have to bite my nails until then.

I can't work for worrying about Felix. The only answer seems to be to get tight, which I do with an elegant young estate agent, from Knight, Frank and Rutley, who's come to talk about selling our house. He admires the sign saying 'Lost Children', which I pinched from the Putney Show, but says the best sign he ever saw was at the Game Fair, and said: 'Shooting Dogs Lavatory'.

At five to twelve Leo comes through the back door, and falls over the doorstep. He looks like a thundercloud, so I realise there's no hope and Felix hasn't made it. Then he grins and puts his arms round me, and says:

'It's all right, darling, he's in.'

I burst into floods of tears, and rush round the house waking Mabel, Barbara, Emily and Maxine, who are all thoroughly over-excited. Then I ring my mother. Evidently when Leo arrived, the headmaster said, 'Can I have a word with you after dinner?' so Leo had to bite his nails throughout the committee meeting and dinner before he knew. This means Felix is the fourth generation Cooper to go to the school, and it means so much both to him and Leo. Keep waking up all night in a daze of happiness – all this and Gloucestershire too.

Wednesday, June 23rd

Walk very late to avoid the regulars, as I'm terrified of telling them we're moving. I don't know why the hell I should be, but having never dropped any hint that we might be leaving London, it seems rather a bombshell to suddenly say we've found a house and we're off. Everyone will probably be thrilled.

Meet Molly and Mrs Tomkin, Max's wonderful owner, who is wearing lots of face powder, and in a high state of excitement.

''Ave you heard,' Mrs Tomkin asks, 'about the Activities? The police 've raided the brothel in Rocks Lane. Absolutely disgusting, the owner was using his own son – and he's only thirteen.

'And there's a house full of "those men" four doors down the road from the brothel,' Mrs Tomkin goes on, 'and they said to me this morning, "'Ave you heard about the Activities, Mrs Tomkin? It gives us such a bad name – we're not like that with kiddies you know; we thought the police was after us, when we saw all the flashing lights and all," and they're all such nice quiet fellows and very artistic.'

We then have lots more lovely lurid details about vicars and M PS caught *in flagrante* running out of the brothel into the night in their underpants.

Molly and I try very hard not to giggle.

The 'Activities' takes us three-quarters round the Common, and then Mrs Tomkin confides she thought the police and the flashing lights were after Max her dog.

''E used to bark at passers-by, and they complained to the police, and they came round and told us to keep Max under control. I mean it's not very nice to have a big black face looking over the fence at you, is it?'

I pat Max and says it depends very much on the face.

Friday, June 25th

Everyone is excelling themselves over our move to the country. It's as though we've committed some frightful crime like going over to the Russians.

'But we thought you loved Putney,' they chorus accusingly.

I still haven't had the guts to tell Clarissa and Rachel. This morning they descended on me, and Clarissa said: 'I saw your letter in the *Richmond and Twickenham Times*.'

'I haven't,' I said.

'Oh well, I'll cut it out for you,' said Clarissa, and makes no other comment.

Saturday, June 26th

Come back from a night in Yorkshire. Maxine says she walked the dogs, and was joined by Rachel.

'Isn't it exciting?' said Maxine.

'What?' said Rachel.

'About Jilly and Leo moving to Gloucestershire?'

'When?' snapped Rachel.

'In the autumn,' said Maxine, 'they've bought a house.'

Next moment they were joined by Clarissa, and Maxine said Rachel couldn't wait to shake Maxine off, so she could impart this piece of news to Clarissa.

Sunday, June 27th

Out with a hangover. Bump into Henrietta, who is at her most bossy and unlovely.

'I hear you're moving to Gloucestershire,' she says. 'Why Gloucestershire – it's so unfriendly? Why not Wiltshire? But I suppose you want to be near the Royal family. What about your contacts?' she goes on.

So I wearily point out that there are telephones and letter boxes in the country, and the cheap day return fare from Gloucestershire is less than a minicab to Fleet Street.

'Won't you miss all those brilliant witty remarks you always claim to hear at London dinner parties?' says Henrietta sarcastically.

'What's the point,' I say, 'if I'm too plastered to remember them next morning?'

Wednesday, June 30th

Our house goes up for sale. Two men from Knight, Frank and Rutley put up the 'For Sale' sign. Between hammer blows, like the end of *The Cherry Orchard*, they ask me why I want to leave a lovely house like this.

Feel slightly sick, and take the dogs out on the Common, trying to work out really why we're leaving. Because I'm sick of living in the Gold-fish Bowl; because I can't get any peace; and because people pour through the house all the time drinking our drink, and I never have any time to see Leo or the children. And because I hate seeing Leo come home white with exhaustion every night having spent two hours in traffic jams on the 22 bus. And because I never get a moment really to think about work – particularly on the Common because of all the people that come up and talk to me; and because if they don't and if I have to walk alone I'm frightened of rapists and murderers and flashers.

Above all I miss Fortnum. Every time I return to Putney I half expect to see him on the look-out, rootling round the churchyard, waiting to throw his portly body on me in ecstasy. Every blade of the Common is etched with his memory. I know it sounds melodramatic, but until I get away from Putney, I don't think I'll really get over his death.

Saturday, July 3rd

Now that we are selling our house the locals divide into two camps: those who say gleefully that the bottom has fallen out of the market, and those who try and make us push up the price of our house as high as possible, so that when it sells they can bask in the knowledge that their house round the corner will go for twice as much.

Sunday, July 4th

The Common is nearly back to normal after Putney Show, except for a bare brown stretch, where the King's Troop had their horse lines, and the six brown hopscotch squares, where the six officers' chargers lived in their loose boxes.

Monday, July 5th

As a result of a piece in the *Standard* mentioning that we are selling our house, prospective buyers are pouring in. I don't think I'm very good at selling. I keep pointing out loose floor boards here and saying the cellar's a tip. The only stipulation I make is that anyone who buys the house shouldn't dig up Fortnum's grave. Two couples, both very nice, seem extremely keen. I don't mind who buys the house, as long as they really love it.

Tuesday, July 6th

The house is sold to a family I really like, so that's that.

Wednesday, July 7th

Find first toadflax on the Flower Garden, but no pink soapwort yet. Red admirals are guzzling themselves silly in the knapweed. Find Rachel picking elderflower heads. She says they're delicious with gooseberries. She makes no comment about our move, so I don't.

Out at lunchtime, the tennis courts by Barnes Graveyard are absolutely packed with people playing with post-Wimbledon vigour. In a week or two they'll revert to their usual pat-ball. On the way home I bump into Ken the Common ranger. Suddenly see black smoke belching out of the hospital chimney.

'How do they get away with it in a smokeless zone?' I ask.

'They've got a new incinerator,' says Ken. 'All the sawn-off limbs from Queen Mary's, Roehampton come down here in a van to be burnt. Now that they've installed the incinerator they've got to use it.'

On such a macabre note, I am quite pleased to see Frances the feminist, and her vegetarian dog.

'I hear you're moving,' she says. 'I suppose you'll keep a place in London?'

'No,' I say.

'What about Leo?'

'Leo's got a bed in his office,' I say. 'He'll go up to London on Tuesday, and come back on Thursday night.'

Whereupon an almost lascivious look comes over Frances' face.

'Do you trust him,' she says, 'with all those predatory separated women on the loose in London?'

Snap back that soon, no doubt, I'll have M F Hs falling out of my ears.

On the way home, I meet a local who works on the *Financial Times*. He says he can't decide whether us leaving the area will make house prices in Putney go up or down.

Friday, July 9th

Notice fleets of goldfinches swooping in and out of the thistles. I never realised before what a heady delicate buddleia smell thistles give off after rain. After a very hot day yesterday, it is a sweet sight to see all the butterflies swimming through the light drizzle and enjoying the green cool after the baking heat. Melted butterflies, I suppose.

In fact, three days of heat wave have triggered off the great autumn caravanserai. The balsam has suddenly popped out and the east end of Barnes Graveyard is lovely: lavender, foxgloves, evening primroses, swathes of cranesbill and veronica in white flower, all held together by the long arms of the brambles.

Meet Clarissa who is singing the praises of Jennifer Bailey, a new Richmond councillor: 'Jennifer and her husband are very fine citizens, and have a strong sense of public duty. Jennifer Bailey has never not done anything she said she would, [how unlike me] and what's more,' continues Clarissa, 'the Baileys have never produced an ugly kitten.'

Saturday, July 10th

My mother rang today to say that my father is dying in the

nursing home in Haslemere. I must get down to see him. Oh God, that I weren't so hellishly busy – and I keep putting it off on the excuse that he probably wouldn't recognise me anyway.

His must be the cruellest of all deaths: the slow torturing erosion of a brilliant brain. I remember how he used to do *The Times* crossword in a few minutes, then gradually it took him longer and longer until he couldn't complete a single word in the book of children's crosswords that my mother had bought for him; and the endless heartbreaking lists he made of things not to forget in a desperate attempt to keep some control of life. And he was so brave, never a word of complaint or a grumble at the frightful pain that slowly curved his spine over like the handle of a walking-stick. No one could have a better father; I wish I were worthy of him.

Musing on the king my father's death, I go out on the Common and meet a pretty foreign lady in her sixties with a plump and genial dachshund, who she says belongs to a friend who is bedridden. It is seven years, she tells me, since she fell in love with Putney Common, and there has been no sign of an itch.

Then she says she's sad I'm going to live in the country.

'The whole of Putney will mourn when you go, Miss Cooper,' she adds. 'Every tree on the Common will hang its head down and cry.'

I almost cry too. I am so touched. It's not true. There are loads of people who'll be only too happy to see the back of me, but it's lovely of her to say that.

Sunday, July 11th

Today I was woken by Emily saying, 'Granny's on the telephone.' I saw it was only 8.15, and said 'Oh God.' 'Granny sounds quite cheerful,' said Emily. For a second I thought egotistically that she might have got up early and liked the piece I'd written on Henley for *The Mail on Sunday*. But she just said that Daddy had just died. Evidently he sat up, shook hands with the nurse, then lay back and died. How typical: courteous, kind and formal to the last. He was such a dear, brave man, totally without vanity or duplicity. I shall never look upon his like again.

Feel bitterly ashamed of myself for not getting down to Haslemere to say goodbye to him.

Arrange to go straight down to Brighton to be with Mummy, but take the dogs for a quick cold walk first. Wish I could take them too to comfort me.

Notice, despite weedkiller, the heartsease is blooming again in the stricken Graveyard – but not for me. Two magpies for joy rise out of the blackthorn copse – the same as they did the day Fortnum died. Their credibility has really gone for ever now.

Crossing the Fair Triangle, I see the woodspurge is out, with its acid-green flowers, with their three cups. I am reminded of Rossetti:

> From perfect grief there need not be
> Wisdom or even memory;
> One thing then learnt remains to me–
> The woodspurge has a cup of three.

I am also bitterly ashamed that I feel a stab of disappointment at having to go to Brighton and missing my last Putney street party this evening. Is grief ever perfect?

Thursday, July 15th

Daddy's funeral. He was buried on his birthday, St Swithin's Day, and it rained and thundered as it did the day Fortnum died. Mummy was wonderfully brave, and the service was lovely. The priest read out a fragment which seemed to sum him up so well:

> He nothing knew of envy or of hate,
> His soul was full of worth and honesty
> And of one thing, quite out of date, called modesty.

which was evidently written by the Duke of Buckingham of his father-in-law General Fairfax.

He was such a shy man; I keep worrying he'll be lonely in heaven.

In the late afternoon I came back to Putney, went out on the Common in my black dress and gumboots, got absolutely soaked, and felt a little better.

Notice horseradish leaves have been eaten to tatters by caterpillars this year. Is this because there are more butterflies about this year laying eggs?

Friday, July 16th

There are already a lot of green sloes on the blackthorn. I am going crackers trying to identify plants. Cannot decide whether tall ugly purple nettle growing along the Brook is downy woundwort or black horehound. It is probably the former, as the leaves are pointed and the trumpets that hold the flowers are clustered together, but it doesn't look pale or downy enough.

Nor can I identify a yellow clover-like flower growing in a huge clump on the north-east corner of Barnes Graveyard; nor a hideous shocking-pink flower, near Flasher's Point, which I think is possibly pink toadflax.

Feel I should produce *An Inconcise British Flora* by Feeble Martin.

Saturday, July 17th

Some men with swords have reaped the horseradish, gouging out the roots and discarding the leaves, which are already turning yellow at the bottom of the Flower Garden.

Meet jolly barman from local pub with new Jack Russell called Henry. Henry, he tells me, was acquired for two bottles of Scotch. I said Henry was worth at least half a dozen bottles.

Meet Clarissa at Lurker's Paradise. She is in fits of laughter because yesterday the retired Barnes district nurse, Miss O'Brien, was flashed at on the Common and didn't bat an eyelid.

'I've seen enough of those things in my time,' she told the flasher scathingly. He retreated abashed.

Rachel joins us, and we pass Horsey Miriam, and Sampson her red setter. After they've gone, Rachel makes some disparaging remark about how callous it is of Horsey Miriam to keep Sampson alive, when he's so old and frail.

I snap that Sampson is fine, and the best-looked-after dog in Putney, and they're a lovely family. Clarissa tactfully changes the subject, and says that she nearly walked slap into Scottish Molly at the Barnes Fair, and had to pretend to be endlessly counting the number of balloons in a taxi to avoid talking to her.

We then try to identify tall shocking-pink flower by Flasher's Point. Rachel thinks it's sticky catchfly, which sounds rather dubious, bearing in mind its location.

Then Clarissa and Rachel say they saw Rosie and David the sculptor, wandering hand in hand across the Common yesterday.

'He has a neurotic face,' says Clarissa bleakly.

'So he should have,' I say, 'after all the hassle he's had with his wife.'

Rachel says, 'He looks like a fallen angel.'

I say, 'He's certainly fallen for Rosie.'

Suddenly realise Barbara has vanished. Return to Squirrel Wood, and spend five minutes trying to catch her as she whisks round and round, eyes sliding. Finally she collapses at my feet.

'That dog,' says Rachel acidly, 'is just like her mother.'

For a second, I think she means me; then realise she is referring to Barbara's mother, Skip.

Can feel great waves of disapproval breaking over me.

Rachel then raises the subject of chasing sheep.

I say I really must find a farmer when I get to the country to lend me a ram, to butt Barbara about to put her off sheep.

'You must,' says Rachel bullyingly, 'or she'll get shot.'

I say that farmers are bloody trigger happy.

'It's a farmer's right,' goes on Rachel, sanctimoniously. 'I don't blame them. I hope,' she adds heavily, 'that your fences in the country are secure.'

Go home in vile temper – why can't she leave me alone?

In the afternoon, Rosie rings up and says that she and David the sculptor bumped into Clarissa and Rachel yesterday. 'They couldn't even bear to smile at us,' she says.

I tell her about Rachel asking if my fences were secure.

'Quite secure enough,' says Rosie, 'to keep out bitches like her.'

She then tells me what Molly actually said about me last year, which Rachel and Clarissa flatly refused to pass on to me because it was so dreadful, and which triggered off the great row, and which I'd always assumed was that I was an adulteress or had maladjusted children or something. Apparently she remarked that even if I walked round the Common with three crocodiles on a lead, Rachel and Clarissa would still rush and walk with me. Not entirely sure that I believe this.

Friday, July 23rd

Identify disgusting shocking-pink flower near Flasher's Point as purple loosestrife. Strife seems the operative word on the Common at the moment but no one seems to be losing it.

Saturday, July 24th

The slain horseradish leaves litter the Common like chamois leather.

Meet my dear friend Mrs Murdoch, with the straight back, and the two golden retrievers. Today she looks very furtive. When I ask her what's up, she says she's just graffitied a bench. Someone had carved the words: 'Gays loved here' on it, so she crossed out the word 'Gays' and wrote: 'Don't you mean perverts?'

Sunday, July 25th

Walk across the Yarrow Meadow; fronds of the wavy hair grass voluptuously caress my bare legs. The catkins are turning brown on the silver birches. Lots of meadow-brown and chalk-blue butterflies are fluttering around. So thrilled they're coming back; a few years ago one never saw a butterfly all summer on the Common.

Enchanted, too, to find the harebells again, a little way up on the East side of Common Road near a little sycamore. They are such an exquisite drained purple with their delicate taffeta petals. In folklore they are known as witch's thimbles.

Make dramatic discovery – no doubt obvious to everyone else – that each cherry-red finger of the willowherb eventually splits open, rolls back into four curls, out of which sprouts the feathering. On the way home I find two wrens, with their little tails up, in an oak tree. As I approach they send out that strange burglar alarm rattle.

Tuesday, July 27th

Autumn is here, but has been kept at bay by the rain. See painted lady in the long grass by the bog. It is absolutely beautiful, but notice it has a very boring brown underside. Perhaps it closes up its wings, when it meets another butterfly it doesn't fancy.

Walking late I meet Mrs Willis and her jolly mongrel Spot, who Rachel thinks is too fat.

Spot, she says, won't touch tinned food, but always enjoys a Sainsbury's steak and kidney pie, potatoes and peas of a Saturday night.

Sunday, August 1st

Deeply gloomy – people keep telling me how wrong we are to move the children to the country, just at the beginning of their teens, when all they'll crave from now on is parties, bright lights and the King's Road.

Cheered up in the afternoon because Emily returns from staying with cousins who live in the depths of the country. She had a glorious time, she says, rode a pony called Robin, and dyed her hair purple, but it came out in the swimming pool.

Out on the Common there is no sun. Despite the punishing heat, the trees have a flat matt heavy look. Walk with sweet girl who works for Capital Radio; she says her husband runs a radio station in Cardiff, which employs a token gay, a token black and a token feminist. He found one secretary in floods the other day, and said, 'What's the matter?' She said all the typing pool were being bloody to her because they said she was sexist, for wearing lipstick.

On the way home I pass Frances the feminist, who is picking blackberries – presumably for her vegetarian dog's supper. 'What are you going to do about schools in the country?' she asks beadily.

I stand on one leg, then say boldly that both children are going to boarding schools. Frances the feminist instantly becomes the personification of outrage and disapproval.

'Because you're too selfish to look after them yourself,' she says.

I then get a twenty-minute lecture about my deeply 'uncaring behaviour'.

I mutter that I went to boarding school myself, and I survived.

'Hardly,' says Frances dismissively.

I feel so cross with her that I finally resort to below-the-belt tactics of asking what has happened to her book on sisterhood.

'No publisher is brave enough to publish it,' she replies. 'It's too far ahead of its time, so I've decided to shelve it for five years.'

Instead, she says, she's decided to start a feminist workshop in

Putney. Thank God we're leaving. There is something infinitely dingy about the word workshop. Pray that England doesn't become a nation of workshop-keepers.

Monday, August 9th

Rosie and David the sculptor come to lunch. It's the first time I've seen them together; they are at the white-heat stage of sexual attraction when they cannot keep their hands off one another. He strokes her forehead in wonderment and reverence, as though he were an archaeologist who'd just unearthed the skull of Helen of Troy.

He asks me about the new house. I say that it's lovely but getting horribly overgrown, and we've had to spray to keep back all the nettles and thistles.

David looks appalled: 'You can't do that,' he says, 'You'll kill all the butterflies, and anyway nettles and thistles are so beautiful.'

Reply that they lose their charm when you can't see out of your windows. But secretly feel cruel and life-denying, and spend sleepless night worrying about the dogs dying from poisoned grass, and wonder if there is any difference between me and the Zombies who sprayed all the wild flowers in Barnes Graveyard.

Tuesday, August 10th

Rachel points out linum, an enchanting blue flower, which she has found growing on the spot where the King's Troop chargers were stabled.

In the afternoon, I meet Tony Phillips jogging. He says Effie, his big blonde mongrel, had to be put down this week. She was drinking two bowls of water an hour and the vet diagnosed cancer. She was fifteen.

'Every time the doorbell goes,' he says dolefully, 'I can't get used to no bark.'

I say truthfully that a bit of Old Putney has gone.

Effie was a great blonde survivalist, a mafia momma, wise, crafty, tyrannical, and always out on the streets. She and Fortnum ran Egliston Road between them and had total monopoly of all the dustbins. Fortnum was devoted to her, and always popped in to visit her every morning, after he'd paid his respects to Rachel's Bridie. He'll be awfully pleased to welcome her in heaven.

Wednesday, August 11th

The situation is becoming ridiculous. Although I walk with Rachel and Clarissa every day, apart from Rachel's crack about my fences being secure they haven't mentioned our move to the country at all.

Today I take out a few photographs of the house to show them. Clarissa makes absolutely no comment at all; Rachel says that it looks nice, and she'd love to get her hands on that water garden.

I give up and hastily change the subject, saying isn't it sad about Effie, and how much I loved her. 'The family,' I go on, 'are utterly devastated.'

'They couldn't be,' says Rachel dismissively. 'They used to let her out in the morning. I've seen her roaming along the Upper Richmond Road. No one who lets his dog out can possibly love it.'

So I say through gritted teeth: 'I let Fortnum out. Are you implying therefore that I didn't love him? You're talking rubbish. Effie came from Battersea and she was already a street dog, like Fortnum, before they got her.'

There is a long pause. Feel tempted to quote Hamlet. The bit about,

> I loved Ophelia: forty thousand brothers
> Could not, with all their quantity of love,
> Make up my sum.

Then realise it goes on: 'Woo't eat a crocodile;' remember Molly's remark about me with three crocodiles on the lead and stop just in time.

There is another long pause, and I stalk off.

'I do like your house,' Rachel calls after me.

Friday, August 13th

Clarissa corners me. She is in a confiding mood. She passed Molly in the street in Barnes yesterday, and as she was in a good temper and it was such a lovely day she smiled and said 'Hullo' before she realised who she was talking to. She is worried Rachel

will be furious with her for letting the side down, and hopes Molly will not try and walk with them again.

Sunday, August 15th

Say to Maxine I am going to avoid trouble by walking to Barnes Station today. Maxine says isn't that where everyone gets raped? Say that I'd rather be raped than bullied. Maxine thought for a few minutes, and said that she thought she'd rather be bullied.

Walking across the Yarrow Meadow, it is a Resolution and Independence Day; everything is sparkling in the sunshine after the heavy rain. Hairbells, crushed by the downpour and by lovers, are strewn like amethysts in the long blond grass. Chestnuts are turning in the wood by Barnes Station. All the oaks look very poorly; their leaves are diseased, and so many of them have that strange lime-green sealing wax formation instead of acorns. Notice sticky buds already forming in the chestnuts. Suddenly feel desolate that I won't be here next year to see them burst open.

Friday, August 20th

Admire a huge clump of white soapwort on the north-east corner of the Flower Garden. Usually soapwort is pink, but notice some of these white flowers are tinged with pink.

'You're going to find it awfully quiet in the country,' screeches a voice, making me jump out of my skin.

It is Frances the feminist. She tells me that her sister lives in

Gloucestershire, and was so badly snowed up last year that all her pipes froze and the village was cut off for ten days.

'How will Leo get home if that happens?' she says happily. 'Imagine him spending ten days on his own in London.'

Tempted to reply that the one spare woman with whom Leo will not dally is Frances.

But go home depressed. I'm beginning to feel Otis the portly black mongrel is my only fan. Let off his long lead, he pursues me all over the Common for handfuls of dog biscuits – a sort of Follow-my-Larder.

Wednesday, August 25th

I am starting to ring up people who've been friends over the last ten years, and asking them to go for last walks on the Common with me. Today I bid farewell to Doreen who was once my secretary, who used to have two perfectly trained Alsatians, one of whom has died. We have a lovely walk together, then Clarissa joins us.

'I've got a perfect leaving present for you,' she booms, 'a tabby kitten.'

'No,' I reply on a note of rising hysteria. 'NO NO NO NO.'

Then I point out more politely that we've already got four cats coming to the country, and that's enough. I then introduce Doreen.

'OH,' says Clarissa jovially, 'you must be Doreen the Alsatian.'

'I am not an Alsatian,' replies Doreen tartly.

Atmosphere becomes very tense. I feel like a piece of beetroot slapped between two very scratchy pieces of wholemeal bread.

Thursday, August 26th

Bump into Vic, the printer. As well as his two Dobermans, he has acquired a lovely bulldog puppy called Enid, who is totally unafraid, waddles up to every dog she passes, and tries to kiss it. Barbara does not approve of Enid, whom she thinks is very plain. When she approaches, Barbara turns her head away in horror, rather like the peeress who allegedly put her hands over her face whenever Cyril Connolly approached because she thought him so ugly.

Friday, August 27th

I can already smell the poplar scent on the boundaries and on the north-east top of Putney Cemetery. I love the way Barbara flattens her ears against the stings as she runs through the nettle tunnel.

I bump into Henrietta in the local off-licence.

'What are you actually going to do in the country?' she says. 'You won't have any of your friends to gossip to.'

I reply frostily that I intend to take up polo and gliding and to join the Women's Institute. Henrietta's derisive mirth follows me down the street.

Saturday, August 28th

Bump into Mrs Bond. She says that she's got to go and tidy up after Henrietta and the pale children who've gone to Cornwall for a month. You can't help being fond of Henrietta, she goes on, despite her funny ways. Find that I can help it all too easily.

Monday, August 30th

Toadflax and soapwort are still out in the Flower Garden. And there is a terrific crop of berries, sloes, haws, hips and blackberries.

Coming home, I notice that the silver willow in front of the hospital has lost yet another huge branch; only a quarter of it is left now. I suppose it will last my time. So busy examining it that I do not see Rachel coming and go slap into her. Would like to have preserved an icy silence and moved on. But instead, pusillanimous, placating, terrified drip that I am, I stammer out an apology, and say I've been offish recently because I'm having all the strain of moving. Why the hell do I always say things like this, instead of telling her the truth – that I'm utterly fed up with her, and will never forgive her for implying that I didn't love Fortnum? Rachel is very gracious, and nods understandingly.

Tuesday, August 31st

Matthew, a friend, comes for a drink in the evening, and is terribly funny about the tarts in Wandsworth ministering to the needs of the commercial travellers in their cars parked along the Common. Suddenly you see a shuddering *Daily Telegraph*, then a large bum emerges from the car, and the bum moves onto the next one. Nothing like this happens on the Eternal Triangle.

Sunday, September 5th

Mayweed has flowered in lush squares and in a long oval on the space where the King's Troop stabled their horses.

Go out in the afternoon to take a farewell signed book to Mrs Willis and her mongrel Spot.

Her sister has just died, she says, from cancer. 'It was very sad, but she felt no pain – she just slipped away.'

Mrs Willis adds that she's so pleased to see me, because she thought I'd also slipped away without saying goodbye.

Oh dear. Is that what going to the country will be like – a kind of death?

Monday, September 6th

Autumn is here. Michaelmas daisies are out. Jays, blue wings flashing, are screeching in the trees; the grass is strewn with gold leaves. The chestnut, two down from the slide, is turning first as usual. Yellow sedum that crawls over the gravestones is just a cluster of grey stars.

Thank God I am terribly busy writing a book which has to be handed in the first week in December, which at least stops me brooding on leaving Putney. I find my moods are terribly up and down, but today I was cheered up by a friend of Leo's who tells me that the tobogganing is terrific in Gloucestershire.

Tuesday, September 7th

Walk with Emily. Want to spend as much time with her as possible, as she's off to boarding school in a week.

She says in a disgruntled voice: 'I have a lovely life, but I don't like anything on me.'

She is referring to two spots on her forehead, and her hair which won't stay brushed upwards.

Wednesday, September 8th

Because I want to savour my last few walks on my own on the Common, I've been getting up very early to avoid other dog walkers. Instead I seem to spend most mornings doing a four-minute mile round the Common keeping up with Syd the carpenter, who walks terribly fast. As we whizz round I have no time to appreciate turning leaves or cobwebbed gorse. All the same he is a sweet man. He says he's been lonely since his wife died, and feels particularly sad because his daughter is about to have a baby, and his wife would have so loved being a grandmother. He is very right wing, and loves to talk about politics, so we have dreadfully fascist conversations.

In the afternoon, Leo and I take Felix back to his new school. He is nearly as tall as me now, and I have annexed all his prep school uniform – and can see myself striding round Gloucestershire in grey flannels, a green peaked cap and a hockey shirt.

Thursday, September 9th

Less than three weeks left. I walk early with Rosie, because we never seem to have time to see each other. She is thinking of getting another dog, and moving in with David the sculptor – evidently his wife has pushed off. I say I think both are splendid ideas.

To avoid the Heavy Brigade we walk across the Yarrow Meadow, and find delicate cobwebs all silvered with dew spread over the grass like table mats.

'And you're really happy?' I ask.

'Oh yes,' sighs Rosie, 'I never want to get out of bed.'

Returning via the Flower Garden, we find yellow tormentil, with its four heart-shaped petals. Its Latin name, says Rosie, is *potentilla erecta*, which brings us back to David the sculptor, again.

Friday, September 10th

Beautiful morning. Why does this particular September have to be so lovely just to torment me, with its soft low sunlight, and the amazing, opaque bands of mist rising above the golden grass? At night it is heartbreaking. Pegasus gallops above the church, and Andromeda stretches over the hospital, but it's been too misty to see the Pleiades.

Saturday, September 11th

Go out with Emily and see three magpies for a girl rising out of the blasted oaks on the edge of the Flower Garden. Syd the carpenter comes rushing up, red-eyed from lack of sleep, and says that he's got a granddaughter: he's so excited.

'It's a little girl,' he keeps saying.

As soon as we are out of earshot, Emily says in shocked tones: 'Isn't he rather old to have a baby?'

Tuesday, September 14th

Out on the Common, breathe in heady autumn smell of moulding leaves. I am joined by Rachel and Clarissa. We proceed along at a solemn pace. Suddenly tempted to sing that Joyce Grenfell song about 'Stately as a galleon I sail along the floor'.

'I caught you on television the other night,' says Clarissa heavily.

I brace myself and say: 'Oh yes?'

'I caught you too,' says Rachel.

Clarissa said: 'You should sit in the middle.'

I protest that I couldn't have, unless I'd sat on Lord Norwich's knee.

'You didn't get into the camera at all,' said Clarissa, 'and you ought to get another chairman.'

I protest that the chairman is lovely and a new friend.

'I don't care if he *is* a new friend,' says Clarissa. 'He's so patronising.'

By second post I get a lovely letter from Felix. He is OK. 'As Daddy predicted,' he writes, 'I am very occupied.'

Wednesday, September 15th

Emily's last day. We walk clockwise round the Common together, in the hope that people will leave us alone. Walking towards Beverley Brook, we meet Rachel and Clarissa. Rictus grins all round.

'Is this the day of execution?' says Clarissa.

They both wish her good luck and have the sensitivity not to turn round and walk with us.

Before Emily goes off there are the usual photographs in the garden. She looks very glamorous with a new punk hairstyle, wearing new jeans with red braces and a dark blue shirt. How different from the hideous navy blue coat and skirt, and red tie which I wore when I first went away to school.

It was a lovely day for the journey down. I held Emily's hand – those lovely smooth hands of childhood; her trunk in the back was like a coffin in a hearse. Her housemistress gave us a lovely welcome.

'I'm not going to look when you drive off,' said Emily. 'It's unlucky.'

My last glimpse of her was standing very tall, slim and smiling and looking speculatively round rather like Barbara, and deciding which of the other little girls she was going to bounce up to.

Now it is night time. I went into Emily's room at midnight, and found the needle had stuck on the record of *Fame* and was still playing. The room looked so bare because all her ornaments are now in packing chests. The bed was stripped and a moth was bashing against the window pane. Even worse, there is no one anymore to leave a light on in the landing for, to ward off the nightmares and the hobgoblins.

Oh please God make her safe, and don't spoil her lovely merry nature. Slightly relieved that I feel far far worse than I did when Barbara went to kennels.

Thursday, September 16th

We are having an Indian summer. Wonder if Indians have English winters? The little alders below the rowans on the second Hillock are wilting from the heatwave. I don't think they've been planted near enough to the Brook. The clover is shrivelling; the everlasting pea is still in gaudy bright pink flower.

Walking through Barnes Graveyard, I find a man gathering up the fragments of Maria Ayoub's tombstone which was smashed by the vandals. Although no one has found the bronze of her face, which must have been stolen, I am delighted to hear that her tombstone is to be stuck together again.

Rachel and Clarissa bear down on me.

'What about Grace Kelly?' asks Clarissa.

'What about her?' I say.

'Dead,' intones Clarissa.

'How dreadful!' I say, very shocked.

'I don't see it's dreadful,' snaps Rachel, 'just because she's famous.'

Friday, September *17th*

We have a very nice new next-door-neighbour: a widower with an ancient springer spaniel. The only problem is that he is between jobs, spends a lot of time walking his dog on the Common, and always seems to combine his lunchtime walk with mine. What with Syd in the morning and the widower at lunchtime, I have absolutely no precious time on my own to take leave of the Common.

Sunday, September *19th*

Have lunch at Langan's with an eighty-eight-year-old Dutchman, who's been writing to me about my books and pieces since I joined *The Sunday Times* thirteen years ago. The place is dripping with chums, and a lot of inter-table gassing goes on. Wonder for the millionth time whether we're making a lunatic mistake leaving London?

On the way home I go to the loo in Green Park Tube Station. See fat blonde with red face, dressed in black trousers and a shirt; turn sideways, she's still fat, and realise to my horror it's me. I look like a provincial lady before I've even got to the country.

We have to change buses at Parson's Green. Sitting down on the new bus, I drop and smash the bottle of hock given to me by the eighty-eight-year-old Dutchman. Consequently, the bus absolutely reeks of drink. Suddenly, sitting opposite, see Matthew Roberts who used to be at All Saints' with Felix, and who, according to Felix, couldn't climb ropes because his willy was too big. He now goes to Wandsworth Comprehensive and is rather sexy looking. Feel that this is where I came in.

Friday, September *24th*

Pickfords turn up to talk about the move, which is going to be hell. With two massive fish tanks, two dogs, two cats, 8000 books, and more than 100 plants to transport to the country, it's going to be like conveying the Pacific Ocean, the zoo, and the Bodleian Library, as well as Birnam Wood to Dunsinane.

Pickfords scratch their heads, and say 'We'll need three pantech-nicons, plus an extra van for the plants, but we won't take the goldfish; and the actual move will take four days.

Leo, who has dazzling powers of organisation, runs the whole thing like a military operation, and draws up a movement order.

Thursday, 10.00 hours: LC leaves for the country with two fish tanks.

Friday, 06.00 hours: Cats to be caught, drugged and boxed by JC. 06.45 hours: LC to convey cats to Gloucestershire.

His able adjutant in this undertaking is Maxine. I spend my time getting in the way and court-martialled.

Saturday, September 25th

Last walk with Crispin. I shall miss him very much. I'm sure one day he'll be very famous and a budded artist, and earnest young reporters will come and interview me in my dotage about having known him.

We discuss moving to the country. I say at his age, when one has no ties (which always sounds like an incomplete wardrobe), one is better in London where the action is.

On the way back, we meet Buster, the collie, and his mistress. She says that Buster still barks at Fortnum's ghost in the church-yard. Feel stab of anguish that he may still haunt the Common, desperately searching for me after I'm gone.

Sunday, September 26th

Everyone keeps telling me that after bereavement and losing one's job the experience likely to cause most stress is moving house. Having lost my father, Fortnum, *The Sunday Times* and Putney in six months, I suppose I can be excused for being slightly uptight.

Certainly moving has many of the trappings of death: the flowers and good luck cards (today I got one from Otis the rotund black mongrel), the farewells, the feeling of total unreality and being endlessly chilled to the marrow, the agonising sorting out and throwing away.

Then there are the ridiculous tears which keep sweeping over me – when Putney Garden Centre gave me a farewell plant this morning; and when Ossie, who runs the local delicatessen, and who shares Leo's passion for highly-spiced food, announced that he had created a special Leo and Chile salad in our memory.

Monday, September 27th

What I hate most of all is seeing our darling house stripped of its riches. Go out on the Common to escape pictureless walls, tables without ornaments, bookless shelves. The mirrors were packed up this morning. Unable to see myself, I shed even more of my identity.

At home in a jelly of indecision, I try to sort out my bedroom and study, failing to throw away any clothes, in case the children need them for dressing up; or toys, because the way I feel I may be a grandmother any minute; or make-up, because Emily, or worse still Felix, might want to use it one day. After hours of sorting, I only manage to jettison fifteen Biro tops, and page one of Mozart's *Rondo in A Minor*.

Tuesday, September 28th

Ludicrous day. Full of spats. I go out on the Common having arranged with Molly to meet her by the Eternal Triangle so we can have a last walk together. As I leave by the Yarrow Meadow, the heavens open. I get absolutely drenched. I hover for about twenty minutes by the Eternal Triangle, looking at the revolting triffid

burr marigold and watching the sun rush in and out, and all the grass dancing and sparkling. I have a nice farewell chat with the man who reads the *Sunday Telegraph* in a deck chair in the Squirrel Wood; then suddenly to my horror I see Rachel striding towards me.

I am too frightened of her to say that I am waiting for Molly; instead I move off, praying that she will go in the other direction – but she follows and walks with me round the Common.

Suddenly as I reach the ranger's hut, I see Molly waving in the distance, and say to Rachel that I think that as it's my last Sunday, and I really want to take a last proper look at the Common, I'll walk round again.

'I'll come with you,' says Rachel.

To my eternal shame I am too chicken to say that I'm off to see Molly, so I say, 'Oh well, I've changed my mind, I'm going home after all.'

So Rachel says: 'Well I will too.'

And poor Molly goes unmet.

As soon as I get home I telephone Biffo, to ask him to explain to Molly what's happened. He says he's never heard anything so ridiculous in his life, and I can't be *that* scared of Rachel.

'I am, Biffo,' I say sadly, 'I am.'

Leo, meanwhile, is cooking lunch.

He says will I pack up all my underwear into a big plastic bag, as I don't want the removal men rifling through it?

'Oh they won't mind,' I say. 'That's why it's called a Pant-technicon – ho, ho! Anyway, they've seen worse things than my underwear.'

'I doubt it,' says Leo heavily.

Brisking about and trying to be efficient, I throw away what I think is vegetable water in the sink. It turns out to be the marinade, in which Leo is intending to braise the beef. He hits the roof. I burst into tears.

'A brawling husband in a wide house,' I sob. 'I don't want to live all by myself in Gloucestershire with you shouting at me.'

So we make it up. Then I laugh because he'd told Maxine to pack all the kitchen equipment and there's nothing to carve the beef with; so we start rowing again.

In the afternoon there is yet another row, because we do the change-of-address cards, with Leo roaring round the kitchen, saying, 'If you send one to that bore, or that bore, I'm leaving home.' When I point out that he's leaving home anyway on October 1st, it improves his temper even less.

Out on the Common in the afternoon, I bid farewell to everyone I meet, just in case I don't see them again before we go.

Wednesday, September 29th

The move proper begins. I rise early, find empty dustbins and burst into tears because I haven't said goodbye to the dustmen. Go out on the Common, and meet all the people I bade fond farewells to yesterday. Returning home my heart sinks to see two huge pantechnicons outside the house. Next moment the Pickfords foreman comes out staggering under a packing chest full of books:

'You ought to see the bleedin' lot we've got to shift here,' he grumbles, then realising it is my house, straightens up hastily, saying: 'Good morning, Madam.'

Evidently he'd asked Maxine earlier what kind of dogs we'd got, and when she said mongrels and not very big, he said: 'Thank Gawd for that – from the size of them baskets, I thought they was bleeding polar bears.'

In fact all the removal men are marvellous, very giggly, and after being primed with Party Fours by Leo, incredibly accommodating.

There is Ralph, the foreman, who has the soul of a poet. Danny, the handsome clown from Fulham, and Derak from New Zealand who tells me that his father, also a removal man, had once dropped a piano into Sydney Harbour, which was never found again.

All day it pours with rain. Maxine and David, our cleaner, clean and clean. The cats have a ball jumping in and out of packing chests. Mabel and Barbara shiver miserably, trailing me, their only constant, from room to room, as each familiar object disappears and their world seems to crumble round them.

By 4.30 I am so bombed producing endless cups of tea that I decide to have my first drink of the day, pouring out gin, then tonic, putting in ice and lemon then solemnly taking a bottle from the fridge and topping up the whole thing with milk.

Brilliant sunshine – a two-edged blessing. Everything sparkles after the rain. The Common has never looked more seductive. Keep re-meeting all the people I bade farewell to on Monday, Tuesday and Wednesday. Feel rather like Tosca, hurling herself to her death over the battlements onto a trampoline and bouncing back into view again and again.

Jump out of my skin as I see Rachel and Clarissa coming striding across the Flower Garden. They turn round and walk back with me to the ranger's hut. I bombard them with questions about their respective families, anything to keep off the subject of our move, as Leo has told me not to give them our new address – not that I expect that they'd want it. As we get to the hut, Clarissa says she won't see me tomorrow as she's going to the country, but am I coming out today at my usual time at lunchtime? I say not today because I'm knee deep in packing chests. There is a long pause.

'Well goodbye then,' I stammer, and turning on my heel, cross the Lower Richmond Road so quickly that I'm nearly run over.

Go home feeling bitterly miserable; what a shabby way to take leave of them after so many years of walking together.

I'm very fond of Clarissa. If she hadn't become so thick with Rachel, I'm sure we'd still be friends. Even Rachel could be very nice on occasions; I just don't want to be a whipping girl any more.

Back home I find Maxine and David still cleaning and cleaning. I drift about dispiritedly peeling off glow stars, and getting on everyone's nerves like a spare Pickford at a wedding. The drawing-room sofa is removed to reveal a disc of ancient cat sick dating back to the seventies.

At 10.00 hours Leo departs for Gloucestershire with two half-full fish tanks. David, our cleaner, looks at the slopping water with concern and suggests the fish would travel better packed in ice. Have grisly visions of the tanks leaking on the motorway, and the water rising over Leo's chin lke *Morning Departure*.

The removal men are very skittish. Danny, the handsome cockney from Fulham, unearths a huge naked four-foot-high doll of Emily's from the attic. He christens her Erica, after the stripper at Twickenham, and sits her on a little sofa outside our house with her legs apart. From the upstairs window I watch the reactions of the passers-by. Rachel comes past with Bridie, I can see the word 'disgusting' forming on her tight lips.

Danny, getting thoroughly carried away, puts a beer can in one of Erica's hands, and a lighted cigarette in the other.

All day a stream of people pour in for farewell drinks: Tommy and his boyfriend; Rosie and David; Scottish Molly; Horsey Miriam; and Mrs Bond, who gives me a card wishing me Good Luck in my New Home. Various other Putney friends turn up. Some haven't met before and get on very well, arranging to meet next week. Feel wildly jealous. Why the hell am I leaving Putney?

Next minute Frances the feminist waltzes in uninvited. I give her a drink, and she takes me aside, and says is it really necessary to have that naked doll sitting outside, and don't I realise how it degrades women?

By the time she leaves, Danny has dressed the doll in a Pickfords jacket, which flops open like a flasher's mac. Frances, who doesn't seem to feel this is any kind of improvement, goes off also with pursed lips.

Just before she leaves, Rosie takes me aside, and says that she's moving in with David the sculptor next week. She looks radiant; I'm so pleased for her.

The tank corps then rings from the country to say that the goldfish are ensconced near the Aga simmering nicely and Gloucestershire is looking magical.

By nightfall, Leo is back again and the house is nearly stripped, so we take the dogs out to a touching farewell dinner arranged by six best friends in Lower Common South. Teeter home at three in the morning, and express mawkish satisfaction that all the winter stars, Orion, Castor and Pollux, and the Dog Star have come out to say goodbye.

'There'll be perfectly good stars in Gloucestershire,' says Leo acidly.

Make pilgrimage to the bottom of the garden. Moonlight floods Fortnum's grave.

'Rest, rest, perturbed spirit,' I whisper.

According to Leo's itinerary, L C and J C are supposed to spend the remaining hours sleeping rough with cats and dogs in drawing-room. It turns out to be very rough indeed. The next three hours are spent shivering on a mattress shared with two equally shivering dogs, worrying about the future, and despairingly watching the sun rise for the last time over the mulberry tree.

Frdiday, October 1st

07.00 hours: woken from punishing hangover by Leo saying he is late, as he's got to let the first Pickfords van into the Gloucestershire house at 09.00 hours, and the cats have been drugged, boxed and loaded.

As his car disappears, senior cat can be seen furiously wriggling out of his Pak-a-Pet box, and peering drunkenly cross-eyed back at the house.

I have more grisly visions of the first Pickfords van with its 8000 books stalling on the steepest hill in Gloucestershire and Leo looking at his watch like Michael Caine in *A Bridge Too Far* saying:

'This is actually the wide bit.'

The whole day, in fact, becomes a farce. I set out with the dogs, feeling very ropey and hungover indeed. Am just wondering whether to be sick behind an acacia tree, when Syd the carpenter hovers into view, very full of his new granddaughter.

Belting round the Common beside him makes me feel slightly better. He says he'll drop in and see us, if he's ever doing a house in the area. Would like to have taken leave of the Common, but not in a fit state for aesthetic appreciation.

We are scheduled to lock up and leave by nine o'clock. But as Ralph, the foreman, has disappeared to Gloucestershire with the first van, and the expected reinforcements haven't turned up, poor Danny and Derak are left to load the 'ast two vans single-handed.

By 11.00, out of sheer despair, Maxine and I join the work force. Maxine lugs up boxes and chairs from the cellar. I help Beau Derak load the plants. Steadying the necks of huge rubber plants, I feel like Alice playing croquet with the flamingoes.

Next minute Rosie rolls up to have a quiet weep over the Cooperless house, and is rather irritated to find me still *in situ*. From the downstairs loo comes a scream that we've run out of loo paper. I knew I should have hung onto page one of Mozart's *Rondo in A Minor*.

Finally, at one o'clock reinforcements arrive, furious at being taken off another job. Through gritted teeth I ask when we'll be away.

'Well, the men have to have lunch. About three, I should think.'

At two o'clock I take the dogs out for yet another 'last walk'.

At least my hangover has receded and I now have a chance to say goodbye to my darling Common at my leisure.

I am just crossing Peter's Meadow, looking at the little oaks for the last time, and quoting Housman to the empty air:

> For nature, heartless, witless nature,
> Will neither care nor know
> What stranger's feet may find the meadow
> And trespass there and go,
> Nor ask amid the dews of morning
> If they are mine or no?

when a voice says: 'Haven't you gone yet?'

It is my nice new next-door-neighbour, the widower with the ancient springer spaniel. As we walk through Mugger's Tunnel, he tells me he is thinking of buying a new car. All the way back to Barnes Graveyard, we have the relative merits of the Ford Sierra and the Metro. I have hardly time to pick a sprig of heartsease to

press between the pages of my diary before we progress onto the Leyland Princess. This carries us through my precious Flower Garden, whereupon we move onto the advantages of a second-hand Cortina, which last until we reach the ranger's hut.

'Then, of course, there's the Toyota,' he adds as we cross the first Common.

As we reach Egliston Road, David the sculptor drives past radiant, no doubt from Rosie.

'I thought you'd gone,' he yells slowing down.

'That's a nice car,' says my companion. 'Italian I suspect.'

'How are you?' asks David.

'Fed up with Bloody Putney,' I shout, whisking into the house.

'That's the spirit,' says David driving off.

But inevitably, as I check through Pickfords' list of last-minute instructions, there is the lightning change of mood. 'Have you remembered to turn off the main cock? Have you left anything behind?' Only my heart, oh Putney, Putney.

Overwhelmed by contrition, I rush out and post change-of-address cards to Clarissa and Rachel. On the way back, I look into the removal van. There's my wedding dress in its polythene bag, and the doll's house Daddy made for me with such loving care for my fourth birthday, and Felix's hobby-horse, with the nose chewed off by Maidstone, propped against Fortnum's old basket. Suddenly all my past seems to be unrolling before me.

But finally the last room is empty, the last van with its forest of plants has rolled away. Maxine and I lock up, place a last milk bottle of Michaelmas daisies on Fortnum's grave, bid farewell to the dear gallant house which had sheltered us so bravely and pile into the car.

As we drive off, the Brigadier saunters back from his lunchtime visit to the pub, blows us a last kiss, and I lose sight of him in a mist of tears.

What was that poem we learnt at school?

> Crack goes the whip and off we go.
> The trees and houses smaller grow.
> Last round the woody turn we swing.
> Goodbye, goodbye to everything.

But as the dogs fall into their first sound sleep in days, and the car clocks up the miles, we begin to perk up. Slowly the country gets lusher, the dogs wake up and start sniffing frantically at the crack of open window, and suddenly there's the church spire, and the valley, 'deep-meadowed, fair with orchard lawns and bowery hollows,' and our house, lying back, golden against its dark wood with its arms out to welcome us.

Leo, who's been supervising operations all day, and humping furniture around like Atlas, has already got the 8000 books up in their shelves, and all the furniture from the first van in place.

It is nice, too, to see familiar faces. The senior cat is purring in a kitchen drawer near the Aga. The junior cat miaows piteously behind a block of furniture in the cellar – in danger of getting boarded up like the Canterville Ghost.

At that moment, two beaming Gloucester removal men stumble in with Felix's fruit machine.

'Upstairs in the nursery,' I say.

They've just staggered up two flights of stairs when Leo appears, and says tartly that the fruit machine is supposed to go in the downstairs loo and will the men please take it down again, and that things will get unloaded much quicker if I make myself scarce.

In the hall, I meet a third beaming removal man carrying my feather boas.

'This is the loveliest move I've ever had,' he says dreamily, cannoning off the wall, 'I've never tasted whisky before – hic – and I've really taken to it.'

Gloucestershire – it seems – is going to be exactly like Putney.